SHEPHERD OF SOULS

Shepherd of Souls

Faith Formation through Trusted Relationships

David W. Anderson

SHEPHERD OF SOULS
Faith Formation through Trusted Relationships

Copyright © 2018 Milestones Ministry, LLC. All rights reserved.

Except for brief quotations in critical articles or reviews, no part of this book may be reproduced in any manner without written permission from the publisher.

Scripture quotations are from New Revised Standard Version Bible, copyright © 1989 by the Division of Christian Education of the National Council of Churches of Christ in the United States of America. All rights reserved.

Publishing Consultant: Huff Publishing Associates, LLC

Cover images: Bible study © Monkey Business/Adobe Stock; coffee shop friends © Rawpixel.com/Adobe Stock; grandfather and child © Noam Armonn/Shutterstock; boys studying © Edward Lara/Adobe Stock

Cover and book design: Jessica Ess, Hillspring Books, Inc.

ISBN 978-1-7320074-0-6

With an eye to the future of the church,

I dedicate this book to six young souls that lift mine every day,

my six granddaughters:

Solvei, Lucia, Freya, Sonja, Silje, and Karina.

Contents

Preface	9
Introduction	13
Chapter 1 Reclaiming the Ministry of Shepherding Souls	25
Chapter 2 Pastor as Shepherd	49
Chapter 3 A Basic Guide for All Shepherds	77
Chapter 4 Shepherding in the Home	107
Chapter 5 The Lay Leader as Shepherd of Souls	139
Chapter 6 Milestones Ministry: A Model for Shepherding	159
Chapter 7 Confirmation as Shepherding Souls	181
Chapter 8 Congregational Life Equips Shepherds	209
Conclusion Shepherd of Souls: The Life of All Christians	231
Notes	235
Appendix 1	241
Appendix 2	243

Preface

Shepherd of Souls: Faith Formation through Trusted Relationships is the culmination of thirty years of pastoral work as speaker, preacher, teacher, trainer, and coach with congregations across the United States. This book has also benefited from numerous occasions to work for the church in other countries, especially in Norway and Australia. To be sure, many of those experiences were with Christians from the Lutheran tradition, but I have also gained many insights and much joy from an ecumenical community. In a larger sense, this book reflects a lifetime of experiences in the church going back to my days at St. Timothy Lutheran Church in Lakewood, California, from Sunday school, confirmation class, and my youth group, that gathering of young people and counselors where I first remember experiencing what I now call a shepherd of souls ministry.

Along the way I have been blessed by brothers and sisters in the faith who have cared for me in ways that have shaped who I am and have guided my understanding and practice of how the church serves as the body of Christ in the world. There were pastors and other church leaders who influenced my future life as a child of God and as a pastor in ways that would take me decades to appreciate fully. There were the people in congregations and the larger church who walked alongside me and groomed me as a parish pastor. There have been a number of colleagues in ministry along the way who have left their indelible mark on my faith and work in the church.

Indeed, I have been nurtured by a cloud of witnesses too large to name individually. While the church has changed in many ways over the years, the people who make up the church have remained the same forgiving and forgiven saints and sinners who seek to understand and trust the God of grace and mercy, the God who defies our full human grasp, but who gives us our life and calling in the world. And in the midst of it all, what holds true is that I have been cared for and guided—shepherded—to continue the journey of love and faith with family, friends, and a world longing for love, hope, and faith. For this I am thankful.

Shepherd of Souls is the outgrowth of many relationships and experiences. My colleagues at The Youth & Family Institute of Augsburg College, later known as Vibrant Faith Ministries, and the congregations we served, were major sources of learning and inspiration. Of particular help were the pastors and program staff that I coached over the years. Being able to work directly with congregations and their staff allowed me to benefit from field-tested observations, insights, and strategies, without which this book with its numerous stories and examples simply would not have happened.

An international contribution to this book is a particular joy for me to mention. My contacts with the Church of Norway over the decades have blessed me with a number of people who have been shepherds in the church. Oddbjørn Evenshaug, the former head of the Church of Norway, has been a particular gift to me and to many others. Menighetsfakultetet (MF), the Lutheran Seminary in Oslo, the Norwegian Teachers Academy (NLA) in Bergen, and the Institute for Christian Education (IKO) have all blessed my ministry and my growth to understand and live as a shepherd of souls. Pastor Runar Liodden, pastor in Modum, Diocese of Tunsberg, Norway, has faithfully and lovingly taken the ministry presented here and made it his own in the community he serves. His feedback, questions, pastoral wisdom, encouragement, and strategies have served me and this ministry well.

From another part of the world, Grow Ministries, the child, youth, and family division of the Lutheran Church of Australia, has helped this effort greatly. They invited my wife Gloria and me to

Preface   11

work with them for three months to teach, coach, and generally support their burgeoning efforts on behalf of the church in Australia. The invitation provided a unique opportunity to partner in ministry with brothers and sisters—Grow Ministries staff, various congregational staff, families and individuals—who welcomed us into their lives and homes and have blessed us beyond measure. We were there at a critical moment in the writing of this book. Serendipitous conversations and experiences made their way from that time and place to these pages. A special word of thanks to the leaders at Grow Ministries— Jodi Brook, Leah Cronin, Vikki Rochow, Nigel Rosenzweig, Rachel Schilling, and Tim Wiebusch. They and many others, including people from the Australian Lutheran College and the national offices of the LCA in Adelaide, extended warm hospitality and collegiality to us. These cross-cultural experiences, and others like them, are ample evidence that shepherding souls has common needs and possibilities wherever hungry souls exist.

A word of gratitude goes also to my former colleagues at Vibrant Faith Ministries. When I retired from VFM, the staff graciously bestowed on Gloria, Debbie and Burt Streicher, and me the resources to establish our Milestones Ministry, LLC. They gave the four of us the Milestones Ministry website, Milestone products and copyright, and the encouragement to continue the development of Taking Faith Home bulletin inserts. We at Milestones Ministry are indebted to Nancy Going, Paul Hill, Leif Kehrwald, Jim LaDoux, John Roberto, and Tom Schwolert for their support and generosity. The joy of that generosity has only grown since 2014 as we have continued to develop Milestones Ministry, Taking Faith Home, and related resources. The ongoing ministry of resource development is clearly evident in the following pages. All that we produce for the church in the home and the church in the congregation represents a vision and tools to support and equip shepherds of souls. Also, a special word of appreciation and thanks goes to the hard work of Debbie and Burt Streicher and their partnership in ministry that we have enjoyed at Milestones Ministry; I thank them for their help with the shepherd of souls ministry through the development of more resources than we ever anticipated.

The shepherd of souls concept has been ruminating in my thoughts for more than a decade and in the writing of this book for the past three years. There are a host of people who have directly influenced the book's fruition, including readers who have contributed helpful critique, affirmation, and suggestions. Dick Bruesehoff, John Matthews, and Craig Nessan served as primary readers, offering detailed, helpful, and inspired thoughts. Each of them made contributions that directly influenced what the book has become. There have been other people like Nathaniel Gustafson, Timothy Johnson, and Runar Liodden who also made meaningful contributions that are evident in the work.

Two other people need to be named. One is Mark Asleson, partner in ministry and friend for over forty years. His parish ministry and passion for confirmation and milestones ministry give the chapter "Confirmation as Shepherding Souls" its substance and credibility. His pastoral wisdom and compassion stand out in the text with very helpful illustrations from his congregational ministry. I am quite confident that his vision and concrete and detailed strategies for confirmation ministry will make its mark (no pun intended) on the life and vitality of confirmation ministry for all age groups and for years to come.

The other soul that I want to recognize is that shepherd of souls with whom I have lived for more than four decades: my wife Gloria. She not only embodies so much of what is in this book, but I pray that her words, actions, and love of Jesus Christ, the church, and the world God loves are reflected in these pages.

Introduction

So teach us to count our days that we may gain a wise heart.
Psalm 90:12

At a staff meeting of The Youth & Family Institute of Augsburg College, a colleague once asked, "Did any of you imagine doing the work we are now doing?" Our answer was a simple chorus of laughter. Of course we didn't. After subsequent years at The Youth & Family Institute, then its future evolution known as Vibrant Faith Ministries, and now, for me, as part of Milestones Ministry, LLC, I slowly began to understand what our ministry was really about: promoting faith formation and evangelical outreach, primarily by equipping homes through the ministry of congregations. What started as youth and family ministry emerged into congregational renewal that included all generations. That in turned evolved into a ministry of Christian formation that encompasses the entire faith community, not just the ordained, elected, and appointed servant leaders and supportive parents.

Ever so slowly I have realized that what began as an isolated ministry to youth and families is actually about how to help all Christians nurture one another in faith, not just for the sake of the church, but for the sake of a world that God so loves.

This book is the outgrowth of four decades of that kind of personal and vocational growth: of studying, conversing, praying, teaching, learning, coaching, repenting, preaching, worshiping, leading, grumbling, and following the Spirit of Christ. I have come to realize that if we as the church do not seek in some meaningful way to personalize and care for the Christian life of each follower of Jesus, we are doing Jesus' followers, the church, and the world a disservice. If we are not building up the church, the body of Christ (1 Corinthians 14:12; 2 Corinthians 10:8; 13:10; Ephesians 4:12), then we are not fulfilling our baptismal calling to believe in Christ Jesus our Lord and follow him in loving service to others.

 The doors of our own homes, cars, work places, and coffee shops serve as the front door to the ministry of the church.

Forty years ago, this is not what I thought ministry in the church would be like. When I graduated from seminary in 1979 I had the distinct impression that the Christian faith and the denomination of which I was a part was well established and I had better not screw it up. I though my task was church maintenance rather than growth and formational ministry. I was to care for—in a sense be a chaplain to—parishioners so that they and I would continue to adhere to the Scriptures, Christian tradition, and the Lutheran confessions. That was it.

Back then, because the well-intentioned leaders of the church believed that all real ministry emerged from the life of the congregation, such thinking promoted sacerdotalism, the belief that priests or clergy have a preferential place in the church. That assumption not only put inordinate pressure on pastors, it also fostered a subtle and often unnamed dependence and resentment on the part of congregants.

Now, forty years later, I see things differently. What was missing then is that the life of the church experienced through primary life relationships has a critical role to play in faith formation and outreach to the world. In other words, the front door to the ministry of the church is most often not the door to a congregational building. It is the door that leads people to intimate relationships of care, exploration, and faith that happen not on schedules dictated by congregational events but anytime and anywhere lives are touched by the Spirit and touched by God's word. Such faith formation happens "when you are at home and when you are away, when you lie down and when you rise" (Deuteronomy 6:7). Caring for, guiding, encouraging, and correcting people in the life of faith happens anytime and anywhere. It cannot be limited to what happens in a single weekly hour of worship. Where Christ is present in faith, the doors of our own homes, cars, work places, and coffee shops serve as the front door to the ministry of the church each and every day, whenever we attend to one another with God's grace, justice, mercy, and peace.

The conviction that faith is formed by the power of the Holy Spirit through personal, trusted relationships in partnership with the ministry of local congregations marked a significant shift in my pastoral work. In this book, I develop that conviction about the importance of caring for others as the shepherd of souls ministry. It names the essential work of the church that can't be confined to the work of pastors, other congregational leaders, and the programs and efforts of congregations. The care of souls is simply too encompassing for that. The work of the church happens when we are home and when we are not at home, when we lie down and when we get up. Shepherding souls happens all the time and everywhere. A congregation can do a lot to promote it, equip it and support it, but shepherding souls cannot be contained only in congregational settings.

A Reformation Theme

Shepherding souls can be understood through the Reformation theme of the priesthood of all believers, also referenced as the spiritual or universal priesthood, language that is particularly related to the work of Martin Luther and subsequent Protestantism. As the church is now observing five hundred years of Reformation history, many have seen how this theme deserves renewed attention. However, interest in this focus is not new. In his 1951 book, *The History of the Cure of Souls,* John T. McNeill (in the language of his era) reflected that

> What is potentially the most important phase of the Lutheran personal ministry has been the cultivation...of the mutual

cure of souls on the part of laymen. Each man was his brother's keeper in a spiritual fellowship. . . This is the implementation of the doctrine of the spiritual priesthood of all Christians—a doctrine often erroneously interpreted in an individualistic sense. There are still undisclosed possibilities in the application of this principle in the Church, both in the direction of brotherly correction and of mutual enrichment.[1]

McNeill goes on to point out that the Reformation doctrine of the priesthood of all believers "constitutes one of the most important aspects of the whole movement. Yet, the doctrine has sometimes been inadequately prized and curiously misconstrued, so that its full significance has not been realized. It still calls for wider and freer application than it has received."[2] This book explores the "wider and freer application" of that vital contribution of the Reformation for the vitality of the work of the church today.

Five hundred years after the Reformation, the theme of the priesthood of all believers has stimulated church leaders to emphasize faith in daily life once again. That is a Reformation theme that is developed in this book through the specific language of shepherding souls. Christian vocation involves more than serving one's neighbor as a parent, bus driver, or student, for example. For the danger is to limit that work to the physical and emotional needs of one's neighbor and neglect their spiritual needs. Instead, Christian vocation means encouraging all Christians to care for the very soul of others. It means "the mutual cure of souls." It means being a shepherd of souls.

One Pastor's Transformation

The language of shepherd of souls emerged slowly in my own teaching and coaching. With an eye to the Bible, church history, and modern research on how people are formed in faith, I have taught the Five Principles of Faith Formation, the Four Key Faith Practices, and the Three Characteristics of Christians.[3] They defined my earlier books, articles, and leadership manuals.[4] Long engagement with these *principles* and *practices*—especially as a coach to congregational staff—has convinced me of the vital importance of shepherding one another in faith.

The Five Principles of Faith Formation

1. Faith is formed by the power of the Holy Spirit through personal, trusted relationships—often in our own homes.

2. The church is a living partnership between the ministry of the congregation and the ministry of the home.

3. Where Christ is present in faith, the home is church, too.

4. Faith is caught more than it is taught.

5. If we want Christian children and youth, we need Christian adults who practice the faith with them.

The Four Key Faith Practices

1. Caring Conversations

2. Devotions[5]

3. Service

4. Rituals and Traditions

Three Characteristics of Christians

1. Authentic

2. Available

3. Affirming

The Five Principles of Faith Formation promote the importance

- of faith formed through relationships
- of a church that has an intrinsic partnership between congregation and home
- of a church that can be and needs to be experienced in the home
- of faith that is experienced in daily life and not just taught in congregational settings
- of a cross+generational church life committed to nurturing the younger generations by equipping the older generations to live the Christian faith

18   Shepherd of Souls

The Five Principles of Faith Formation and the Four Key Faith Practices direct us to practice the faith (rather than *learn about* the faith in hopes that we will live the faith). Instead of an approach to faith formation that believes insight will lead to action, the Five Principles and Four Key Faith Practices promote a deepening commitment to and understanding of the Christian faith *by living it, by practicing it.* The Four Key Faith Practices identify essential and irreducible faith practices of the Christian faith embedded in all other Christian practices. They form the foundation of any other Christian practice such as worship, evangelism, acts of justice and mercy, stewardship, and dying well.

The Three Characteristics of Christians could be named the Three Characteristics of a shepherd of souls. A shepherd of souls is authentic, not perfect. He or she is flawed, forgiven, and real, not pretending to live up to some kind of ideal Christian prototype. A shepherd of souls is available, meaning present to the needs of others, not absent from real encounters and people's real-life needs. The shepherd is also affirming of God's saving and gracious presence that makes all the difference in the world. The result of a focus on the Five Principles and the Four Key Faith Practices leads to a shepherd of souls who is imperfect yet caring, graciously present to others, and willing to trust Jesus Christ's triumph over all that separates us from the love of God.

In my various roles of congregational trainer, consultant, and coach over the years, I learned that something was missing at the heart of my work with the servant leaders of the church. I learned that this ministry had to inspire the people who *did* show up before it could inspire "those people" who were not showing up in the life of the congregation. The gospel message and life needed to be deeply rooted in their daily lives as well as their congregational work or it would end up being generic leadership training, eventually falling flat as a way to nurture the Christian faith and empower and renew the church.

Even when I said this, church members routinely came back to me with questions like, "But how do we get new members to be more involved in the church?" or "How do we get our kids and young families to come back to church?" I am not unsympathetic to such concerns. But I am convinced that the foundational mission of the church is to present the grace and mercy of the crucified Christ in word and in deed. That is a different starting point than how to get people more "involved in the church" (meaning for some, "How do we keep our congregational doors open and enough people showing up often enough to feel good about what we are doing?"). When the starting point is showing up for worship, involvement in the congregation, and paying bills, a very different spirituality is enhanced, one that is more institutional than relational, more "bottom line" than transformational, more civil religion than Christian.

Over the years I have therefore made a rather strategic shift in my work regarding how to nurture faith in homes and congregations and how to expand the ministry of the church to those not yet or no longer connected with the body of Christ. I emphasize that we must be relational, not just organizationally effective. Isn't that how Jesus did his ministry? Didn't he shepherd, heal, teach, and talk to his followers and all who would listen? Didn't he welcome all, insiders and outsiders alike? It is time for all disciples of Christ to serve as shepherds of souls, people who reach out to others with gospel promise, hope, and courage, often one person at a time.

Expanding the Understanding of the Life of Faith

The ministry of the shepherd of souls offers us a way to imagine and explore the life of faith, day in and day out. It affirms the ministry of all the baptized on behalf of all the world for the sake of Christ. It offers a way to speak of the Reformation theme of the priesthood of all believers, a focus on being the church in the world and for the world that God loves. It perceives the church not just gathered around word and sacraments in a congregation but also scattered to serve in the world. It also assumes that Christian servants gather not only in congregational sanctuaries but in homes and other intimate settings to be fed and nourished by God's word and then to be scattered again, not just from congregational buildings but from other locations as well. This scattering is an essential task of the missional church. The ultimate goal is not to gather Christians in a sanctuary more often. The goal is to be the people of God and bring God's reconciling work of Christ to everyone.

Through God's call to them in baptism, all Christians are sent out into a world that needs healing and hope. The shepherd of souls ministry means that all of us—and not just clergy and other congregational leaders—participate in the call to serve in the church for the common good through the power and mercy of God in Christ Jesus.

Such a life of faith endorsed here through the metaphor of shepherding acknowledges not only the loving service done in the world to care for daily needs and our common good, but the work of all Christians to nurture one another in faith in Christ. This means all Christians share in proclaiming in word and deed the message of Christ to the world. This means not only hands of service, but hands gathered in prayer; not only our words and deeds as doctors, plumbers, accountants, and school teachers, but our words and deeds that encourage one another to follow Jesus with hope and confidence. Shepherding souls does all the above. And it does so with particular attention to listening, praying, reflecting, and serving others so that they do not lose heart and become discouraged. Shepherding souls helps us all to hold fast to the hope that is promised in Christ Jesus. Shepherding souls is about loving God and neighbor on behalf of Christ Jesus our Lord. Shepherding souls marries the Great Commandment to love and the Great Commission to make disciples.

 Scattering is an essential task of the missional church.

Speaking the Faith Out Loud

Yet the challenge for the church is not simply to understand this intimate connection between the Great Commandment and the Great Commission, but to live it in such a way that promotes and equips Christians to do both and to do both out loud, not just in the silent recesses of one's heart and mind. To make disciples requires one to engage with the world around us and to speak the faith out loud. The life of such a missionary is based on the love of God and neighbor that propels that person into the world to share the love of God in Christ with others. Christian missionaries serve the world as parents, grandparents, neighbors, friends, co-workers, and more. In all of those roles, there are innumerable opportunities to bless others with God's word. It can happen by simply offering a table grace, engaging in a caring conversation, or blessing a child when she goes to bed.

This book helps congregations take on the shepherd of souls ministry to help Christian brothers and sisters in everyday life. That means encouraging people anywhere and anytime to be for others the love, undeserved kindness, encouragement, and hope that Jesus gives. The attention given in each chapter to the life of the congregation and the home is, therefore, not intended to make the congregation or the home the ultimate end point. Each of these essential settings serves the larger work of faith formation and outreach that touches all lives in all places through shepherds who not only care for others through loving deeds, but who also speak the faith out loud with their prayers, questions, reflections, doubts, wonderment, songs, and more. It is one thing for the church to lift up the importance of faith in daily life. It is quite another for congregations to organize and function in a way that actually encourages faith in the midst of daily life. This book promotes the Christian faith in the midst of daily life.

An Overview of What Is to Come

The following chapters will delve more deeply into the shepherd of souls ministry and give examples of how that ministry can assist the life of faith in the congregation as well as in and through the home to the larger world. Intentionally serving as a shepherd affects how pastors and other congregational staff understand and do their work. Serving as a shepherd influences the goals of various programs and activities in the congregation. And, most certainly, serving as a shepherd means understanding and appreciating how Christians live their lives of faith beyond the congregational setting, especially with family, friends, and others to whom they relate.

22   Shepherd of Souls

Reclaiming the critical importance of the priesthood of all believers through the "mutual cure of souls," in the language of McNeill, is the focus of chapter 1. The chapter on pastor as shepherd (chapter 2) precedes a more detailed look at what a shepherd does (chapter 3) to emphasize that if the pastor is not leading as a shepherd and is not helping others to be shepherds, it will be very difficult for people in the congregation to engage effectively in the cure or care of souls. However, this is not to put responsibility solely on the shoulders of pastors. Yes, their role is critical, but it is not exclusively theirs. Yet how a pastor acknowledges the importance of soul care will deeply influence the life of the congregation.

The life of the home (chapter 4), another important expression of the church, appears early in the book because people's primary supportive and sustaining relationships (the meaning of "home" used here) needs attention to keep the focus on shepherding that takes place outside the congregation. Knowing that a pastor cannot be the sole proponent and exemplar of shepherding in and through the congregation, other congregational leaders will have a vital role in implementing this ministry in the life of the congregation for the life of faith beyond the congregation (chapter 5). Other leaders in the congregation have the opportunity and capacity to bless lives on a one-to-one basis with the power of the gospel and to serve as a model for others. Milestones ministry (chapter 6) offers a template for shepherding that can influence all other congregational faith formation activities. Milestones ministry promotes faith spoken out loud through each of the Four Key Faith Practices. It identifies a ministry that is cross+generational, focused on faith practices, and that understands the importance of follow-up or checking with people to see how the word of God is blessing and challenging their lives. It teaches how all in the church are called to be shepherds and identifies important priorities and actions for serving as a shepherd. Confirmation ministry (chapter 7), as a critical milestone ministry itself, is given a chapter all its own to emphasize that confirmation ministry done well is a formational, shepherding ministry before it is an informational (or teaching *about* the faith) ministry. Many congregations still have some form of confirmation ministry. That ministry is a strategic way to implement shepherd of souls ministry in the life of many congregations. To be clear: shepherding is not to be pigeon-holed into isolated congregational programs and activities. Therefore, a final chapter (chapter 8) suggests how the principles and practices of shepherding can influence other areas of the life of a congregation so that the shepherd of souls ministry can be promoted and lived in the world by the body of Christ.

The Appendices support the contents of the book by offering an accessible list of the Five Principles, Four Key Faith Practices, and Three Characteristics of Christians in Appendix 1. Appendix 2 gives a sample Taking Faith Home bulletin insert, a weekly resource that sustains Christians with daily faith practices to enrich their lives as shepherds.

Questions for Reflection and Conversation

1. What insights have you gained over the years about how the church can do its ministry more faithfully and effectively?

2. What do you think when you hear the words *shepherd of souls?*

3. How do the Five Principles help define the life of a shepherd of souls? (See the Five Principles on pages 17 and 243.)

4. How do the Four Key Faith Practices guide and equip the life of a shepherd of souls? (See the Four Keys on pages 17 and 243.)

5. What is the difference between wanting people to show up to worship and wanting people to live lives based on faith in Christ?

6. What does the priesthood of all believers mean to you? How can being a shepherd of souls serve as an integral part of the priesthood of all believers? What would most help a shepherd to live out her or his calling?

7. How are you a shepherd of souls? What would help you be a more prepared/effective shepherd of souls?

1

RECLAIMING THE MINISTRY OF SHEPHERDING SOULS

Strengthen the weak hands, and make firm the feeble knees. Say to those who are of a fearful heart, "Be strong, do not fear! Here is your God..." For waters shall break forth in the wilderness, and streams in the desert. *Isaiah 35:3–4, 6*

How might we care for one another on a more personal level? Shepherding souls is about caring for one another within and beyond the body of Christ. It is about nurturing and promoting the Christian faith and life. Shepherding souls is the personal care of others through caring conversations, faith-filled reflections, and prayerful engagement. Such care can happen in one's home over a meal. It can happen at work or on the bus or at a ball game. In fact, it can happen anywhere people feel safe to open up to one another and where they are open to the Spirit's leading in reflection and prayer. A shepherd of souls also demonstrates a commitment to his or her lifelong faith formation by welcoming the care and support of others.

A shepherd of souls is best described simply as a Christian friend. Shepherding souls is a ministry that includes all who are ready to offer the comfort and guidance of the Christian faith. The language "shepherd of souls" names a person who is open to explore and respond to the faith odyssey of another person. Ultimately, like the priesthood of all believers, the daily ministry of all the baptized, the ministry of the shepherd of souls includes at some level everyone who claims the name Christian. It is a model of discipleship that needs to be reintroduced—or at least re-emphasized—and expanded for today.

 Shepherding souls is the personal care of others through caring conversations, faith-filled reflections, and prayerful engagement.

The ministry of a shepherd of souls emphasizes the essential task of caring for others through trusted relationships. It gives human form to the work of the Holy Spirit for faith formation, care, healing, and outreach. It complements local congregations' work through their public worship, educational opportunities, service projects, and much more. A good shepherd is born, fed, and nourished at the font, table, and fellowship of the congregation. The ministry of the congregation, in turn, is strengthened and made more visible in the world through the faith and daily life efforts of shepherds of the soul.

I am using the term "shepherd of souls" rather than "spiritual director" because the latter refers to a trained person who engages with another through a formal relationship with established, periodic, and timed visits, a relationship that is mostly one-directional from the director to the one directed. By contrast, a shepherd of souls lives in a world of mutual growth and care. He or she can be a trained pastor, but can also be anyone else in the church who has a trusted relationship to the one receiving care. That care includes focused listening and prayerful attention, and the care is typically more episodic or occasional than scheduled, more personal than professional,

Reclaiming the Ministry of Shepherding Souls   27

more informal than formal, more listening than advising. The training of the shepherd of souls is primarily community based and occurs through congregation and home. Such shepherds bring faithful wisdom and experience instead of formal training in the history and techniques of spiritual practices. A shepherd of souls can be a family member, a friend, or some other well-placed sojourner who receives as well as offers faith-filled and personal support to another.

The shepherd of souls ministry describes the work of the church to promote the vital service of a Christian mentor. There is a mutuality about mentoring, at least as it is exemplified in the Bible. The care goes both ways: brothers and sisters in the faith support one another in the life of faith with all its nuances, joys, challenges, questions, doubts, and motivations. For example, Jesus refutes hierarchical relationships in his community by noting that those who are first are also servants of all (Matthew 20:24–28), and the model for the life of faith extolled by Jesus is that of a child (Mark 10:13–16). In Leviticus 19:17–18 the command to love one's neighbor includes the need to correct that neighbor when that person has strayed. In Colossians 3:12–17, a follower of Jesus is clothed with qualities of compassion and humility to love, forgive, and even "teach and admonish one another in all wisdom" (verse 16b). In Hebrews 10:24–25, Christians are reminded to "to provoke one another to love and good deeds" and to encourage one another to gather together for worship. And then there is that passionate Pauline description of mutuality: "Rejoice with those who rejoice, weep with those who weep. Live in harmony with one another; do not be haughty, but associate with the lowly; do not claim to be wiser than you are" (Romans 12:15–16). The ministry of the shepherd of souls serves on behalf of the larger community of faith and promotes mutual respect and care as well as an attentiveness that is willing to intervene on behalf of others.

The motivation for being a shepherd of souls is the command to love others, enemies included. In the post-resurrection account of John 21:1–19, the threefold question of the resurrected Lord to Peter portrays this model of love. Three times Jesus asks if Peter loves him. Three times Peter affirms that he does. Three times Jesus tells Peter to feed or care for his sheep. For followers of Jesus, says Frank Crouch,

[t]his kind of love, whether it is called *philos* or *agapē*, involves an inherent expectation of "doing." Love is as love does. This is love as courage, love as risk, love as not wavering, regardless of what we are called to do. Christ calls Peter and us, as individuals and as communities of faith, to follow him even where we would not otherwise go, even where we might not want to go. The times in which we live are no time for "we have never done it that way before," no time for returning to what we are used to. These times, more than ever, are times that call for the best love of God, friends, neighbors, and enemies that we can muster. Or, better yet, these times cry out for the love to which God calls us and that God will bring to life within us for the sake of others.[1]

Serving others with love—including the willingness to be a shepherd of souls—is not necessarily easy. It requires courage and risk to reach out to another in need, especially when that need is not yet apparent to the other person.

Although any moment in life can be served by the ministry of the shepherd of souls, people gain particular benefits from such ministry while experiencing life milestones, like going to school for the first time, developing a close friendship, moving away from home for education or work or military service, making career choices, getting married, intentionally remaining single, having a baby, losing a loved one, experiencing a crisis in personal identity or meaning, and having a major health concern. For a person to have someone or a group of someones walking alongside them and offering support and deep listening about the meaningfulness of the experience in that person's life is an invaluable though often overlooked gift. Such deep listening includes candid conversations, imaginative reflection, and prayerful attentiveness that explores the spiritual dimensions of life. This kind of caring relationship involves a significant level of trust and personal concern.

There are countless shepherds of souls out there in the world. Naming the ministry as vital to a healthy life and resilient faith, and intentionally equipping people for this ministry makes an important

Reclaiming the Ministry of Shepherding Souls

contribution to the overall work of the body of Christ, the church. The woman with two teenage daughters going through the pains of divorce is well served by the tight group of Christian women who meet with her periodically and check in with her individually. The man who loses his job and fears the prospect of his family being homeless can certainly benefit from others who will be devoted to his wellbeing with prayer, conversation, and perhaps material support. Parishioners who struggle with questions and practices of faith will welcome seeing in their pastor and others in their faith community faith-filled guides who can help them wrestle with issues close to the heart and deep in their souls.

 The motivation for being a shepherd of souls is the command to love others, enemies included.

For the ministry of the shepherd of souls to flourish today, we need a clearly articulated vision in the church for this kind of care, a vision for ministry that includes support, resources, and modeling along the way. Such support includes congregational leaders claiming and valuing the role of shepherd of souls as a ministry of the church. Without their encouragement and teaching of this vital service, it will not likely become part of the culture of a congregation. It is not that clergy need be the ultimate experts or practitioners in this field. In fact, others may naturally be more gifted to serve as a shepherd of souls. But clergy must value the communal task of helping one another explore and develop the spiritual life, the life that integrates the Christian faith with personal practices, meaning and purpose, hopes and dreams, and the daily decision-making that we all long to be shaped by the kingdom of God revealed in Jesus Christ.

The following true and recent account gives an example of the importance of the shepherd of souls ministry for today.

Jeff is active in his local congregation. He has been a part of the same congregation for more than forty years. He has served on his church council several times, been an active part of the congregation's small group ministry, assisted in worship services, and participated in a number of mission trips and congregational work projects. He cares about his congregation and is committed to his faith life in a variety of settings, including home, congregation, and workplace.

Jeff had a recent exchange with his congregation's senior pastor. He had heard his pastor give a sermon on predestination, a topic with which this parishioner has wrestled for years. He emailed his pastor to ask for a time to talk about the sermon because it really hit home. He asked in the email, "Do you have some time today or tomorrow to talk and exchange ideas and interpretations?" The pastor wrote back that the pastoral staff and elected leaders had "decided to forgo email conversations on theological issues. A couple of bad experiences (misquoting, reposting, etc.) has led to this. So, to be fair and consistent we don't venture into these waters. With the load we carry, there just aren't enough hours in the day. Thanks for understanding." There was actually never confirmation that Jeff had understood the response. In fact, the pastor's response left this parishioner hurt, angry, and with a "heavy heart," to quote Jeff.

This story of Jeff and his pastor offers a good example of the challenges in caring for people beyond the confines of worship, study, or a host of programmatic ministries of local congregations. Historically in the church, *cura animarum*, or cure or care of souls, has been central. The care of souls includes the ministry of Christian worship, preaching, and the sacraments but also nurturing people's lives of faith through supportive, mentoring relationships. Today, the more intimate setting for *cura animarum* tends to include wedding and funeral preparations, visitation of the hospitalized and others whose mobility is restricted, and the occasional pastoral care and counseling sought by individuals. The general absence of other ways to provide for the more personal dimension of the care of souls is leaving an untold number of people with a "heavy heart" or simply a lonely, isolated, and anxious life of faith. If someone from a congregation is sick or hospitalized, in a care facility, or living alone without much chance to get out in the world, that person is very likely to receive pastoral care upon request, if not from a pastor then at least from someone from the congregation designated, ready, and able to respond to the individual's need. But if someone is experiencing the existential drama of life and wonders about the deeper questions, where can they turn? Jeff in our story it seems can't turn to his pastor, and finding someone else was apparently not an option for Jeff.

And yet, to be fair to the pastor in this narrative, the initial request for time to talk was couched in language of a rather academic discussion, "to talk and exchange ideas and interpretations." What the pastor did not read in the request was that there was something more pressing to Jeff's faith going on here. It appears that Jeff did not know how to ask for or clarify that he wanted something more than a discussion or debate of the history and theological implications of predestination. It is also evident from the pastor's response that he overlooked Jeff's request to talk, not to email.

It is likely that this pastor, like many if not most pastors in the church today, has not been well prepared for this aspect of the historical work of the care of souls that is more akin to the language of spirituality and pastoral care or spiritual direction than traditional pastoral ministry in the recent Protestant tradition. And since few people in the church actually ask for such spiritual care, the pastor probably thought the request was simply to have a theological debate about predestination, something for which he simply had no time. Why? Because, as implied by the phrase "the load we carry," his calendar was likely filled with planning and executing any number of other tasks of ministry.

Yes, there is a bit of irony here: Jeff's pastor and congregation seek to engage people relationally, socially, and spiritually through worship, retreats, Bible studies, prayer groups, hospital visits, and service projects, but offer little space in which a person feels free to wrestle aloud with his deepest questions, concerns, and anxieties, the kind that are best disclosed in a one-to-one conversation with a trusted and capable confidant.

To be fair to Jeff, he wasn't asking for an email exchange, something the pastor said he would not do. Jeff wanted to talk, hoping deeper, more personal content and clarity would emerge in the conversation, but it appears he didn't know how to ask for that something more. When someone pointed out to Jeff that his request was for spiritual care or the care of souls ministry, he said that was exactly what he would have liked. However, before that recognition, Jeff had not known what to call or how to identify what he needed. He simply knew that his pastor's email response felt like rejection at a rather personal and deep level.

Jeff's story is only one of my more recent experiences of the need for a greater emphasis on the role of shepherd of souls. As a congregational trainer and staff coach over the years, I recognize that this area of ministry has been surprisingly underdeveloped: caring for individuals in their journey of faith beyond worship, Bible study, and other group settings in the congregation. I believe that void contributes to part of the current critique of the church by those who are not affiliated with it. That critique expresses people's observation— right or wrong—that the church is more concerned with institutional survival than with care for and attention to people's spiritual lives. Perhaps one reason for this predicament is that it is easier to quantify, measure, and report the numbers of worship services, Bible studies, and participants than to record and evaluate the personal care of others and the impact on their lives of faith.

So, where does a person go who is not wanting help with an emotional crisis or with the in-depth work that a spiritual director typically offers? For centuries, attention to people's lives of faith was addressed through individual confession and absolution before receiving Holy Communion. However, that has been replaced largely by the corporate confession in worship without individual attention or support. Much of the personal dimension of the care of souls has morphed into the role of pastoral care and counseling, something that is often informed more by modern psychological categories and counseling methods than the church confessional and other established spiritual practices. Attention to the individual has also been reprised by spiritual directors, people who are trained to assist those who want a deeper spiritual exploration and experience. Since the practice of one-to-one spiritual care is talked about rather

Reclaiming the Ministry of Shepherding Souls   33

infrequently, especially in the Protestant church, parishioners are not primed to ask for such care, and pastors are not primed to note when people want it or are in a particular need of it. And yet, helping individuals and their loved ones address the spiritual life is surely a central ministry of the church.

The Care of Souls, Faith Formation, and Outreach

Currently there is serious discussion within the church about the relevance and effectiveness of its ministry. Some of the key concerns expressed today relate to the ability of the church to extend the faith to future generations, to provide faith formation for all generations, and to reach out to the surrounding community in meaningful ways. There exists more and more clarity about the need for the church to serve the larger world as a robust faith community that knows the biblical story, serves the community and world, and seeks to live the Christian faith as a distinct subculture within the larger society. And yet, for decades a dramatic drop in the number of children and youth involved in Sunday school classes and youth groups has continued, challenging the church's self-understanding of its ability to nurture the Christian faith in subsequent generations. That alarming trend continues as youth move out on their own, often to a college or work environment and leave church life behind. Increasingly, church leaders recognize that it is no longer enough for congregations to upgrade their existing Christian education programs or a youth ministry that rallies teens around an inspirational young adult or two. As a result, today's church is on a learning curve to become proficient on how to care for children, youth, and adults in a way that is more cross+generational and reaches out to those not affiliated with a local congregation. As it does so, many—if not most—congregations struggle to adapt to these changing times and to reach out to younger generations.

The ministry of the shepherd of souls—that one-to-one spiritual care—has a role to play as part of a vibrant and relevant church in the twenty-first century. It can make a significant contribution to the faith formation and outreach of the church. But where does the need for *cura animarum,* the care of souls, fit into the church's self-critique

34   Shepherd of Souls

and search for relevance? How exactly does the church promote the importance of the faith journey of an individual or a small group of people like a family, for instance? Where in the church are people personally assisted in the task of being "transformed by the renewing of your minds, so that you may discern what is the will of God— what is good and acceptable and perfect" (Romans 12:2)? Where is a person like Jeff, the woman getting a divorce, or the man who just lost his job to go to be grounded in the life of faith and the "peace of God, which surpasses all understanding" (Philippians 4:7a)?

Rarely does the current critique of the church's relevance and effectiveness include the need for the care of souls in a way that has just been illustrated by Jeff's story. When the church engages in its ongoing self-critique and reformation (a legitimate task of the church of all generations), it is good to include examples from the history of the church to look for paradigms, language, and vision that might offer insight and direction for the church of each new generation. The language of *cura animarum* is one example. Another comes from Theodore Tappert, a church historian who was the translator and senior editor of the 1959 edition of *The Book of Concord*, the resource that includes the confessional documents of the Lutheran Church. As an eminent church scholar and voice worthy of attention, he represented the mainstream of theological thought in the heart of the twentieth century.

Tappert translated and edited a volume of Martin Luther's writings entitled *Luther: Letters of Spiritual Counsel,* first published in 1960. In the introduction Tappert writes,

> Martin Luther (1483–1546) is usually thought of as a world-shaking figure who defied papacy and empire to introduce a reformation in the teaching, worship, organization, and life of the Church and to leave a lasting impression on Western civilization. It is sometimes forgotten that he was also—and above all else—a pastor and shepherd of souls.[2]

For Tappert, Luther's example impacted more than orthodox teaching, worship, and organization. Luther served the church as a "pastor

Reclaiming the Ministry of Shepherding Souls   35

and shepherd of souls." From the perspective of the early decades of the twenty-first century, that Luther's contribution is "sometimes forgotten" may be rather an understatement. What Luther represented as a shepherd of souls may be a lost treasure of the reformation heritage that the church of today would do well to reclaim and redefine as it lives out its mission diligently and faithfully.

More recently, Stephen Pietsch offered a similar assessment of Luther's contributions to the church. Pietsch writes,

> As a monk, then a theologian, Luther had prayed, meditated, studied and lectured on the Bible for decades. He knew Scripture intimately. This biblical scholarship together with his deep experiential knowledge of Scripture enabled him to pastorally apply biblical texts with great insight, integrity and skill, especially to those whose melancholic struggles he himself shared.[3]

Pietsch perceives that in Luther we have a person uniquely qualified to offer pastoral wisdom and care to others. Luther did so in personal conversations, many of them recorded from discussions at the table in his home with family and friends, and many others saved through the thousands of pastoral letters that he wrote to people experiencing depression, spiritual questions, and other occasions that became the impetus for a letter to encourage faith and confidence in daily life. Luther knew the Bible intimately, not only as a scholar of the Bible, but as one who applied the Bible to his daily life experiences through prayer and meditation. Luther suffered from physical and emotional trauma that he reflected upon and used as a source for his aid to others, especially those in some form of personal distress. Thus, to use Tappert's language and Pietsch's description, Luther served the church as a shepherd of souls by combining biblical knowledge, an experiential understanding of the Bible through his personal life of prayer and reflection on the Bible, and his own experiences in life that he talked and wrote about to offer comfort and guidance to others. Biblical insights, faith-filled and experiential wisdom, personal reflection, and using the practices of the church as a monk combined to make Luther an exceptional pastor and shepherd of souls, the kind of leadership needed for any age of the church.

To elevate the ministry of being a shepherd of souls as critical to the relevance, credibility, and integrity of today's church is to promote the importance of nurturing people's lives of faith through relational faith formation, sometimes one person at a time. In today's world of efficiency and time management, this may not seem prudent, but in the world of soul care, it may be essential. Can anyone imagine what the church would be like if Jesus had not taken three years to groom his inner circle of followers who would then become the first generation of church leaders? Where would we be without Jesus' soul care for his own disciples? He listened to their hopes and dreams (Matthew 19:27–30; Luke 10:17–20; 22:24–27; John 6:66–69). He knew and addressed their fears and shortcomings (Mark 14:37–42; Luke 5:8–11; 22:31–34; John 6:16–21; 6:70–71). He knew their thoughts and confusion (Matthew 9:38–41; Mark 10:41–45; John 4:27, 31–38; John 14:1–14). He confronted their misguided quests and judgments (Mark 10:35–40; Luke 22:24–27), and was not afraid to correct them (Matthew 16:21–23; 20:20–28; Mark 14:32–42; Luke 9:57–62). Jesus taught them to pray and he prayed for them (Matthew 6:5–15; John 17). He gave them a mission, a reason for being a unique spiritual community (Matthew 10:5–15; 28:16–20; John 20:19–23; Acts 1:8). He led them to a moment when they would be guided by and rely upon the Holy Spirit to recall what he had taught them in words and actions, the message that presented a vision of the kingdom of God and that would define the church for ages to come (John 14:15–16:33).

To focus on the spiritual care of individuals and small groups (e.g. a family, prayer group, or church council) is not to refute other church work or programing. It is simply to reach deeply into the biblical faith and the history of the church to recall and reclaim the care of souls on a more intimate level as part of all that the church does. This is not an either/or conversation—either the shepherd of souls ministry *or* the public, organized, and institutional life of the church. Both are needed, and each needs the other to serve most effectively. In recent decades, a lot of attention has been given to the larger organizational

Reclaiming the Ministry of Shepherding Souls   37

life and mission of the church. However, without attention to shepherding souls, all the other work of the church becomes dryer and less dynamic. Not convinced yet? Then,

- Ask the faithful pastor who preaches and leads worship regularly yet feels utterly alone and forgotten, parched by a call that does not satisfy
- Ask the congregational board member who agonizes over congregational decisions (hopefully, more about the larger ministry of the church than the color of the carpet) yet fails to feel fed by her fellow decision makers
- Ask another congregational leader whose need for spiritual care the pastor overlooks, incorrectly assuming that he has his spiritual life in order (if one's spiritual life is ever really in order!)
- Ask the Sunday school teacher who begins to feel like just another warm body filling a classroom spot
- Ask someone who has had a deeply personal religious experience but has difficulty discussing it with anyone for fear of sounding crazy
- Ask those who work to make a living and make a difference in the world but are feeling as if lost at sea without rudder or oar
- Ask those who struggle to find work and a sense of being valued
- Ask those who struggle to find a sense of vocation, that confidence that they are gifted with a passionate calling in life
- Ask the person whose gifts and passions for ministry are overlooked as the apparent needs of the congregation dictate how that person can contribute
- Ask the man who is active in his congregation and who has the perpetual knot in his stomach because he has questions, deep, soul-searching questions that do not get addressed, even in his congregation, his community of faith

38   Shepherd of Souls

- Ask the child who is afraid to close her eyes at night because of the monsters in the closet
- Ask the parents of that child whether they even know of those fears
- Ask the child who has no closet or home to call her own

Once you start asking, you gain some clarity on the importance of the ministry of the shepherd of souls.

To be clear, the importance of the care of souls of individuals in the Protestant tradition has been identified for years as essential to the work of the church. Since John T. McNeill's *The History of the Cure of Souls* and Tappert's assertion about the sometimes-forgotten role of Luther as a shepherd of souls, a host of people have also expressed concern to retrieve the ministry of the care of souls. In 1984, the noted pastoral theologian Thomas Oden gave attention to the significance of this ministry in his book *Soul Care in the Classical Tradition*. In 1985, Nelson S. T. Thayer wrote *Spirituality and Pastoral Care*. In 1986, Kenneth Leech, an author, priest, and leader in the spirituality movement of the Church of England, wrote a book also titled *Spirituality and Pastoral Care*. In 1989, Eugene Peterson offered words of encouragement for the future of this ministry in the life of the church in his book *The Contemplative Pastor: Returning to the Art of Spiritual Direction*. Peterson suggested that clergy's role of spiritual direction was on the rise and would grow in its influence in the church. In the chapter entitled "Curing Souls: The Forgotten Art," he wrote, "A REFORMATION may be in process in the way pastors do their work. It may turn out to be as significant as the theological reformation of the sixteenth century. I hope so. The signs are accumulating."[4] He was hoping and even predicting that the role of spiritual direction and the larger work of the care of souls would take on greater meaning for clergy in the years ahead, a role that would impact the spiritual life of the larger church. Did this happen? Since these earlier decades, the literature in the field of spirituality has grown, but not the impact, at least not in any sustained and noticeable way in the life of local congregations. Hopefully, by reclaiming the Reformation history of the priesthood of all believers, the time may now be ripe to see more

Reclaiming the Ministry of Shepherding Souls   39

evidence of the interpersonal work of the care of souls in the life of our congregations and homes.

The Role of the Home for Daily Shepherding: A Reformation Model

The history of the Reformation is the history of those beyond priests and others living under religious vows who also shepherded souls. Earlier, I noted that a major Reformation theme was the priesthood of all believers, meaning that not just clergy but all Christians have an important calling or vocation to serve the church and society. Daily life in and through the home—not the monastery— came to be understood as a primary place to practice one's faith through a broadened sense of vocation that included serving the needs of one's neighbor and members of one's own extended family. Part of that effort on behalf of others includes the role of shepherding one another in the Christian faith through prayer, caring conversations, and reflection on the demands and needs of daily life lived together. Mothers and fathers—not monks and nuns—come to represent the Reformation value of serving the needs of others, especially the needs of children, with sacrificial devotion and dedication that raises the next generations to follow Jesus and serve one's neighbor.

Luther's own home became a testament to this Reformation model of the Christian life that shepherded all who entered the Luther dwelling. Extended family, friends, colleagues, students, and other visitors sat around the Luthers' table to eat, drink, and discuss the Christian faith and life. The conversations would include discussions about current events, biblical texts and their meanings, and how people live the faith daily. His conversations in the home that gave recommendations on how clergy, princes, magistrates, and parents should lead parishioners, citizens, and children in the basics of the Christian faith show what Luther expected the Christian home to be like.

No wonder Luther's Small Catechism was written for the home, for the head of the household![5] Luther's home life provided the environment that nurtured people of all ages in the Christian faith. Martin's vision and Katie Luther's responsibility as his wife

40   Shepherd of Souls

and administrator of the home included a domestic life that was extravagantly hospitable to those beyond kinship ties. Through the Small Catechism, one glimpses the daily life of the Luther home. It suggests how to begin and end the meal in prayer and how to begin and end each day reciting the Apostles' Creed, the Lord's Prayer, and by remembering one's baptism by making the sign of the cross on one's body. The Christian faith was the centerpiece of the Luther home. In a letter written shortly before his death, Martin—with an endearing facetiousness, it is presumed—chastises his wife for her worrying about his health. He writes, "I fear that if you do not stop worrying, the earth will swallow us up and all the elements will fall upon us. Is this the way in which you have learned the Catechism and understand faith? I beg you to pray and leave the worrying to God."[6] He then recites Psalm 55:22 to reinforce his conviction that she need not worry but should give her concerns to God. This and many other examples from Luther serve as evidence that those who came in contact with the Luther home were shepherded in the Christian faith as the Catechism and the Bible were taught, discussed, prayed, and lived.

For people who could not read or did not have access to a copy of the Bible, Luther's succinct catechism gave the essentials of the biblical faith, including how one then lives with hope in Christ and with others in love. Memorization—a spiritual practice and an important didactic method for the masses who could not read—became an important tool through catechetical instruction in sermons, repetition of the catechism in the home, and a long history of confirmation instruction. Luther wrote the Small Catechism to guide the conversations of the home and to be used as a resource for Christian prayer and instruction. Luther's own home life and how he intended the Small Catechism to be used in the home give helpful examples of what shepherding souls looks like: faith-filled conversations, reflection, and prayer that guides the beliefs and actions of one another.

Luther's example is not so different from other Reformation traditions. For example, the tradition of worshiping and learning the faith in the home is also true of the Church of England and the use of the Book of Common Prayer, "common" because the worship book is to be used and understood by the laity as well as the clergy. It was written by Archbishop Thomas Cranmer (1489–1556) in English to make worship more accessible to all, since until then public worship had been in Latin. The Book of Common Prayer gives shape to the life of faith in the home by offering morning and evening prayer. These prayer services include the Creed, the Psalms, other lessons, and the Lord's Prayer. The Anglican Catechism is also in the Book of Common Prayer, so that people can daily recite and reflect on the Christian faith. By using the Book of Common Prayer, individuals and families are joining with fellow Christians around the world in prayer and daily faith formation.

The Methodist tradition has its roots in the Church of England and the efforts of clergy like John (1703–1791) and Charles (1707–1788) Wesley. As children, these brothers and future church reformers were part of a large family that gathered in the home to sing the songs of the faith. For a period of time, their mother Susanna (1669–1742) provided worship that gathered family, friends, and parishioners in the Wesley home. On a regular basis, their mother taught the faith to John and Charles along with their many siblings while their father Samuel served as a clergyman in the Church of England.

Numerous other Christian traditions that emerged from the Reformation have a history of the faith life of the home as a partner in faith formation with the local congregation, including churches that became part of the pietistic movement. Over the centuries it was common for parents, grandparents, and other caregivers to read from a book of sermons, especially on a Sunday when there was not a local worship service to attend or when weather made it difficult to reach the worshiping community. Through hymns, prayers, intentional Christian instruction, catechisms, books of sermons and a life of service to others, the Christian home has been a foundational environment to shepherd souls of all ages—with special attention to the faith formation and care of the young. While recognizing that there is a clear need to reestablish this history with innovations for today's world, there remain insights and practices that can be gained from the history of soul care in the Protestant tradition that can help the church's ministry today.

Shepherd of Souls and the Ministry of the Congregation

Shepherding souls offers language and a ministry priority that can help the church reclaim some of its value and place in church and society. It is a ministry that far exceeds—but definitely includes—parish pastors. Indeed, as congregational shepherds, pastors will need to be intimately involved with the whole arena of soul care in congregations, but such soul care cannot be limited to clergy. There needs to exist a mentoring process—even a mentoring culture—in the life of the congregation that reaches out to care for all people. Through this congregational culture, council and board members, committee and task force members, catechists, Sunday school teachers, students, parents, grandparents, and others will see how their lives are in some way offering soul care to others. As disciples of Jesus Christ, all have an investment in the faith and daily life of others. For example, even offering someone a cup of soup has a shepherd of souls dimension, for that gift of food conveys the presence of the Bread of Life to others from a friend of Jesus (see John 15:12-15). Or, a child that prays with a parent or grandparent—or overhears that person praying—has just received a life-giving, faith-shaping example of being a follower of Jesus, a Christian. It is all part of a world view that sees God's creative and redeeming work as active in all aspects of life through all persons in the body of Christ.

 Soul care cannot be limited to clergy.

As the church recovers and esteems the ministry of the shepherd of souls, pastors will perceive their mentoring, supportive role in the congregation and community to be as important as that of preacher, worship leader, theologically and biblically trained educator, evangelist, and visionary organizational leader. Pastors and congregations will value how shepherding souls is an integral component of all the other ministry activities. The role of shepherd of souls is one that goes to the core of the mission and ministry of the church: lives blessed, made well, saved, redeemed, sanctified, and, therefore, transformed by the gospel to affect change in the lives of individuals, households, larger communities, and creation. It is a role that fits well with the other essential tasks of the church, and without which the other ministries lose some of their ardor. Being a shepherd of souls uses language adopted from an earlier time, but it is a ministry that has had and always will have its place.

Reclaiming our Biblical Language and Imagery

Shepherd of souls ministry is about walking alongside others in the intimate space of exploring and caring for life at its deepest levels of meaning and purpose. Shepherding is about caring, supporting, feeding, and protecting. Shepherd is the root meaning of the word "pastor," a term used in Ephesians 4:11 to identify part of the church's leadership "to equip the saints for the work of ministry, for building up the body of Christ" (v. 12). Psalm 23 lifts up the Lord as our shepherd who passionately cares for, pursues, and protects us.

In 1 Peter 5:4, the Lord Jesus Christ is described as the "chief shepherd." A few chapters earlier, 1 Peter 2:25 described him as "the shepherd and guardian of your souls." An elder writing this epistle, using an image for shepherding, exhorts other local elders to "tend the flock of God that is your charge" (v. 2). He describes the life of a shepherd throughout the letter. While some are to lead and "tend the flock," their training would have come from within the community as a whole, as all learn to care for others following the example of the Lord Jesus Christ, the chief shepherd.

The soul, *nephesh* in Hebrew and *psyche* in Greek, is about one's whole life. The biblical understanding of soul is very materialistic. It is about matter, the dust of the ground that is breathed into by the Spirit of God to give life, to give *nephesh*, to create a living being (Genesis 2:7). As something that comes from the breath of God and the earth itself, the soul is an all-encompassing reality, more than the sum of constituent parts like personality, mind, emotions, and body. Biblical scholars have pointed out that *nephesh* is only fully understood in community. One's life is only fully understood in relationship to others. The soul refers to a person born out of and living in a community of interlocking relationships, not an isolated individual. As George A. F. Knight puts it, "It is this whole *nephesh* then that is the object of God's love."[7] Combining the two terms, a shepherd of souls dares to walk along the dreamy meadows and frightful cliffs of daily existence. She enters into dark corners of doubt and despair as well as the bright light of joy in God's presence. He reaches into personal journeys and connects them with very public and social agendas. And, at all times, the Christian shepherd of souls does so with the defining premise that reality is measured by the grace and mercy of God in Christ, the power of God's will, work, and reign that ultimately has its way. Without that, the proclaiming, the worshipping, the educating, the leading, the evangelizing, the researching, the counseling, the processing, and the planning all fall short. It is like the biblical example of someone who shares the peace of God with another, yet dares to walk away and not care about that person's real-life needs (James 2:15–16; see 1 John 3:17), including their questions about the God of love and mercy. Without wanting to be too harsh, it may not be so different from Jeff's pastor who wanted worshippers to reflect on predestination but refused to engage with someone whose reflections created unsettled waters. To preach good news effectively sometimes means that the good news also has to be shepherded one soul at a time.

Shepherd of Souls for the Domestic—as Well as the Public—Church

Those ministering as shepherds of souls will want to be mindful of the basic building block of faith and life: the personal life of the home and the formative relationships that go with it. The church of the last half of the twentieth century in America made a fateful leap from individual Christians to the institutional life of the congregation, largely passing over the home, the domestic church, that laboratory of human development that influences language as well as cognitive, moral, social, physical, and spiritual life. All too often, infants and children were brought to the waters of baptism and plunged into Sunday schools and youth groups without much attention to the home, the spiritual environment that shaped their lives by the

Reclaiming the Ministry of Shepherding Souls   45

minutes, the hours, and the days. Today's training for and ministry of the shepherd of souls will find ways to mend the tear between the public and the individual life through the personal, trusted relationships of the "home" that includes blood kin, legal relationships, and emotionally bonded relationships through personal histories. Recalling that the soul involves one's defining relationships with others, caring for another includes attention to the important relationships surrounding an individual.

 A shepherd of souls dares to walk along the dreamy meadows and frightful cliffs of daily existence.

The power of the more cellular and organic level of discipleship in the church is evident in many places for those willing to look. The life of the church in China can give us a rather surprising example. China is on track to become the nation with the largest Christian population, what one might call the largest Christian nation on earth. One of the influencers for this is the Chinese Internet. Weibo is a Chinese microblogging website somewhat akin to Twitter and Facebook and a very popular website in China. As one article states it, "Jesus is getting more love than Mao on Weibo these days."[8]

The other contributing factor to the rise of Christianity in China noted in the same news article is the church operating in private homes. And, like the church of old, it is an expression of the body of Christ that is quite successful at growing disciples. For those who have been exposed to the church in China, the surprising growth of the church there may not be so shocking. For example, in 1993, the late Andrew Chow, at the time president of the Lutheran Theological Seminary of Hong Kong, spoke at a conference entitled "Family Catechesis" hosted by The Youth & Family Institute of Augsburg College. Chow talked about the number of seminary students who came over the border from mainland China. As part of his seminary leadership, he sat down with each of these new students to discuss how it was that these people came to a Christian seminary from a professing atheist society. Again and again, Chow heard these students talk about how they had received the Christian faith from parents and grandparents. It led Chow to conclude that the homes of these parents and grandparents were the Christian seminaries of China. One may add that the parents and grandparents were also vital shepherds of souls.

In addition to an abundance of research presented since the 1980s that identifies parents as the top influences in faith formation of children and youth,[9] one can also see the role of the home in faith formation through the life and work of the Reformation. In his "Treatise on Marriage (1522)," Luther wrote, "Most certainly father and mother are apostles, bishops, and priests to their children, for it is they who make them acquainted with the gospel. In short, there is no greater or nobler authority on earth than that of parents over their children, for this authority is both spiritual and temporal. Whoever teaches the faith to another is truly an apostle and bishop."[10] It should be no wonder that one of Luther's greatest contributions to the Reformation was the writing of the Large and Small Catechisms, resources intentionally written for clergy and for the faith formation of the home to shape the lives of parents, grandparents, children, other relatives, and even guests, boarders, and masters and apprentices. All of these people are shaped by daily experiences in and through the domestic life.

Finally, the ministry of a shepherd of souls emphasizes the essential task of caring for others through personal, trusted relationships. It embodies the work of the Holy Spirit for faith formation, care, healing, and outreach. It is essentially the ministry of every Christian. It complements the work of a local congregation through its public worship, educational opportunities, service projects and much more and is an important part of the church's cutting-edge connection to the larger world.

Questions for Reflection and Conversation

1. In the story about Jeff's email request, how might Jeff have asked for what he really wanted besides asking for time "to talk and exchange ideas and interpretations"?

2. How might Jeff's pastor have responded besides sending an email indicating he was supposed "to forgo email conversations on theological issues"?

3. When have you felt like Jeff or Jeff's pastor in our story?

4. When have you experienced the care of a shepherd of souls? How did having a Christian caregiver affect your life then?

5. How does the ministry of the shepherd of souls affect the relevance of the church in America today? How might it influence those who say they are "spiritual but not religious"?

6. Describe a life situation you have experienced or know that could benefit from personal, spiritual care.

7. How can a pastor, Sunday school teacher, or other congregational leader impact the faith of others in the congregation by being a shepherd of souls?

8. How does the ministry of shepherding souls support all other activities in the life of a congregation? in the life of one's home?

9. How does your congregation help parents, grandparents, and other primary caregivers serve children as "apostles, bishops, and priests" and as a shepherd of souls?

10. What key ideas come to you from reading this chapter? Write them down on the blank pages at the end of the book.

Pastor as Shepherd

The gifts he gave were that some would be apostles, some prophets, some evangelists, some pastors and teachers, to equip the saints for the work of ministry, for building up the body of Christ. *Ephesians 4:11–12*

Obey your leaders and submit to them, for they are keeping watch over your souls and will give an account. Let them do this with joy and not with sighing—for that would be harmful to you. *Hebrews 13:17*

"And, one more thing you can do . . . . " That's all pastors need to hear! If being a shepherd of souls becomes one more thing added to a long list of tasks they already have to do, then this proposal is doomed from the start. However, if being a shepherd of souls becomes a lens through which one sees most everything one does, then it just may become the one thing that lightens the pastor's load with a reminder of why he or she felt called to be a pastor in the first place.

If being a shepherd of souls is to work for pastors and the church, it needs to permeate the very fabric of the life of faith, of being Christian, of being part of the body of Christ, that life that reconciles instead of divides, that heals instead of sickens, that gives life instead of death, joy instead of torment. It needs to be perceived as essential to the Christian faith and the community of faith. That focus gives energy, meaning, and excitement for ministry. As one senior pastor confided, refocusing his ministry to shepherding souls added years to his ministry. Instead of preparing for retirement, he wanted to—and did—keep going. In addition to the gains it offers individual pastors, imagine how shepherding souls can strengthen the witness of the church to a world in need of divine care and hope.

Exploring Uncharted Waters

Precisely because the care of souls too often has been restricted to milestone moments like marriage, divorce, birth, death, illness, or occasions of emotional crisis, the shepherding of souls ministry is necessarily experimental. Life is filled with uncertainties, and each life and community is unique. How each person responds to the variables of life cannot be prescriptive. The trial-and-error nature of this ministry can therefore be frustrating. But it can also be exciting to wonder and explore various means to connect with others on a deeper, more authentic and enduring level. That itself will require candor, humility, courage, and a commitment to the gospel and to a partnership in the gospel amongst the faithful.

This openness to explore options and experimentation can be seen in the example established by that shepherd of souls Martin Luther as he sought to care for others with the solace and confidence of the gospel. In July of 1530 Luther wrote a letter to Jerome Weller, the tutor for his son Hans. Jerome was struggling with melancholia, what we might call depression.[1] It appears that Luther was concerned about Weller's scrupulous piety that recoiled from doing anything wrong for fear of condemnation. In that letter, he encouraged Jerome to be outside and with people because, as Luther noted from his own personal struggles with depression, the devil loves solitude. Luther went on to give this pastoral counsel:

> Whenever the devil pesters you with these thoughts, at once seek out the company of men, drink more, joke and jest, or engage in some other form of merriment. Sometimes it is

necessary to drink a little more, play, jest or even commit some sin in defiance and contempt of the devil in order not to give him an opportunity to make us scrupulous about trifles. We shall be overcome if we worry too much about falling into some sin."[2]

Here Luther gives Jerome a number of options to consider, including a rather humorous recommendation to commit sin to annoy the devil. Clearly Luther is reaching for something that can connect with the melancholic Jerome. Understandably, these are not the recommendations pastors would likely offer today. However, Luther's suggestions do demonstrate his willingness to engage a hurting soul with the experiential wisdom and worldview of his time.

In another letter, Luther writes to Bernard Von Doelen, a pastor in Saxony who is experiencing some unhappiness whose source is not clear to Luther. To him Luther writes, "Perhaps your temptation is too severe to be relieved by a brief letter; it can better be cured, God willing, by a personal encounter with me and my living voice."[3] The idea of the healing power of a person's voice was prominent for Luther. He believed that one's living voice spoken with the power of faith offered the means of grace, the very presence of the living God. One's voice spoken in faith to another served as a vehicle for the work of the Holy Spirit. This point is also evident in his 1537 Smalcald Articles, where he speaks of the "mutual conversation and consolation of brothers and sisters" as a means of grace to "help against sin" through the work of the gospel.[4] This spirit of uninhibited freedom to reflect on and speak the faith to another in love and prayer is important for every age and is at the heart of a call to serve as shepherds of souls today.

A number of years ago I was exploring uncharted waters in my own ministry when I was coaching a pastor via a phone call and said for the first time, "I want you to work with your staff as though you were their spiritual director." I had misgivings about using the term "spiritual director" because I was not wanting to import all the possible implications of that model of care. But at least the term "spiritual director" was a term people recognized, even if it did not necessarily fit every person's pastoral or theological predisposition. The pastor at the other end of the call laughed, which was not exactly what I was hoping for. Being a bit uncertain about initiating this course of action and about using a term that was a hot button for some, I asked, "What's funny?" The pastor's surprising answer was that he, in fact, was a trained spiritual director. However, he had never thought about using those skills and passions with the congregation's leadership—paid staff, elected, or appointed. He was actually delighted by the idea and agreed to give it a try.

> One's living voice spoken with the power of faith offered the means of grace, the very presence of the living God.

Prior to that conversation, it had never dawned on this pastor to connect his training as spiritual director with his work as a pastor who was leading a staff. He had reserved the training as a spiritual director for the few who were interested in exploring their Christian spirituality in an intentional and scheduled relationship of soul care. But once the idea had been birthed, this pastor was fully on board with this new way of thinking about his work as a spiritual director and a parish pastor, one that would include working with and caring for his staff and other key leaders through caring conversation, reflection, and prayer.

The pastor decided that he would begin by asking each of his staff members in private conversations three basic and faith-focused questions, questions that the pastor quickly identified from his work as a spiritual director: 1) Where does God seem to be most present in your life? 2) Where does God seem to be most absent? and, 3) What might God be saying to you today? The plan was to report back following those interviews at the next coaching session a month later.

The questions were framed in a way that did not ask for or expect answers presuming absolute knowledge. The questions are about what "seems" to be the case and what "might" be happening. This line of questioning relies on the theological conviction that we are not God and do not have the mind of God, a perspective that can deceive a person in subtle ways. We do not have the mind of God, but we do have God's living word in Scripture, in sacraments, and in the community of the faithful to guide us. We can and need to wonder, using our kingdom-of-God thinking caps to guide our imagination and actions. Such conversations have a different center and tone than those that say God is doing this or that in my life with the kind of regularity and certitude that suggests we have God in our pocket, a god that looks a lot like our own life experiences and prejudices. Life in the kingdom of God is filled with confidence in God—but not confidence that we know God completely.

A month later the pastor and I had our next coaching session. He was eager to report his experience of having spiritual direction—or what might be called shepherd of souls—conversations with each of his staff. His report: they didn't believe him. It was such a departure from how he had related to them as their supervisor and head of staff that they assumed it was simply a manipulative ploy to get them to do something he wanted done, even though no such agenda had been placed before them. As with the exchange between Jeff and his pastor in our previous chapter, there was a breakdown in expectations and assumptions about the kind of communication or ministry that can take place between pastor and parishioner or pastor and staff member. Once again, a congregational community did not expect this kind of care. The staff saw this pastor, trained in spiritual direction and now excited to apply his training and interests to his role as pastor and head of staff, as a manipulative boss because he had never addressed them like that before. Clearly, we had entered into troubled waters. Either the idea of one-to-one soul care needed to be relinquished or new expectations and experiences would be required to serve people's formation in faith.

It would take some time, but the pastor's persistence and genuine desire to care for his staff's faith life led to a new level of relating and of pastoral care. He noted that all staff members were nervous at first, including himself. To be fair, being a supervisor who wants to walk alongside a staff member's spiritual journey, especially as it relates to their work on staff and in the congregation, is a delicate maneuver. It will not always work, especially if there are tensions between the pastor and a particular staff member. However, simply to avoid the spiritual arena of the work of the staff is also a challenge and danger to the spiritual life of the staff and, therefore, to the larger congregation.

The pastor continued to have individual spiritual direction conversations with his staff. He also developed individual conversation time with each of his council members and worked with them to develop a council devotional as part of that one-to-one time. The gains developed slowly. For example, it took time for some council members to know what to do with the new level of pastoral care given to them. The pastor developed a routine with staff and council that included lighting a candle and sitting in silence for two to three minutes. One of the opening questions he began to ask was put as simply as possible: "How is it with you and God?" After the genuineness of the exercise was established, one staff member responded, "I am so glad you asked." She jumped in with her own question, asking about an appropriate way to pray. She wasn't sure how to do it or how it should be done on her own. The pastor's question opened up a faith formation journey for this person that she had longed to enter but was not sure how to begin.

For his staff, a follow-up question the pastor began to add was, "How is it with you and God in your work here?" He wanted to explore with his staff members what it meant to their lives of faith that they were part of the congregation's staff that faithfully and humbly sought to lead the community of faith with the word of God. He was learning much he had not known before. He learned about marital struggles that he had no idea existed for one of his staff members, a stressful situation that was affecting the person's home life, work life, and relationship with God. As their pastor, he was learning about and able to address with them deep issues of faith, the practice of their faith, and the challenges of daily living.

During a later coaching session when it was evident to him that combining his passion for individual soul care and his pastoral work was doing something new and very meaningful in his ministry, he asked, "What have I been doing the past twenty-three years?" That is a good question, especially since twenty to thirty years earlier people like Eugene Peterson (author of *The Contemplative Pastor* and the very popular *Message*), Kenneth Leech (Anglican priest and author of *Soul Friend*), and others were suggesting that a new era was upon us. It is a fascinating question that I have been asked a number of times since. It is a kind of confession that acknowledges that something very important to their ministry had been missing but is now claimed or reclaimed.

 How is it with you and God in your work here?

Story after Story

That initial coaching session with the pastor who was also a spiritual director prompted a learning curve for me that continues to this day, one that has planted enough seeds for insight that I believe it is time to set down in writing what I have learned and continue the discourse with a larger audience. Over the course of working with clergy and other program staff for some years now, basic questions of faith and practice have entered into our conversations again and again, especially as clergy and other staff work with a number of servant leaders in the congregation.

Clearly, the church needs to become more comfortable exploring and discussing the Christian faith in daily life relationships. It is one thing to value, assume, or even profess the Christian faith in worship. It is another to integrate Christian faith into personal conversations and decision making in settings that go beyond congregational agenda, settings like home, workplace, and school. If the church can increase its everyday fluency with conversations regarding the Christian faith and life, then it will be easier for grandparents, parents, and children to have meaningful and faith-forming interactions. Friends and neighbors will more easily enjoy each other's core identity as a gift that blesses. Co-workers and fellow citizens will be enriched by

56   Shepherd of Souls

God-bearing lives all around them. All of this would reflect a Christian spirituality that enters into all areas of life so that faith is actually experienced as the substance of conversations, daily routines, personal relationships, and decision making.

What began as an experiment with one pastor has become a routine focus of my work with pastors and other leaders (see chapter 5 on lay leaders as shepherds of souls). Early on in the transition to focus on a more personal spiritual care of leaders in the congregation, I asked pastors (and sometimes other program staff) to work with council members to develop a church council devotional. Each month a different council member gave the devotional, something created by them with the assistance of the pastor. The preparation time would begin with the three spiritual care questions listed above, questions that many pastors were quite intent on having in writing as a clear guide for the pending conversations: 1) Where does God seem to be most present in your life? 2) Where does God seem to be most absent?, and 3) What might God be saying to you today? From there, the pastor and council member would explore the council member's own experience of faith in the context of the congregation's life, ministry gifts, needs, and mission. The result would be a devotional experience that would address pertinent faith issues in the life of the congregation with the integrity of the person presenting the devotional. Usually the devotional would include the Four Key Faith Practices: a conversation starter for the group to discuss (perhaps in groups of three), a devotional text from the Bible, a connection to Christian service (often linked to the work of the council itself), and a ritual and tradition as simple as lighting a candle or closing with a blessing.

Often the planning for the council devotional would be aided by recent Taking Faith Home sheets.[5] These are congregational resources that take the Bible passages from the Revised Common Lectionary, worship texts used by many denominations, and also include all the Four Key Faith Practices, suggested daily Bible readings, a Scripture verse for the week, prayer of the week, mealtime prayer for the week, a hymn for the week, and a blessing for the week, all based on the Scriptures assigned for that particular Sunday in the church year. The Taking Faith Home sheets can be placed in the worship bulletin and be available in other places like the entrance to the sanctuary or church office. Taking Faith Home encourages people to continue to digest the weekly worship service and to use biblical texts and themes throughout the week. It has also become a familiar piece to revisit with council leadership and a meaningful aid in developing the council devotional.

The heart of the pastor-council member conversation is the spiritual care provided by the soul-searching questions. Most often for the council member, the real issue is putting together a devotional for the next council meeting. Some are nearly petrified by the request to come up with their own message, their own voice for the council. Others are quite comfortable with the task and wonder why they need to meet at all with the pastor. On those occasions, the pastors try to make it clear that it is important for them to support that person—as well as the council and congregation—by knowing something about that person and supporting his or her own journey of faith. That clarification is usually enough to satisfy the council member's initial resistance. So, month by month clergy begin to see a side of council members, other leaders, and the larger congregation that had not been so apparent before such conversations.

One frightened council member was really hesitant about presenting his own devotional. To his credit, he trusted his pastor and youth and family director enough to sit down together with them to write the devotional. Although it is not the typical process, sitting down with both these people together gave him more courage. The three had good conversations and learned more about each other, especially each other's life of faith. The council member opened up about his own joys and struggles in the faith. Together they used recent Taking Faith Home bulletin inserts as a guide, and he wrote down his own devotional. Immediately after he presented the devotional at the next council meeting, there was a holy silence. Finally, one of the other council members asked, "Can I get a copy of that?" The person who had once been panic stricken thinking about leading the council devotional had stepped forward with the support of his pastor and youth and family director and presented something that moved his fellow council members to silence, reflection, and appreciation—not a bad example of risk taking in one's life of faith.

Encouraging clergy to be shepherds of souls presents challenges for clergy as well as the recipients of that care. As a process that is new to most clergy and council members alike, neither is really sure what to expect in the exchange. One fairly new and courageous pastor began to have the one-to-one conversations with her council. She strategically began with the council president. Her goal was to ask questions that fostered deeper conversations about the individual's faith and daily life and then direct the conversations to the development of a council devotional. The council president clearly did not anticipate the kinds of questions she asked. At one point he interjected, "Are you my therapist?" To which she responded, "No, I am your pastor." When she relayed that conversation in the next coaching session, she was not that encouraged by the pastor-council president exchange. However, at the following coaching session she reported to me that at the next council meeting, the president commented that his experience of a personal conversation with the pastor was amazing and he looked forward to the other council members experiencing that too.

That kind of a response has not been unique. In another congregation, a council member began her devotional time by saying something quite similar: "I was not looking forward to the visit with the pastor to talk about my devotional. Well, after the visit, I want you to know I am excited for all of you to have the opportunity I had with the pastor." Pastors in other congregations report similar transformations from fear to delight.

One particular senior pastor was passively resistant to the pastor-council member conversations. He never really said he wouldn't do it; he just didn't do it. Finally, after months of delay, this senior pastor began to have the focused soul care conversations with the added goal of helping council members come up with a council devotional. This seasoned senior pastor with a family counseling background was nothing less than shocked by the results of the conversations. At the end of his first conversation, the council member said, "Well, now the knot in my stomach is gone." The knot was not due to his fears of the conversation with the pastor but the result of years of faith questions that had not been verbalized to another person. The council member said he had had no one to talk to like this before, and by the end of the conversation he wept and expressed how relieved he was to have overcome that sense of isolation.

This same pastor noted with surprise that everyone on council quickly signed up for their turn with him, even a recording secretary who was not actually part of council and whom he did not expect to participate in the conversations or prepare a devotional. The pastor called me some months after his initial foray into these soul care conversations. He had finished another council member conversation, the one-hour faith-focused interview that went two-and-a-half hours. He was stunned. This particular council member had seemed to him to be a pillar in the congregation and community, someone he did not expect to be in need of or to desire pastoral conversation and prayer. However, this established congregational leader and CEO of a statewide business had lots on her mind. She had issues with her family, her business, and, yes, with her life of faith as well, so much so that she just could not contain it all in a sixty-minute visit. The once reticent pastor was quickly becoming a believer in the value of soul-shepherding.

In another instance, though an associate pastor had committed to engage in one-to-one conversations with members of the church council, for months she did not make them happen. I finally asked her what was preventing her from having these conversations. She paused, thought about it, then said, "I guess I just don't have time for them." I pointed out that not having the time was a way of saying that it just wasn't enough of a priority for her to do them. After some more silence she acknowledged that she felt like a fish out of water conducting these individual conversations as a pastor. It required a big leap for her. Her reflection and openness was itself revealing and not terribly surprising. I acknowledged that her thoughts and reaction made total sense, and she was certainly not alone in her reaction. It truly is a challenge to shepherd souls in this more personal manner when it has not been modeled or promoted in the larger community of faith. It does require a willingness to leap, to trust that one's efforts will be well received and have a positive impact on individuals and larger congregational life.

After that exchange, she recommitted to try the council conversations and began to have the conversations with individual council members. One of the first things she did was to restate the three questions the following way: 1) Where has God been present sometime in your life journey? 2) Where has God been especially present in the congregation? 3) Where might you say God has been absent in your life? With this personal pastoral input, this pastor was owning the process. She soon discovered that the council members were more interested in creating the devotional than engaging in the spiritual care she was providing. However, now she was seeing the need and the benefit of helping the leadership focus not only on providing congregational and community programs but on their own and the congregation's faith formation. She began to add relationship building activities to council meetings to encourage the council to take risks and explore more deeply the purpose of the council and the ministry of the congregation.

Soon, the associate pastor and another program staff member began to report back to council how the ministry of the congregation was blessing people's lives. The stories centered on the faith formation and outreach that took place within the congregation and that moved out to the larger community. She began to use her council reports to point out that the spiritual conversations and devotions were not an add-on to the work of council, but were at the heart of who they are as a council. She also pointed out that their congregational constitution spoke of the council's responsibility to be guided by the word of God in the spiritual care of the community. The pastor's underlying goal was to help congregational leaders see beyond program development, something they already did very well, to the larger but often overlooked goal of forming and nurturing faith through relationships and faith practices. What began as a challenge for both the pastor and council eventually became part of the routine life of the pastor-council relationships. That model of care also expanded to how the pastor related to others in the congregation and surrounding community.

Within two years the senior pastor retired, and after a thorough call process, the associate pastor became the newly called senior pastor. Her commitment to be a shepherd of souls had changed how she went about her pastoral work. The shift from being a program congregation to a congregation that offered programs and soul care took years, but it marked a profound change in the ministry of the congregation and its impact on people's lives.

In another congregation I coached, I encouraged the senior and associate pastors to have personal, faith-focused conversations with the program and support staff. The senior pastor had been in the congregation for more than fifteen years, the associate pastor for ten. Both were motivated to conduct the interviews, especially the associate pastor who was a trained spiritual director and had wanted to find ways to support and promote prayer and other spiritual practices on the part of parishioners. Yet they had never ventured into this kind of spiritual care before.

The senior pastor discussed with me his difficulty at having the planned conversation with one particular staff member, the faith formation director who had been on staff for more than a decade. They had a good working relationship, yet each had strong and often differing opinions about faith and practice. When the two sat down for their one-to-one care of souls conversation, the pastor ditched the three questions he had in front of him and blurted out, "So, how is it with your soul?" From the pastor's perspective, it began the kind of conversation they had never had before. They laughed and they cried and they ended the conversation in prayer. The pastor believes it turned a corner in their working relationship, one that has an even deeper appreciation of each other, their work, and their journeys of faith.

The associate pastor subsequently jotted down the following points about having one-to-one spiritual care conversations with staff members:

- *It felt initially awkward, but also really important. For we talk about so many things, and I know so much about their families, etc., but so little about their faith.*

- *It serves as a corrective to that prevalent feeling among church staff that it's all about getting the tasks done. It's easy to lose track of the "why" beneath the "what."*

- *We all have such unique stories and such unique ways to practice our faith!*

- *I learned some things that helped me support the unique prayer life of one person, at least. One of our staff is a runner and prays while she runs. So I forwarded an article to her about running as prayer.*

- *I think it helped some of the staff members feel like they have a pastor. So often they don't feel that they do.*

- *I was able to share some ideas/resources about prayer, God images, etc.*

Here was another instance of a pastor trained as a spiritual director and not sure how to use her passions and skill in the congregation. Through this experiment in pastoral work, she learned how her work with staff and other key leaders could be served by her background in spiritual direction. Although it felt "awkward" at the beginning, it also felt rewarding to get to know the faith lives of her fellow staff members and be able to support and encourage them with conversation, prayer, and resources.

A Pastor's Changed Perspective

Once pastors have been encouraged to pursue the role of shepherd of souls, their view of their role in the life of the congregation often shifts. They emphasize the importance of equipping others for ministry and of others having a deepened experience of faith in daily life. Their anxiety about programming tends to lessen as they perceive the relational work of soul care as a valued foundation for subsequent programming. Their enthusiasm for ministry tends to go up, and, at times, they even say they want to push back retirement or changing calls because they have new energy and excitement for pastoral ministry where they are. After engaging staff and council members on a more personal, faith formation level using the shepherd of souls model, one pastor blurted out what has come to be a familiar question: "What have I been doing the past thirty years?" He went on to write down his thoughts with the following assessment:

For too long—for most of my nearly thirty years of ordained ministry—the focus has been on getting people in the door, caring for their needs, and recruiting them to do the work of the church. I think I've understood that cultivating disciples is an important part of this work, but have never really had good tools to do this in a way that can extend into much of congregational life, which is what [this coaching] has provided us. Doing this work has helped me/us find a way to cultivate disciples that isn't intensive Bible Study, but something that literally persons of any age can do.

The pastor's observation that this is something that "persons of any age can do" is critical for the larger ministry of the church. Yes, pastors are important for the modeling and equipping the ministry, but it is, finally and fundamentally, something all can do at some level and all are called to do as part of their baptismal journey. More than one congregational leader has responded to the pastor's care of soul ministry with them by saying, "I can't wait to ask these questions at my next committee meeting," or "I want to go home and have similar conversations with my family." Through the pastor's modeling, others gain a sense of permission to go and do likewise.

How Shepherding Souls Influences Other Pastoral Work

The pastor's task is to encourage and equip others in the church, the body of Christ, to be disciples to the world. The examples given thus far have focused on working with staff and board leadership, whether it be designated as a council, vestry, session, board of elders, or other denominational nomenclature. As defined in chapter 1, "*Shepherding souls is the personal care of others through caring conversations, faith-filled*

64   Shepherd of Souls

reflections, and prayerful engagement." Therefore, being a shepherd of
souls contributes to this larger work of the pastor. It influences most
everything the pastor does. Working with the congregation's leadership is a strategic and good place to begin the shepherd of souls ministry. However, being a shepherd of souls can and needs to impact the
pastor's preaching, weekly worship, Christian education faith formation, administration work, pastoral care, outreach into the community,
and more.

For example, the pastor's sermon can include a number of elements that impact the ministry of the care of souls. The pastor can
remind listeners that faith is more than a doctrine to which one gives
assent. In fact, the word "creed" (as in the Apostles' Creed or the
Nicene Creed) comes from the Latin word "credo" and means "I
believe" or "I give my heart to." A creed implies more than what one
believes as cognitive assent, but is that to which one gives one's heart.
Believing in the Christian faith indicates a way of life and commitment of the heart formed by the Holy Spirit working through shepherds who work through personal, trusted relationship. This requires
a host of mentors in soul care including parents, other family, and
friends. A pastor can point out that shepherding souls is part of their
Christian life, too, not just something the pastor does. Sermons can
refer to and recommend the faith practices observed in the Bible,
practices like regular worship, benevolence, faith-building conversations, service to others, a life of prayer and Scripture reading, and
the observance of faith-nurturing rituals and traditions referenced
throughout the Bible. Sermons can promote a daily attentiveness to
God's word that also includes attentiveness to others through prayer,
small group discussion around life choices, and personal conversations
that offer consolation and encouragement from the gospel. Including
in the sermon stories and examples of soul care that occur in the Bible and today reinforces the importance of the shepherd of souls ministry for individuals, households, congregation, and the larger church.

The pastor can encourage soul care conversations by practicing such conversations in the sermon. The pastor can take a minute
during the sermon so that people can turn to someone near them
and respond to a question that fits with the message for that day. It
is a good idea to ask people (perhaps prepped in advance for the

Pastor as Shepherd   65

question) to respond publicly during the sermon. Encouraging the
participation of people of various ages offers the added dimension of
a multi-generational wisdom to the sermon.

Recently a pastor engaged worshipers in conversation in his
sermon. The text was Luke 7:36–8:3, the story of the woman who
anoints Jesus' feet. The theme for the day was "Forgiveness leads to
love." The pastor took the first two questions from the Taking Faith
Home that was in the bulletin. Worshipers were to turn to their
neighbor and discuss one of the following: 1) "Recall a time when
someone forgave you. How did you feel?," or 2) "Is it sometimes
hard to forgive others? Why?" The people were given a minute to
tackle one or both of these conversation starters. The pastor's own
conversation partner was a professor emeritus from the seminary.
The professor delighted in the conversation and connected it immediately with the sermon preached thus far. After a minute or
so, the pastor interrupted the conversations and asked a woman—
someone whose permission he had elicited before the worship service—what it was like for her to have the conversation. She could
talk about her experience or focus on her answers to the questions
or both. She had talked with her husband. They had acknowledged
how hard it is sometimes to forgive each other and how painful it is
when you don't receive a word of forgiveness. That idea the pastor
then brought into the sermon by noting that because Christ lives in
us (Galatians 2:20 from the second lesson for that day), our voices
do offer the forgiveness of God. The pastor then continued with
his sermon and ended by having people use "A Blessing to Give"
from Taking Faith Home to bless one another right then and there,
another example of Christ living in and through us to others. He
then strongly encouraged people to take the Taking Faith Home
insert home with them to continue to experience the word of God
through prayer, conversations, blessings, and more. At the end of
the sermon, he returned to his seat next to two acolytes. As he ap-
proached them, one was softly applauding the sermon and the other
gave the pastor two thumbs up. Both had big smiles on their faces.
The presiding minister concluded the service by using "A Blessing
to Give" both as the benediction and also as a sending word before
the people left the sanctuary.

After the service, one man said to the pastor with a wink, "Don't you know we aren't supposed to talk during worship?" When the pastor responded with a playful apology, he retorted, "Oh, no. We need to do that." The woman who contributed to the sermon with her own thoughts came up to the pastor afterward and said, "Oh, I should have mentioned how hard it is to forgive myself!" Who knows how those pew conversations and blessings continued into the day and week? Such a homiletical and liturgical approach not only gets people's attention, it tends to continue to ruminate in the thoughts and hearts of worshipers after the service is over. All of this contributes to the equipping of the saints as shepherds of souls.

The worship bulletin and inserts can also equip people to engage with the word of God in their daily lives as shepherds of souls. The bulletin includes information on people and organizations in need of prayer and support. It can help people consider various ways to be of service to others. The bulletin can be used to help people continue to meditate on the sermon texts. It includes hymns that can be prayed and sung at home. This is all part of the care of souls by making worship the beginning of a weekly journey of faith, one that begins with the resources offered in worship and that can be experienced in the home (or coffee shop or anywhere else) day in and day out through conversations, prayer, and the interpersonal care of others.

Encouraging people to live the Christian faith intentionally through everyday activities is a good way to use the worship service to support people in their journey of faith. It also provides a way for them to reach out to others with the word of God. Worshipers can be reminded that faith practices can be done with others—including those who have not worshiped recently or ever—to nurture their faith as well. For example, parents and grandparents can help grandchildren and children (including adult children) hear the word of God by simply offering a table grace or by engaging in a conversation with open-ended questions based on the sermon or the Caring Conversations in Taking Faith Home. Friends can connect with friends with similar easy-to-use practices that fit into daily routines. These are examples of how proclamation can take many avenues outside of worship and reach out to more people with the soul care of the church.

Children's sermons can help children (and later their families at home) do some of these same faith practices. The children's sermon can be used to teach faith practices like giving someone a blessing, using table graces, memorizing Bible passages, offering service to others, and much, much more. Pastors and others can check in with these children and their families during the week to see how the faith formation practices are working in the home. There is nothing like a little extra support, encouragement, and accountability to create new habits that bless the faith life of the home.

The Value of Follow-Up Contact

The pastor's worship leadership promotes a climate and an example that can be replicated at leadership meetings, Bible studies, youth group and service events, and most everything else associated with the congregation's ministry. A basic ingredient of all such gatherings can be follow-up discussion and evaluation. Simple questions to find out how the event impacted the person and their life of faith is beneficial to shepherding people in faith.

The added element of follow-up, of checking in with others to see how the word of God impacted their lives, can be a major turning point in the life of a congregation. It begins with the pastor, and it takes some courage to initiate. As one experienced pastor put it, "It's not easy to check in with people. That's intimidating. I sometimes suffer from a lack of self-esteem." For checking in with others might reveal that the ministry moment actually didn't have a great impact on people. No one wants to hear that. At the same time, valuing people's thoughts and feelings can promote engagement and benefit the ministry of the congregation. Many a pastor and other congregational leader have been pleasantly surprised by how the care of souls through checking in with others has blessed the leader, the person being asked, and the larger congregation. Yes, there is an element of risk involved. Yes, there is an element of trial and error about going forward as a shepherd of souls, especially for the pastor. However, what better example can the spiritual leader of a congregation offer than to lead a life of candor, humility, courage, and commitment to the gospel and embark on a partnership in the gospel amongst the faithful?

A multitude of other pastoral care contacts can benefit from such follow-up conversation and serve as meaningful soul care. For example, when a council or staff member finishes a task or resigns his or her position, it is an excellent time to check in and support that person's life of faith following their service to the congregation. Using an exit interview, the pastor can ask the following kinds of questions:

- "What was it like to serve in the congregation?"
- "What blessed you by being in your leadership role?"
- "What was difficult?"
- "For what experience do you want to give thanks to God?"
- "For what do you want forgiveness?"
- "Who needs your forgiveness?"
- "How does this experience shape your life of faith going forward?"
- "Of what grievance or pain do you need to let go?"
- "What do you need to say, experience, or hear so that you can now enter the life of the church refreshed and ready to continue your journey of faith in the church?"
- "What can we in the congregation learn from your experience here?"

Being on staff or in another servant-leader role in a congregation can be filled with many joys as well as pain. The joys need to be named and expressed with a thankful heart. The pain needs to be released so that healing and a new beginning can take place. Such release and healing can prevent former leaders in congregations from becoming inactive, former members of the congregation and larger church. Taking time to offer the care of souls ministry can apply the balm of Gilead, the healing word of Christ, so that wounds can heal and a new, even deeper, experience of faith in community can emerge.

Grief work can also benefit from follow-up contacts. Whether it is the death of a loved one, divorce, or serious decline in health, any experience of serious loss can be well served by a follow-up conversation, reflection, and prayer to explore how the grief experience is going and how the faith journey is intersecting with the loss and grief. Helping people see the experience as a faith experience can serve as a powerful moment along life's path. Ignoring the faith content of the loss and grief or simply ignoring the person grieving has left many a person to drift from the community of faith and feel alone and abandoned by others and by God. It is not that the pastor needs to be the person who does all shepherding of souls during times of loss and grief, but the pastor's leadership can orchestrate such care and the expectation that others will share in such caregiving and soul shepherding as well.

Pre-Marriage and Marriage Care

Pre-marriage counseling and marital crisis care present other prime occasions for the shepherd of souls ministry. The love and anger, dreams and disappointments, joys and sorrows experienced in all intimate relationships contain deeply spiritual material that leads people to places of hope and faith as well as despair and disbelief. While pre-marriage work benefits from good knowledge of marriage dynamics and family systems, there remains the need to discuss the faith component of the marriage covenant. Yes, it is wise to talk about the couple's families of origin, their hopes, expectations, and even fears for the conjugal partnership. It is also deeply important to discuss how their image of God and practice of faith connects them as a new family unit—or does not. It is helpful for a couple to reflect on why they want to get married and why they want the marriage blessed by God and in the company of family and friends. Couples benefit from a candid conversation with each other and in the presence of another about their faith traditions and practices or the lack thereof and how they experienced or did not experience the faith in their prior home life.

Nowadays, most couples have not experienced the life of faith in the home. Pre-marriage and marriage care and counseling can introduce the topic of faith, how to talk about their core values and faith, and how to live out those values through a variety of simple faith practices. Practicing faith conversations together and giving them prayers, scripture readings, and other examples of Christian traditions for the home will get the couple to wonder about their faith lives and how they may use faith practices as a foundational part of their marriage. If the pastor does not help the couple do this now, when will it ever happen?

The wedding sermon can likewise promote and use Christian practices. Couples can be given conversation starters, prayers, Bible readings, and blessings to use with each other as part of their honeymoon. Yes, it will lead to some chuckling when the pastor asks, "Well, what else do you have to do tonight when your family and friends are gone?" However, it can also be a wonderful gift—both quite seriously and playfully—handed to them right in the middle of the sermon and contained in a simple envelope.[6] Why not? And by placing some of the same or similar information in the wedding bulletin or other convenient location, the worshiping community can be encouraged to use some of the same faith practices as they remember the couple in prayer in the days and years ahead. By talking about the church in the home and how to live as a faithful couple in daily life, the wedding service becomes soul care not only for the couple but for all who witness the marriage and walk away with examples of how to begin or enhance an active faith life in the home.

Being a pastor and shepherd of souls impacts almost every other ministry in the congregation as well. From visiting the hospitalized and home bound to Christian education faith formation, community outreach, social justice, and community service, a rich variety of occasions become opportunities for people to engage with one another through caring conversations, faith-filled reflection, and prayer. The pastor as shepherd of souls and model for others in this vital work offers the spiritual dimension to the faith community in the congregation and the home that is foundational to the church and Christian faith. Such care and concern serves as an essential element to the pastor's and congregation's leadership and function in the community and world.

The Priesthood of All Believers in Home and Congregation

The shepherd of souls ministry impacts daily life, not just congregational activities. Partnering the ministry of the congregation with that of the home (those relationships nurtured regularly by family, friends, and peers) is a guiding premise for the ministry of the shepherd of souls. It is not a ministry of clergy or other staff in isolation from the larger communities of faith. It is the lifeblood of the church experienced in a number of diverse yet symbiotic relationships and communities. When the church has parents and other family members, mentors, and peers serving and caring for each other, then there is a greater likelihood that God's living word will impact young and old alike. When the focus of congregational and home life is to attend prayerfully to the life and faith of all people, then we are ready to embrace the Reformation theme of the priesthood of all believers, Christians seeing their daily lives and their life's work as caring for the world God loves.

 The shepherd of souls ministry impacts daily life, not just congregational activities.

For decades, the Lutheran church has described the priesthood of all believers as the unfinished Reformation, that creedal and strategic movement in the church that claims all in the church as disciples sent out into all the world. It is a focus that still needs attention. The church's gospel care and outreach to the world is only restricted by the number of people who participate in the "partnership of the gospel" (Philippians 1:5). However, this does not need to mean more people serving on committees and signing up for more congregational activities and programs. What the world needs, what the "spiritual but not religious" need—and what the church has to offer—is a community of people sent out with good news to care for others as shepherds of souls.

Neglecting ways to support the priesthood of all believers in daily life limits the church's impact on society. The trends are evident. Fewer people are actively involved in congregations. While many grandparents remain faithful to the church, many grandchildren live far from it. More people advocate that one can be spiritual without the religious life of congregations. In the changing spiritual landscape of America, atheists are gaining their own voice and witnessing to their beliefs more fervently. Other world religions are clearly more visible in American communities.

Precisely because of this wilderness moment, many servant leaders in the church are recognizing that it a good time to be followers of Jesus Christ with hands wide open to receive what the Lord Jesus gives to quench our thirst and feed our souls. The church may be in the midst of a vital and exciting renewal that clarifies the core ministry of the church, one that seeks to distinguish the language and work of the church from the language and work of corporate power, bottom-line thinking, political parties, national creeds, or the morality of the outspoken masses. Current events are leading congregations to reclaim their roots, their mission, core values, and identity as the body of Christ that serves the world. In fact, there is a growing and audible voice claiming this time in the history of the church as a time of repentance and readiness to be restored, refreshed, and reinvigorated. One of those thirst-quenching streams, part of what God has always called the church to be, may be a community nurturing, mentoring, shepherding, provoking "one another to love and good deeds," and "encouraging one another" (Hebrews 10:24–25) in faith, love, and service.

We have already seen that the pastor as the spiritual shepherd to staff and other servant leaders in the congregation is a good place to begin the care of souls ministry in this time of church renewal. The pastor serves as model, mentor, and leader for the congregation's faith formation through soul care that affects such activities as worship, preaching, Christian education, leadership development, and caring for the sick and hurting. The pastoral office offers leadership and guidance for the shepherd of souls ministry with servant leaders and finally to the larger congregation through the public ministry of worship, study, service, advocacy, outreach, and general fellowship. The pastor can be an example of how anyone can experiment with doing soul care. The risk-taking and a trial-and-error approach to the spiritual care of others is based on the gospel that allows Christians to make mistakes and learn from them for the sake of caring for others. The pastor is in a strategic position to promote this ministry in a variety of ways. But such work can be exhausting. So who cares for the pastor?

So Who Cares for the Pastor?

As significant and beautiful as the work of a pastor can be, it also drains the soul. The time required, the energy needed to initiate and follow through, the prayerful reflection on the essentials, engaging with so many people on so many levels, serving a community with many different—even contradictory—convictions and assumptions, and the need for professional development and personal time as well as time with family and friends, these all contribute to the need of the pastor for a shepherd of the pastor's soul. One aspect of how pastors model being a shepherd is to make clear that the pastor also needs care. It can be in the form of having a spiritual director or a colleague in ministry who commits to the care of the pastor. It can be a trusted, savvy Christian friend who can maintain confidentiality. It can be an intimate and designated group of elders who give top priority to caring for the pastor. Whoever it is, the pastor needs a shepherd, too.

Such support is important for the pastor, but it is also important for the congregation to know about it. The pastor needs to enjoy life with the Good Shepherd, to reflect and pray with our Lord without those tasks being directly related to sermon or meeting preparation. To do that, the pastor must risk being vulnerable and humble, able to engage prayerfully in God's word as well as receive encouragement, warmth, and kindness from the community she or he serves. It can be tempting for a pastor to play the part of a shepherd who only gives and does not need to receive. The wiser pastor and the wiser and more compassionate congregation know better. It will be difficult for the congregation to celebrate and own the ministry of the care of souls without the humble acknowledgment that all, including the pastor, are in need of such careful attention.

74   Shepherd of Souls

Questions for Reflection and Conversation

1. What most captured your attention in this chapter? Why?

2. What do you see as the essential role or tasks of the congregational pastor?

3. Caring for others can at times benefit from creative ideas and risk taking. When have you benefited from the risk taking of others on your behalf? When have you taken risks to care for another person?

4. Martin Luther wrote thousands of letters caring for other people. What is surprising about his care for Jerome Weller and Bernard Von Doelen? What do you find helpful? What do you find confusing or unhelpful?

5. What did you learn from the stories about the pastors' initial attempts to shepherd souls? What story or stories did you find particularly meaningful? Why? What examples do you have regarding pastors offering the ministry of a shepherd of souls?

6. How do you see the shepherd of souls ministry being emphasized in the life of your congregation? For example, where do you see it happening in worship, education, leadership teams, weddings, funerals, working for justice and mercy, or fellowship groups? Where would you like to see the shepherd of souls ministry emphasized in the life of your congregation? Give concrete examples.

7. When have you attended a wedding or funeral and left the worship service wanting to live the Christian faith more fully? What did you do with that desire? What was it about the worship service that led you to a desire to renew your life of faith?

8. How does your congregation care for its pastor(s)? What areas of care for the pastor could be suggested? What kind of care does your pastor seek for himself/herself?

Pastor as Shepherd 75

9. How is the shepherd of souls ministry more than the work of the pastor or other congregational leaders? How is it your ministry? What support do you need in order to be a more effective shepherd of souls?

10. What questions do you have about how to be a shepherd of souls? With whom can you talk to get answers to those questions?

11. If there were to be a couple of small steps you might take after having read this chapter, what might they be? Write them down in the back of this book. Offer prayer. Listen for the Holy Spirit.

A Basic Guide
for All Shepherds

> Above all, maintain constant love for one another, for love covers a multitude of sins. Be hospitable to one another without complaining. Like good stewards of the manifold grace of God, serve one another with whatever gift each of you has received. Whoever speaks must do so as one speaking the very words of God; whoever serves must do so with the strength that God supplies, so that God may be glorified in all things through Jesus Christ. *1 Peter 4:8–11*

Prior chapters have given examples of interactions that befit a shepherd of souls. This chapter will explore the kinds of conversation, reflection, and prayer that exemplify the work of a shepherd of souls and review some guidelines and parameters that make for effective shepherding.

Who Can Be a Shepherd of Souls?

Being a shepherd of souls in the Christian community is an activity of care in which all Christians are encouraged to engage as part of their vocation, their own priesthood. It is a way of life that follows Jesus, the Good Shepherd. This connection is made in the pastoral words of 1 Peter. It is a letter addressed to Christians suffering for their faith, some as slaves or wives of nonbelievers. In chapter 5, the text reads, "And when the chief shepherd appears, you will win the crown of glory that never fades away. In the same way, you who are younger must accept the authority of the elders. And all of you must clothe yourselves with humility in your dealings with one another" (1 Peter 5:4–5). Yes, there is an expectation to "accept the authority of the elders," but there is also a conscious awareness of how all are to conduct themselves "with humility in your dealings with one another." In this letter, Jesus is the model of caring with humility and suffering. Shepherding is a practice that requires deep humility and trust in the Christian faith passed down through the centuries. Instead of being a practice of the faith assigned exclusively to specialists like an elder, pastor or bishop, shepherding souls identifies a practice of the Christian faith for all to exercise for the sake of nurturing and promoting the Christian faith and life in one another. It exemplifies the important partnership between the ministry of the congregation and the ministry of individuals and households in daily life, each supporting and strengthening the other.

Being a shepherd of souls means being a person who offers a trusted relationship to another that involves caring conversations, faith-filled reflections, and prayerful engagement. It can be expressed through loving service to another as well as by a demeanor that promotes calm, warmth, patience, and reconciliation rather than a desire to dominate, berate, cajole, or abuse. That preferred attitude and behavior is affirmed throughout the New Testament letters and is seen in the gospel accounts as well. It reflects the contemporary focus on spirituality, that is, the living out of one's faith through practices and routines that, in turn, shape one's life and understandings of the Christian faith. Part of that spirituality suggested here is that all followers of Jesus in some way serve as a shepherd of souls to others through their caring, their words, and their actions.

Shepherding souls describes an essential component of the spiritual life of Christians. It demonstrates a way to love God and neighbor and how we love God by loving our neighbor. The Gospel of Matthew makes this point when Jesus identifies the love of God through the words of Deuteronomy 6:5 and links it to the love of neighbor in Leviticus 19:18. Jesus then concludes, "On these two commandments hang all the law and the prophets" (Matthew 22:37–40). By arguing from a negative perspective, 1 John makes the same point by noting that "those who do not love a brother or sister whom they have seen, cannot love God whom they have not seen. The commandment we have from him is this: those who love God must love their brothers and sisters also" (1 John 4:20b–21). Shepherding can be active by doing things like feeding the hungry, giving water to the thirsty, showing hospitality to strangers, clothing the naked, caring for the sick, and visiting the imprisoned (Matthew 25:35–36; James 2:14–17). By doing so, people have experienced the love of God through the people of God. Shepherding souls takes place in public worship through Scripture reading, sacraments (ordinances in some traditions), meditation, prayer, passing the peace, and more. Shepherding souls is also what occurs once people leave public worship and it is a factor that brings them back.

In these Bible passages, being attentive to the lives of others with support, love, and faith is clearly not perceived as being the exclusive work of church leaders. In fact, for the sake of the community of saints, it dare not be. Trained, called, elected, and appointed leaders in the church cannot be available to the larger community of believers at every turn and every moment of need. Everyone has a role to play in the support of others in the life of faith. As Ephesians points out, Christ gave a variety of gifts to build up the church: "The gifts he gave were that some would be apostles, some prophets, some evangelists, some pastors and teachers, to equip the saints for the work of ministry, for the building up of the body of Christ" (Ephesians 4:11–12). The text continues, "But speaking the truth in love, we must grow up in every way into him who is the head, into Christ, from whom the whole body, joined and knit together by every ligament with which it is equipped, as each part is working properly, promotes the body's growth in building itself up in love" (Ephesians 4:15–16). While recognized leaders guide the equipping and the building up of the body, all the saints engage in the enterprise of strengthening one another in the Christian faith.

Building up the body of Christ requires endless shepherding, a commitment to the ongoing wellbeing of the community of faith and to the individual members of it. As the Apostle Paul notes, "Now there are varieties of gifts, but the same Spirit; and there are varieties of services, but the same Lord; and there are varieties of activities, but it is the same God who activates all of them in everyone. To each is given the manifestation of the Spirit for the common good" (1 Corinthians 12:4–7). Building up the whole body of Christ, caring for the faith and life of one another is the work of all "for the common good." As a ministry that equips, edifies, and builds up the church, at some level it needs to be the ministry of all Christians. Why? Because life is difficult, complex, messy, and filled with temptations and alluring powers that can weaken, deceive, or blind someone each and every day. The complexity of life requires help from all of us.

 Everyone has a role to play in the support of others in the life of faith.

The Humble Beginning Point for Shepherding

Christianity has been described beautifully as "one beggar telling another beggar where he found bread."[1] That description is also apt for the work of a shepherd of souls. It represents the mutual quest to experience hope and the courage to endure over time. A shepherd of souls does not present herself or himself as the master of all wisdom or the provider of solutions to life's ills. The shepherd is true to the Good Shepherd, the one who lays down his life for the sheep (John 10:11). Jesus joined us in our humanity and "humbled himself and became obedient to the point of death, even death on a cross" (Philippians 2:8). Jesus, the Good Shepherd, serves and redeems by suffering with us that we may be made whole. The Apostle Paul acknowledges this theme when he tells of God's word addressed to him when he was looking for a healing regarding something he described as a "thorn . . . in the flesh" (2 Corinthians 12:7). Paul writes, "My grace is sufficient for you, for power is made perfect in weakness" (v. 9). The shepherd of souls, as a servant of the Good Shepherd (the chief shepherd according to 1 Peter 5), likewise is able to enter into another person's pain and by his or her presence, care, and attentiveness offers hope that there is bread to be found.

The spirit of the shepherd of souls is heard in the words of the Apostle Paul, a shepherd for the ages, when he wrote,

> Let love be genuine; hate what is evil, hold fast to what is good; love one another with mutual affection; outdo one another in showing honor. Do not lag in zeal, be ardent in spirit, serve the Lord. Rejoice in hope, be patient in suffering, persevere in prayer. Contribute to the needs of the saints; extend hospitality to strangers. Bless those who persecute you; bless and do not curse them. Rejoice with those who rejoice, weep with those who weep. . . . do not claim to be wiser than you are (Romans 12:9–16).

The shepherd of souls humbly walks alongside another person with acts of love and the appropriate bearing to go with the care of souls. In Philippians 4:4–14, Paul speaks similarly of a gentleness that rejoices, prays to God, believes God is near, and pursues a life that moves one beyond worry and distress to a life of faith filled with care for others and hope and joy for the goodness and mercy of God shown through the Lord Jesus Christ.

The Gift of Being Present and Listening

A good beginning point for the Christian as a shepherd follows the Hippocratic oath to "do no harm." This means not trying to say or do more than one can safely say or do, it means no attempts at bombastic and quick fixes to people's pains, questions, concerns and predicaments. Doing no harm certainly suggests that one be aware of personal limitations. The intent of soul shepherding is not to give good advice but to breathe hope and encouragement into lives through Christ's living presence in our midst, through the good news that

God has become flesh, dwells among us, and brings us to a future we cannot arrive at on our own. Recalling these promises can aid the shepherd in helping an anxious person see beyond the clutter of destructive thinking and emotions. Recalling that we have a God who comes to us as a wounded healer can deter the shepherd from the need to comfort oneself or others with a false or premature solution to life's complex questions and challenges.

An important aspect of shepherding is to be physically present, an act that itself offers meaningful support and encouragement, the kind that brings with it an awareness of the very presence of God. Job's three friends Eliphaz, Bildad, and Zophar initially did this well. In the depths of Job's personal anguish and physical plight, the three friends did not even recognize him. They grieved with him and "sat with him on the ground seven days and seven nights, and no one spoke a word to him, for they saw that his suffering was very great" (Job 2:13). Unfortunately, they went from exemplary care and attentiveness to a subsequent and misdirected need to point out Job's failings. They saw themselves as defending God's righteousness with a theology that believed that if Job suffered, he must have done something sinful. The three friends moved from being present to Job with deep empathy for his experience to an argumentative approach that sought to explore the depths of the mystery of God and, in the process, condemn Job for his apparent misdeeds.

The Book of Job rejects a simplistic formula that the good are blessed and the bad are cursed. Instead of praying to God, Job's friends were trying to fix Job's understanding of God and relationship with God. They had wanted Job to repent to God for his sinfulness. However, with more than a bit of irony, God later has the three repent to Job and seek Job's prayers for their forgiveness (Job 42:7–9). Job in his anguish and despair questioned and challenged God in a way that God honored as right and true. His friends had allowed their own anxieties and need for order—instead of their compassion—to guide their way.

A shepherd of souls does not need to be God's spokesperson by offering answers to the deepest questions. One does not need to say that some tragedy has happened for a divine reason. One does not need to offer premature comfort by explaining away life's painful questions. Shepherding is being with people when one does not know what to do or say, remaining with them in prayer, sometimes silent prayer.

Good interpersonal care of almost any sort begins with listening, and good listening becomes an act of prayer, one that brings in the care of God to the relationship and conversation. This kind of listening is not a way to be attentive so that one can figure out when to interrupt and tell one's own story, give one's own suggestions or solutions, or speak one's own mind. The Letter of James gives good advice on this: "You must understand this, my beloved: let everyone be quick to listen, slow to speak, slow to anger . . . Therefore, rid yourselves of all sordidness and rank growth of wickedness, and welcome with meekness the implanted word that has the power to save your souls" (James 1:19, 21). Good listening begins by welcoming the "implanted word," the message of the gospel that grows in us. It does not begin with—or include—a lot of "Why?" questions that often mask the listener's frustration and anger and feels more like an interrogation that makes the responder defensive.

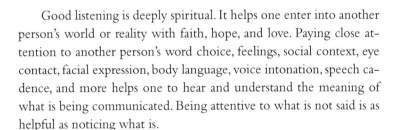

> Good listening becomes an act of prayer.

Good listening is deeply spiritual. It helps one enter into another person's world or reality with faith, hope, and love. Paying close attention to another person's word choice, feelings, social context, eye contact, facial expression, body language, voice intonation, speech cadence, and more helps one to hear and understand the meaning of what is being communicated. Being attentive to what is not said is as helpful as noticing what is.

Such attentiveness, such listening is not easy. It takes work. Just as learning contemplative prayer requires time and patience to overcome one's wandering mind, so too, good listening requires one to learn how to focus one's energies on another soul. In his first lecture, a seminary instructor of pastoral care wrote on the board one word: "Listen." He then turned to the group and asked, "Any questions?" His lecture was over. Listening is that critical.

To listen deeply is a skill worth developing. When deep listening happens during a candid conversation, an intimacy of care can be sensed between the conversational parties. When one party is revealing personal information and emotions, the other person can feel a deep privilege and the speaker can sense deep gratitude for the opportunity of being heard, really heard. Opening up one's deeper issues in life involves a risk that the listener will not trample the moment with inattentiveness or disinterest. When the speaker has offered an occasion to treasure the gift of experiencing another person's inner life, will the listener know she or he is on holy ground?

Listening as an act of a shepherd begins as a prayerful activity, one that seeks not to problem solve but to receive another soul with care, understanding, and faith in the God who became flesh and lived among us—and lives among us now. An individual may have a particular concern and describe it as a problem to be understood a certain way. The speaker may, in fact, want assistance to solve the problem as presented. The challenge is to listen in such a way that the identified problem does not become the whole focus, and to respond in such a way that one does not simply interject one's own situation or solution. If the person has a problem he or she has not been able to resolve, it may be that the problem is not yet fully understood. Giving the speaker time to tell his or her story, entering into the other person's world, is a precious gift rarely offered.

Paying attention to another person's communication gives that other person the opportunity to hear his or her own thoughts. Giving that person the podium and time to speak can help the person expand on her or his thoughts and feelings in ways that allows new insights to emerge. At times like these, the listening party simply needs to nod and say a few "ah-has" to keep the speaker going. It is well to resist the temptation to say, "I understand." When understanding seems to be present and important to announce, one can offer one's perceptions to see if, indeed, one has gained an accurate understanding of the other person's narrative. And then return the focus to the storyteller.

Listening and Reflecting on the Deeper Issues

Conversations regarding faith and doubt are at the top of the list of concerns for a shepherd of the soul. In an age and society that prides itself on independent thinking, opinions, and action, trusting a gracious God epitomizes the basic challenge for the modern believer. How can one know if one truly believes or believes enough to be saved? Such questions emphasize one's own responsibility in knowing, trusting, and loving God in a way that ignores that the primary mover is God knowing and loving us. In addition to the Old Testament assertion that God is the initiator of the covenant relationship with Israel, a whole host of New Testament texts point out God's initiative in faith and knowledge and love of God (e.g., Galatians 4:8–9; Ephesians 2:8–10; 1 Peter 2:9–10; 1 John 4:7–12). The larger question and quandary becomes wondering whether God has chosen or called me. John 6 addresses this by assuring followers of Jesus that those who come to Jesus will not be rejected (v. 37). The pastoral words of 1 John 3:19–20 reassure us that God is more merciful to us than we are to ourselves.

As people grow up, they usually move from childish to mature adult thinking, and need to bridge those maturing thoughts into a maturing faith. In that process, emerging adults often begin to question and doubt the faith of their childhood—though it can happen at any age. This soulful wrestling is not to be feared or discouraged. All four gospels in the New Testament end with issues of fear and doubt. Perhaps one of the most dramatic—and often overlooked—is the ending of Matthew. The resurrected Jesus comes to his disciples and gives them the Great Commission, the command to go and make other disciples throughout the world. However, when the disciples see Jesus, some doubt (Matthew 28:17). What is stunning about this text—according to the standards of those who insist on faith as personal certainty and confidence—is that Jesus does not reject the doubting disciples or send them back to a remedial discipleship course. He sends them all out to build the church with their mixture of worshiping and doubting lives. Somehow, in the midst of very real and human experiences of both worship and doubt, God promises to work amazing things.

A good shepherd of souls need not fear how God is at work in the life of one who wrestles with or doubts God. This biblical acceptance of human fear and doubt gives shepherds of souls the confidence to hear the real concerns without anxiety. The ability to care for lives that struggle with faith is a gift to those wrestling with faith in God. God is greater, more merciful, more loving than our fears and doubts.

Such doubts about God often arise around issues of pain and evil. How can there be pain and evil in a world created by a good and all-powerful God? How come good people experience bad things? In essence, Job asked that question. How could he, one who was described as righteous, experience such pain and suffering? In the end, God honors Job's question but does not answer it. God simply points out that the question leads to a reality that goes beyond Job's human comprehension. The finite cannot fully grasp the infinite.

Despite this biblical reminder about our finite understanding, faithful people still succumb to the temptation to give answers, some of which can sound trite to a grieving soul. Some have responded to the shock of an untimely death by saying that God needed another angel in heaven. Really? Yes, the "answer" seeks to offer comfort, but it is a response that begins to sound like the three friends of Job who were not able to refrain from speaking for God. Sometimes it is better to join the question rather than answer it. It was Jesus who asked the soulful question of the psalmist, "My God, my God, why have you forsaken me?" (Matthew 27:46b). The good news is that Jesus joins our deepest and most painful question by making it his own. He does so by quoting Psalm 22:1, an example of how the prayers of the Bible speak on our behalf. The good news does not grant us the full wisdom of the universe. The gospel grants us a relationship to God, one that can trust God enough to ask the most difficult questions. That itself expresses biblical faith, the faith of Job and the psalmist as well as the faith and trust of Jesus.

If we can dare to ask the deepest questions, questions that express human frailty and doubt, then we can dare to explore a whole host of other questions and concerns as well. A faithful shepherd of souls can tolerate and join the quest for answers to life's deepest questions, knowing that full and satisfying answers will reach beyond our ken. A good shepherd can "[r]ejoice with those who rejoice, weep with those who weep" (Romans 12:15). Being there to join the experience of another and to reflect on that experience with trust and hope is a gift of faith. When someone verbalizes, "Why did this happen?" or "Why did God let this happen?," it is okay, even laudable, not to give an answer. Sometimes listening to the question and enduring the silence is all we need do. Sometimes just responding in a way that acknowledges the question is enough: saying "You'd like some answers," or "It's hard not knowing how this could happen," is enough to join a searching soul in an hour of need.

 Biblical acceptance of human fear and doubt gives shepherds of souls the confidence to hear the real concerns without anxiety.

Not all questions we ask are as painful as the life and death questions that wonder why traumatic things happen to us. Often there are questions about direction for life, for discerning God's will for one's future. Some believers might suggest that God has a specific roadmap for a person and hope that the person will figure it out. Some read that into Romans 8:28: "We know that all things work together for good for those who love God, who are called according to his purpose." However, another understanding of that text is that whatever decisions are made in faith and love, God's will is for good to happen. It is good because God is present in a relationship of faith and trust. Especially when serving as a shepherd of souls, we do well to remember that the core of God's will is for people to believe in Jesus as the Son of God and have eternal life (John 6:40).

With that foundation, a shepherd of souls is liberated to reflect and wonder with another soul what may be in store for that person. The relationships, careers, priorities, and daily decisions to which one commits can all be pursued in faith with a desire to love God and neighbor. How we can do those things to the best of our abilities are issues we are freed to explore as saints who have been liberated by the work of God through Christ. Paul states this well when he writes to the church in Galatia, "For you were called to freedom, brothers and sisters; only do not use your freedom as an opportunity for self-indulgence, but through love become slaves to one another. For the whole law is summed up in a single commandment, 'You shall love you neighbor as yourself'" (Galatians 5:13–14). It is a gift of the body of Christ to have others on the journey with us as we look for what steps to take next. Those loving sojourners in Christ we call shepherds.

> A faithful shepherd of souls can tolerate and join the quest for answers to life's deepest questions.

Prayers That Relate to Common Human Experiences

The Psalms, the prayerbook of the Bible, serves the shepherd of souls well. It gives language to our questions and experiences, to our thoughts and to our feelings whether of rapturous joy or of deep despair. The prayers of the Psalms depict real fears, real grief, real repentance, and real hope and trust. The prayers speak in poetic terms of mercy and make unrefined requests for vengeance and judgment. Above all, such prayers of the Bible are honest prayers, the kind that communicate an authentic relationship to a real God who is able to hear and accept the cries of despair and the praise and thanksgiving of joy.

Grace was visiting Freda, a friend hospitalized for depression after an attempted suicide. Freda told Grace that God could not understand her despair. Every night she went to bed and cried herself to

A Basic Guide for All Shepherds   89

sleep. She admitted she felt utterly abandoned by God. Grace acknowledged how difficult that feeling must be and added that perhaps God could understand her emotions and despair better than Freda imagined. She pointed out how Christ from the cross cried out with the words of Psalm 22:1, "My God, my God, why have you forsaken me?" Grace also noted that people over centuries have used the Psalms to express similar feelings as Freda's. Grace read from Psalm 6:6-7a the lament, "I am weary with my moaning; every night I flood my bed with tears; I drench my couch with my weeping. My eyes waste away because of grief." Grace asked if some of those words expressed what Freda was going through. Freda's eyes opened wide with utter surprise that the Bible communicated her very thoughts and feelings. Grace did not assume that Freda's depression would be overcome by reading a few words from the Psalms. But Grace did want her to imagine that, as alone as she felt, perhaps God did know something of what she was going through, and that others had gone through similar times as well. Even in Freda's despair, perhaps she could hear that God was in her corner.

Grace encouraged Freda to read and pray some of these psalms that seemed to express her grief and came back to visit her over the following days and weeks to talk and pray with her in the hospital. Over time, Grace was able to point out that even the psalms that expressed Freda's deep sorrow also included words of confidence and trust—even praise to God—that things would be better some day. Grace noted that Psalm 22, which begins with an expression of utter abandonment, ends up proclaiming, "I will tell of your name to my brothers and sisters; in the midst of the congregation I will praise you: You who fear the LORD, praise him" (22:22–23a). Without demanding a change in Freda's emotional state, this shepherd of souls walked with this deeply hurting woman to convey that she was not beyond God's care even though it felt like it to her. Freda acknowledged that while she was not there yet, she could see that there were people who had similar pains as hers and who eventually moved beyond them.

Like Grace, a shepherd of souls is a sojourner in faith, whose daily life enables another person to hear and experience a message of hope and find support in their journey. A brother or sister in Christ can be a shepherd to another by showing hospitality and care, by listening and providing support, by responding to the needs of another or a group of people like a family or group of friends. Caring for another person with the love of God helps lessen their anxiety during a personal storm. A caring shepherd can claim the victory of Christ for another who as yet cannot do so. God's word and work are not dependent upon our feelings (recall 1 John 3:19–20).

 God was in her corner.

Shepherding in times of pain and grief means leaving behind more comfortable emotions to walk with another into the valley of the shadow of death. The ability to listen and remain silent can sometimes offer the greatest benefit to the hurting soul. The danger is to avoid the hurting person because one does not know what to do or say. Another temptation is to say too much in an attempt to erase the difficult moment. It is okay, even desirable at times, not to claim answers to the "Why?" or the "How?" of one's painful dilemma. Being present to another during their pain and confusion can itself serve as a prayer of hope.

Supporting Individuals Strengthens the Whole Community

Shepherding builds up the body of Christ by supporting one another in the challenges and the joys of daily living. Such support is not first and foremost about skills, techniques, or having the right answers but about "faith made effective in love."[2] The Christian community, the community of shepherds, is founded on "speaking the truth in love" (Ephesians 4:15), an approach that builds up the body of Christ and pursues life together in unity (Ephesians 4:11-16). Yes, we can become better listeners over time. Our prayerful words can move from trust in the cultural religion of personal success, material possessions, and sporadic happiness to trust in the God of the Bible. Our mastery of language can improve to speak more clearly and our social skills can be refined to know when to listen and when to speak. Our life experiences can grow and help us to see pitfalls on the path of life. Nonetheless, all of that pales in comparison to the faith grounding the shepherd brings to any relationship. That grounding is the solid rock of faith in Christ that moves us to care for others as we have been cared for. It is a faith freed to announce God's loving presence, a faith that acknowledges our forgiveness, a faith that expresses joy at being claimed as a beloved child of God. This mutuality of care is given and received through the community that is known by and that knows Christ. The activity of shepherding souls simply expresses the New Testament directive to care for others with the love of God in Christ. And this means that anyone of any age can do it.

A child can be a shepherd of souls with a hug, a listening ear, a word of comfort, by offering a prayer or by asking for help on behalf of another. Grandmother JoAnne was deeply saddened because her mother was seriously ill and at the point of death. JoAnne's son-in-law Scott, knowing the depth of her sorrow, came to visit her with her three-year-old granddaughter Gabriela, someone whose loving presence he thought would be of help. Gabriela was being held in Grandmother's arms as Grandmother was weeping. Gabriela had never experienced her grandmother crying before and did not know what to do. Gabriela turned to her dad who was in the room and simply said, "Help." That plea from Gabriela expressed concern for her grandmother and her own need of assistance. Scott stepped forward and together the three held each other with a warm embrace. In the midst of the embrace a little laughter emerged from both JoAnne and Scott as they thought about Gabriela's sweet and simple plea for help. A blessing followed that included making the sign of the cross on Grandmother's forehead accompanied by words of love and faith that were deeply meaningful expressions of Christ's care for Grandmother. The intervention of both the little girl and her dad was a simple and meaningful expression of shepherding. JoAnne was cared for, Gabriela gained a valuable lesson in the importance of care, and all three were strengthened with God's love during a sad time.

People who enter into a new Christian fellowship particularly benefit from shepherding. This can be in the form of being mentored or sponsored by someone through an initial period that helps the new person feel accepted as part of the new community. It also happens more informally as the established group understands the importance of hospitality expressed so well in Romans 15:7: "Welcome one another, therefore, just as Christ has welcomed you, for the glory of God."

I think here of Galen, who started going to his congregation's youth group as a new ninth grader. At the time, he was not aware of how his parents' strained marriage was shrouding his own emotions and relationships. To his amazement, he was warmly welcomed into the youth group by the adult counselors and the other youth. He began to experience a sense of joy with others that he rarely experienced at home. A few of the older youth took particular interest in welcoming him and made him feel as though he had gained some older brothers and sisters, people who cared for him, listened to him, and shared with him their own life stories and experiences in ways he had not experienced before. It took him decades to be able to name it, but the support and positive relationships he experienced in the group during his high school years had a life-changing impact on him. Shepherding can look like that, too.

Using Worship and Bible in Shepherding

The act of shepherding changes us when we enter into the uncertainties and darkness of our fragile relationships and our larger experience of humanity. It leads to our own growth in the grace of God as we experience God in worship, in study of and reflection on God's word, and in community. Kenneth Leech expresses this well. He writes that spiritual growth "comes as a result of being opened up and confronted by realities which disturb and transform us: the reality of the word of God, challenging, piercing, shaking us; the reality of the encounter with ourselves, with God and with the depths in other people, through silence and darkness."[3] Entering into the depths of one's own life experiences as well as those of others represents a journey where one loses control of the path and the destination. All that is known—all that needs to be known—is that the Good Shepherd meets one along the way with grace, mercy, and peace. Shepherding one another is an exercise in seeking and trusting the presence of God with the word of God.

 Shepherding changes us when we enter into the uncertainties and darkness of our fragile relationships.

People can attend public worship and study the Bible in groups or alone and still not perceive how they are being equipped and molded to shepherd others in the redeeming and reconciling work of God. Being addressed by the word of God is not a passive experience. It leads to the jarring and joyous life of faith that loves God and others. However, worship and the study of the Bible are ways both to support one's own Christian faith and to equip the members of the body of Christ for ministry. Worship and Scripture are not just private sources of strength. They bless and challenge those who hear and see God's word in action to serve the world as a shepherd of souls.

Ephesians 5:15–20 expresses a deep concern that the community of faith live wisely and not foolishly. It offers sound instruction for wise and effective shepherding. This biblical counsel leads to a life "filled with the Spirit" through communal worship that includes singing psalms and hymns, a life of worship that gives "thanks to God the Father at all times and for everything in the name of our Lord Jesus Christ." For such Christian worship strengthens the Christian community and the care for one another.

The book of Psalms likewise offers a wonderful model for the life of a shepherd. For it covers the gamut of emotion and intimacy with God and neighbor, from joy and gladness to deep grief, from the bliss of life in community to the discouragement of betrayal, from a spirit of genuine confidence in the face of life's challenges to soulful repentance, from gratitude and thanksgiving to a desire for vengeance. It is all there. Through it all, the Psalms aid the shepherd in telling his or her own life of faith. That itself provides a foundation for meaningful contact with others. It serves as a permission-giving script for truth telling. It frees us to be honest with God and before others because we have been reconciled, redeemed, and sent out renewed day by day. It is no accident that the Psalms have been a source of prayer and meditations for Christians throughout the ages.

Shepherding includes telling one's own story as a testimony to the goodness of God through all of life's experiences and emotions. It is important for others to hear someone's story of God's goodness. Psalm 116 offers us an example of this. The psalmist's struggles and God's faithfulness are recounted for others to know so that others may join in the chorus of thankfulness (v. 14, 18–19). The shepherd likewise needs the encouragement of that story to recall God's goodness the next time he or she goes through a valley of despair.

 Shepherding includes telling one's own story as a testimony to the goodness of God.

Of course, the larger biblical narrative helps one pray and tell one's story of faith as well. The Scriptures are filled with human drama that weaves people's joys and struggles in the presence of a righteous and demanding yet merciful God. The human dramas of those who have come before us give us hope and good courage in the face of the unknowns. It is good to know and to reflect on the lives of biblical characters like Abraham and Sarah, Jacob and Esau, Moses, Aaron and Miriam, Hannah and Samuel, Saul, David, Solomon, Ruth and Naomi, Mary and Joseph, the disciples, the women at the cross and empty tomb, and a host of other people and stories that are recorded in the Bible. The better one knows the rich story of faith from the

Bible, the more one can rely on the biblical characters' witness to be a faithful shepherd today.

For example, while caring for someone who has lost a loved one, it is helpful to recall Jesus' own story of grieving with Mary and Martha following the death of their brother Lazarus (John 11:32-44). Jesus exuded confidence knowing he was about to raise Lazarus to life again, yet he was nonetheless moved to grieve and weep with Mary and Martha. Confidence in the presence, work, and will of God and grief can certainly co-exist. Some believers think that Paul is discouraging grieving when he writes, "But we do not want you to be uninformed, brothers and sisters, about those who have died, so that you may not grieve as other do who have no hope" (1 Thessalonians 4:13). For them, grieving is a sign of disbelief. However, in the context of Jesus' own weeping and the depth of grief expressed in other biblical passages, a different interpretation can emerge. Christians are actually free to express the depths of their grief precisely because they know there is an end to the grief, for there will come a time when God "will wipe every tear from their eyes. Death will be no more; mourning and crying and pain will be no more, for the first things have passed away" (Revelation 21:4).

Four Key Faith Practices of Shepherding

Four basic faith practices can assist effective shepherding. Conversation, reflection, and prayer take place through the Four Key Faith Practices of: caring conversations, devotions, service, and rituals and traditions. Being alert to these four practices helps clarify and facilitate the important work of shepherding souls.

The Four Key Faith Practices are faith-nurturing activities of the church. Conversations that emerge from the lives of Christians have a devotional center to them. Whether conscious or not, caring conversations are anchored in the person's own soul that is shaped by grace through faith in Jesus Christ. So conversations offered in faith—and for faith—have a devotional quality to them.

Devotions, the second of the Four Key Faith Practices, connect daily life with the word of God so that people have a sense of hope and faith and love grounded in the love of God most fully revealed in Jesus Christ. To actively engage in a devotional life strengthens one's awareness of the God-centeredness of our lives, including our thoughts, words, and actions reflected in conversations, service, rituals, and traditions of the faith.

Service, the third of the Four Keys, embodies the life of a follower of Jesus. Jesus came to serve and not to be served (Matthew 20:28 and Mark 10:45). He states quite unequivocally that a disciple who wants to be first in the reign of God must be last of all and servant of all (Matthew 20:26 and Mark 9:35). Shepherding another soul is a form of service.

Fourth, Christian rituals and traditions remind us who and whose we are as we reflect on our lives, interact with the world, and care for others. Such rituals and traditions will often involve caring conversations, have a devotional core, and offer service to others as personal experiences are celebrated or mourned.

Though named as distinct and foundational faith practices, these four are inseparable. To do one of the Four Key Faith Practices as a shepherd of souls will likely engage a shepherd with one or more of the other Four Key Faith Practices. What follows is a closer examination of each of these four practices as a way to live as a shepherd of souls.[4]

 Shepherding another soul is a form of service.

1. Various occasions to shepherd another person with caring conversations
At the heart of caring conversations is listening. This listening connects us not only to the voices of others but also to the voice of God. To be a good listener of the soul requires that one pay attention to the word of God as well as to the needs, interests, and passions of one's neighbor. A shepherd of souls listens for topics related to grief and the need for affirmation and forgiveness when people are hurting. The shepherd also pays attention to dreams, aspirations, and decision

making when future action is being contemplated. And through it all, she attends to the soul's search for meaning, especially as it is grounded in the desire for a loving, renewing, and gracious God. A good listener helps another person tell and accept their life story with grace. This does not exclude the possibility of guiding or even correcting another person, as long as that instruction and admonition is done with care, wisdom, and with a spirit of gratitude instead of a punitive or belittling intent (see Colossians 3:12–17).

The power and critical importance of forgiveness cannot be overestimated. From the beginning to the end of the gospels, forgiveness is announced as a central claim of the good news of Jesus Christ. Humans need to hear a word of forgiveness and to extend that same word to others. At times it seems that it is hardest to receive and offer forgiveness to those closest to us. Helping to liberate others by the power of forgiveness is a great gift of shepherding, especially when the person most difficult to forgive is oneself. Having a trusted friend or mentor to help one take that liberating step in life and relationships is a valuable gift.

While the Christian faith recognizes the need for forgiveness as a result of a guilty heart, offering a word of forgiveness may be misplaced if one's situation is not clearly heard. For example, feeling shame has to do with a seriously bruised self-image. It is not so much that the person has done something wrong, something to feel guilty about as that there is something fundamentally wrong with the person's self-worth and sense of belonging. Forgiveness is about guilt for doing something wrong, a wrongful act. Shame is about the unacceptability of who one is, someone not lovable or forgivable.[5] Offering a word of forgiveness does not accurately address shame. In fact, it can be counterproductive. What one needs to hear when the person is struggling with self-doubt and shame is the baptismal message: "You are God's beloved child" (Matthew 3:17 and 17:5; Mark 1:11 and 9:7; Luke 3:22 and 9:35; John 1:12–13; and Galatians 3:26–29). Offering a word of forgiveness can exacerbate a person's sense of low self-worth and isolation. What one needs is affirmation. In such instances, a thoughtful shepherd will remind the person that he or she is someone so loved by God that Jesus would die on a cross to show that love and to reach out and call that person by name.

Grief likewise benefits from shepherding. Experiencing grief when someone dies is its most evident form, but grief has many causes and shapes. People grieve lost or damaged relationships, a changed direction in one's life, or even an altered self-understanding from that which one held in the past. Shepherding people through a wide range of losses benefits from observant listening that includes paying attention both to the emotions being expressed and those that are being ignored or denied.

Being present to hear a person's hopes and dreams is also an important task of shepherding. Listening to one's passions and interests and linking them to a person's skills and abilities serves a crucial role in helping another person make decisions that live out their sense of vocation, their calling in life. This is best done in a community of shepherds who can bring diverse observations and thoughts to the conversation. It is an example of testing the spirits (1 John 4:1) to discern what is faithful to Jesus Christ. Everyday conversations go a long way to help others live lives that are faithful, satisfying, and that serve the world around them.

Giving advice and correcting someone are best when used quite sparingly. When done well and in love, advice giving and admonition can be greatly appreciated and life altering. Done poorly and in anger, they can lessen the impact of the intended soul care. Well experienced elders may come by this a bit more naturally. An older brother offered a younger brother much-needed instruction when the younger brother was being very critical of their dad. The older brother advised the younger to be easier on Dad because Dad, as fallible as he is, is trying as hard as he can to be a good parent. The older brother's words offered important help to the family relationships, especially to a younger brother who needed to hear from a trusted older brother that dads need help, tolerance, and forgiveness too. The one who suggests that a friend go on the congregation's foreign mission trip to expand her horizons on how to value and love others who are different from her can be making a life-changing impact on the friend. This is especially true if that friend stays connected to the parishioner following the mission trip to help process that person's new experiences and emerging insights. Comparing those experiences and insights with the person's assumptions and worldview before the trip can be immensely helpful for personal growth in faith and in acceptance of people who come from a different culture.

2. Devotions: Practicing the Presence of God

Devotions mean different things to people of different Christian traditions. In this book, it means to practice the presence of God with the word of God. The word of God is first Jesus Christ, the Word made flesh (John 1:14), second, the message of Jesus (1 Thessalonians 2:13), and, third, the word of God in the Bible. With this understanding, public worship fits into the practice of devotions. In fact, worship done well provides the examples and resources to continue a daily devotional life in the home and beyond. To "practice the presence of God" is the language of Brother Lawrence (1614–1691) who believed he could worship God as well by scrubbing floors as by joining his fellow monks in the chapel. The devotional life that seeks an awareness of God's saving presence is thus a gift of faith not to be ignored or minimized, a gift that can be employed in public worship, in the home, while driving the car, on a walk, or countless other places and occasions.

To shepherd others with the devotional life is to be present in such a way that God's presence is also acknowledged. A common practice for many Christians is to say to someone experiencing a real concern or crisis, "I will pray for you." This expresses that it is God's presence that binds the individuals together in trust and hope for the future. An extension of that statement would be actually to pray for the person in that moment. Depending on the setting, this can be done with brevity or with a social media text that offers the intended prayer. To promise to pray for someone is good. To stop and pray with or for that person, when the situation permits it, is better, as the following example shows.

Carmen had just lost her young adult son to a tragic accident, and she and her husband Denny were beside themselves with grief. Aaron and Juanita called to extend their condolences and to let them know that Carmen, Denny, and the extended family were part of their prayers. They made it clear they would be at the funeral and would see Carmen and Denny in the near future. At the end of the call, Aaron offered a prayer. Carmen expressed deep appreciation for the prayer and said she wished it had been recorded. Aaron did the best he could to recall what he had prayed and wrote it in a sympathy card to the family. His written prayer was, "Dear God, we thank you for Tony, a sheep of your own flock, a child you have redeemed in love. You called him by name and he is yours. You loved him and you love him still with your promise of life eternal. We thank you for Tony, his life, his smile, his warmth, his care for others, his faith in you through all the ups and downs of life. In Christ's name we pray, amen." Aaron's prayer was filled with biblical images and a clear and loving picture of Tony. At least for Carmen, it was evident that she experienced the grace and presence of God in that prayer.

Besides prayer, there are countless other ways of practicing the presence of God as a shepherd with others. Sharing a Bible passage with someone can inspire trust and courage. Some people have cards in their homes or with them in a purse or billfold that have Bible passages on them with pictures or with related conversation starters, prayers, and other faith practices to initiate personal or group reflection.[6] These are simple yet meaningful ways of connecting others with the word of God to nurture faith, encourage people in daily life, and enjoy the bond of faith and peace that God's word brings.

One of the great—and largely untapped—treasures of the church is receiving God's word in informal settings and, often, with a brevity of words. It can be as simple as offering a mealtime prayer. A prayer is a form of proclamation, words that articulate the faith and trust of an individual or group of individuals. An evening conversation amongst family and friends that includes a reflection on a biblical passage or pursues questions of faith and meaning can go a long way to deepen people's lives of faith and people's relationships within the faith community. Reflecting on the words of a hymn or a recent sermon can do the same. Welcoming others or sending them on their way with words that express the peace of the risen Christ (John 21:19, 21, 26) offers encouragement to the body of Christ.

A Basic Guide for All Shepherds 101

3. Service: being a servant of God's love

The Christian practice of service gets at the heart of Jesus' ministry. He said to his disciples, "whoever wishes to be great among you must be your servant, and whoever wishes to be first among you must be your slave; just as the Son of Man came not to be served but to serve, and to give his life a ransom for many" (Matthew 20:26–28). The church, the body of Christ, is now the hands and feet and voice of God in the world. A follower of Jesus is someone who serves their neighbor (Matthew 25:31-46) with the love of God.

A shepherd of souls serves another person in a number of ways, including conversation, prayer, and reflection. The activity of the shepherd of souls is enhanced by other occasions to be present to serve. Through acts of care, trust is developed to establish a shepherding relationship. If someone has real physical needs and the response is "Go in peace" without caring for the real needs of that person, that reveals a rather empty spirituality and shepherding (James 2:14–17). Just as shepherding is a form of service, serving the physical and emotional needs of others can be the start or deepening of a shepherding relationship.

4. Rituals and traditions

The final foundational faith practice involves rituals (patterned behaviors, gestures, and symbols that convey a deeper meaning) and traditions (routine activities used over time to convey meaning). Our society has just come through an age in which rituals and traditions have often been dismissed as archaic and unimportant. However, a deeper look at human behavior indicates that all humans use rituals and traditions to celebrate and memorialize the life they value. Whether it be chants at a sports event, placards, whistles, cheers and groans at a political rally, birthday parties, meals, hugs and kisses at a family gathering, or the gestures, words, and sequence of events at a religious service, rituals and traditions are expected and relied upon to give meaning, order, and value to the occasions.

A gift of a shepherd is to have a home that values rituals and traditions that reflect the hope and confidence that Christ brings. The use of particular kinds of art and home furnishings adds to one's ability to engage in caring conversations, devotions, and service to others as a part of one's trust in Jesus Christ. Displaying a cross or a picture of a biblical story makes a clear statement about where one places trust and faith. Having a place in the home that displays the Bible, cross, and a place for prayerful meditation (perhaps with a chair nearby or even a simple prayer kneeler) for use in the home also presents a clear message to others and a reminder to oneself that all who enter this home are on holy ground.

When entering people's homes, one expects activities and visual cues about what the residents of that home stand for and treasure. A simple greeting of "Peace be with you," or a hug or handshake gives a clear sense of welcome that the visitor's presence is anticipated with a sense of gladness. Entering these same homes leads others to expect conversations that bond lives around the deeper interests and concerns of life, often marked by a word of prayer and perhaps a reflection on a Bible story or text. These same homes can offer friends and families a table grace when there is a meal and a blessing when the guests leave. Even the word "good-bye" was originally received as a blessing, a contraction of the longer "God be with ye." Giving a blessing to children going to bed or guests leaving with the words, "May the word of Christ dwell in you richly" (Colossians 3:16), promotes a sense of calm as people go to sleep or travel home.

Not all of these options will be equally appreciated by all people. Awareness of who is present and what can serve them the best remains an important skill for the shepherd. However, reclaiming simple yet significant rituals and traditions make a shepherd's home a place of peace, hope, and joy, a place to engage in conversations, prayer, and reflection that touch the valued interpersonal experiences of the Christian faith.

A benefit of the Four Key Faith Practices to shepherding is that these practices fit comfortably into daily life relationships, more so than asking people to sit down and bare their souls. Having a conversation, acknowledging an awareness of God's presence, valuing others through service, and enjoying social interactions through thoughtful rituals and traditions can happen anytime. Such faith practices can offer gentle clues that affirm the centrality of the Christian faith

A Basic Guide for All Shepherds 103

in people's lives and between personal relationships. They establish a setting that makes it easier to support one another throughout life. Whether it be before a surgery, when one goes off to college, while establishing a more intimate relationship, celebrating a new home or job, fretting over unemployment or underemployment, loss of a loved one, having a new child, letting go of a child to an adult milestone like college, military, work or marriage, caring for an aging parent, or countless other moments worthy of attention, care, and faith, the Four Key Faith Practices can make it easier to journey deeper into the world of conduct, character, faith, values, and hope with another soul.

 A gift of a shepherd is to have a home that values rituals and traditions that reflect the hope and confidence that Christ brings.

Things One Might Learn along the Green and Dry Pastures of Shepherding

Listening to and noting the presence of another person as a child of God reflects the ministry of a shepherd. It provides the setting to support one another with a living faith, a faith that rejoices, struggles, and lives with God and others daily. Shepherding brings deep joy to the preciousness and vulnerability of daily life and of being a follower of Jesus Christ. It gives meaning, hope, and courage to life experienced with friends, family, and others one meets along the way.

Yet as we live our lives as shepherds of the soul, we discover that the efforts to listen, stay in touch, and encourage one another in the journey of faith can be difficult. Paying attention is a challenge to our wandering minds. When mindful that you have wandered away from the thoughts being expressed by another, without being overly self-critical, return your attention to the other person. Make a conscious effort not to let your mind wander to your own thoughts, feelings, and activities. Make it your goal to be part of the conversation without trying to take over the conversation. Summarize what you think you are hearing and reflect back to the person the emotions as well as the content of the conversation. Although it is best not to make it into a routine formula, it is okay to begin your comments with something like, "What I hear you saying is . . ." or "I sense you are feeling . . ." Let that be a way to make sure you actually are following the other person's communication. It also helps to assure the speaker that you are, in fact, listening and caring about the other person and his or her concerns. Other simple behaviors can also help, like turning off a screen that can distract you or the other person, and facing the person instead of looking away. It is helpful to maintain eye contact, but without a stare that intimidates.

After you are confident you are hearing the other person with some measure of accuracy, then it is time to dance with the other person using your own wit, wisdom, experience and, of course, living faith and prayers. Be ready to share part of your own faith story, the thoughts, images, and feelings that emerge for you about living the Christian life—not to make yourself the center of attention, but to wonder whether any of your journey of faith helps the other see his or her situation more clearly.

A kind and courageous shepherd can accept difficult and heavy conversations without needing to leave. To stay with the person's stormy thoughts and feelings can be a test of one's ability to be present and support the other. If the listener has the strength to stay and hear the story, the concern, or the crisis, then maybe the scenario is not as scary as the speaker might have imagined. On the other hand, to cut short someone's narrative can suggest to the speaker that the situation is either too boring or too dangerous to hear.

Shepherding is also important during times of joy and celebration. Learning of an engagement or being at a wedding, hearing the announcement of a new job or promotion, joining others in the joy of bringing a new life home through birth, adoption, or foster care, celebrating a graduation from school or the completion of a major task, witnessing the performance of a work of art, all of these and more are worthy of attention and thanksgiving. And while the joy and thankfulness will be real, a good shepherd can celebrate the moment and remain ready for when the relationships are strained, the workload unbearable, or the new joy has faded into the demands and pressures of daily life. An experienced shepherd stays alert to follow a person into the deeper waters of life.

Shepherding trusts that the pastures lead to places far and wide. It is not necessary to resolve personal problems or questions of faith with a brief or one-time conversation. Committing to get back together to continue to explore the topic can give both parties time, space, and freedom to pray, daydream, and imagine ways of seeing the situation in new ways. There is a bit of healing already taking place with the promise to listen and speak again.

It can and does happen that on rare occasions a conversation has entered into deeply troubled waters. At such times, a shepherd needs to know that there are other shepherds to turn to, other shepherds available like family, friends, and mentors and professionals like teachers, pastors, counselors, and social workers.

These and other intentional and learned behaviors and understandings that one will gain over time as part of the body of Christ, the body of the Good Shepherd, will help a person care for and shepherd another soul. Faith encourages a way of life, and that way of life supports one's confidence in the Christian faith. Everything needed for the life of a disciple has been given, so that one may "make every effort" to live the "faith with goodness, and goodness with knowledge, and knowledge with self-control, and self-control with endurance, and endurance with godliness, and godliness with mutual affection, and mutual affection with love" (1 Peter 1:5–7). The life of a Christian moves in the direction of understanding and discipline that leads to the reciprocity of affection. All are to care for—to shepherd—one another in a spirit of love. As 1 Peter continues, "Now that you have purified your souls by your obedience to the truth so that you have genuine mutual love, love one another deeply from the heart" (1:22). A shepherd of souls has a sense of what it means to be freed to love one another from the heart.

Questions for Reflection and Conversation

1. What most captures your heart or attention from this chapter? Why do you think that is?

2. What do you look for in a trusted shepherd? What are the qualities that draw you to a fellow shepherd?

3. Give an example of when you have felt truly heard.

4. Give an example of when you felt you were truly focused on another person's conversation in a caring way. How did that seem to impact the other person? How did it impact you?

5. How has someone responded to you when you were in pain or grief that helped you cope with that moment?

6. What are some Scriptures that comfort you in difficult times? What about some that help you celebrate the joyous times? How have you used those Scriptures to comfort others or to help them express joy?

7. How do you use the Four Key Faith Practices—perhaps without even realizing it—to be a shepherd of souls to others?

8. What is something you have learned about caring for another person that you could pass along to others?

9. One of the challenges in today's world is the intrusion of electronic tools for communication that can, ironically, distract us from personal contact with others. How do these electronic devices and programs help you communicate with others? How do they get in the way of deeper listening to the soul of another? What might you do to limit the intrusion of the technologies and maximize their benefits?

10. Do you feel nudged in some way to more deeply engage or support the work of shepherding souls? In your own life as a shepherd of souls? In the life of another? Who might that be? Jot down your thoughts on the blank pages at the end of this book.

Shepherding in the Home

> Children, obey your parents in the Lord, for this is right. "Honor your father and mother"—this is the first commandment with a promise: "so that it may be well with you and you may live long on the earth." And, fathers, do not provoke your children to anger, but bring them up in the discipline and instruction of the Lord. *Ephesians 6:1–4*

There is a reason why a focus on the home comes now and not after other chapters on how congregational leadership and activities can equip people as shepherds of souls. This chapter belongs here to emphasize that the shepherding ministry of the church often takes place outside the walls of the congregational church. It happens more often in the domestic church, whether that is in a dwelling place or a pub, anywhere people can gather to nurture lives of faith through personal, trusted relationships (See the Five Principles in Appendix 1 for a review of the central perspectives guiding this book).

That the work of a congregation is to support the faith life of the home is eminently expressed in research done in a congregation. A mother stated, "My husband and I . . . can see clearly the difference between our two older children and our two younger children. . . . [W]hen we were raising the older children, the church didn't equip us with any tools. We were kind of winging it on our own; we were trying our best but we weren't taught the kinds of things we are being taught now. You know those Four Keys [Four Key Faith Practices], caring conversation, ritual and traditions."[1] This book hopes to correct that sense of abandonment and confusion on the part of families and others who want to be guided and encouraged by the Christian faith.

For those connected with a congregation, there is no reason for parents and other caregivers to be "winging it on our own." And yet it happens often in the church today. In spite of four decades of research on the importance of parents and other caregivers in faith formation and in spite of the emergence of resources and congregational trainings in this area, the vast majority of households that are actively involved in a congregation continue to have a negligible experience of a faith life in the home. It is a sad statement about congregational life that parents and grandparents confess that they have no idea of how to bring their own Christian faith into the lives of their homes. Countless adults who have been lifelong members of the church acknowledge their deep sadness that their young adult children or grandchildren are not part of any faith community. In the same breath, they also acknowledge with pain that they do not know how to make the Christian faith part of their relationships with their children and grandchildren. Regrettable, indeed.

It is long overdue to recognize the relational, home-centered and lay-led church guided by shepherds of souls that reaches deeply into cross+generational relationships, and creates fertile ground for the Spirit's work for faith formation and outreach to the larger world. The outcome of a faithful—or "vital"—congregation will then be to equip daily life relationships within and beyond individual households to shepherd the world in love, a love that is not first and foremost a warm emotion but rather a commitment to the needs of all for the sake of the reign of God in Christ.

Some people may say that today's church is making strides to overcome the failed programmatic and expert-ridden paradigm of the past decades and move ahead in a way that truly nurtures the

Christian faith and reaches out to others with the gospel of Jesus Christ. However, until individual congregations and the larger institutional church can acknowledge and confess their part in minimizing the role of the home in nurturing the Christian faith, no real progress will be made.[2] True, there are pastors and congregations that are making great strides in partnering with the home. However, overall few value the home as a meaningful expression of the church. The negative sentiments regarding the role of the home are made evident by pastors and other leaders who bemoan the idea that parents are not helping the congregation do its ministry, instead of bemoaning how the congregation is not assisting parents in doing their ministry. Yes, parents are resistant to a model of faith formation that focuses on the home, but what does one expect after decades of messaging from congregations that basically says, "Bring your kids to us and we will raise them for you in the Christian faith"?[3] A positive change will truly happen when congregational leaders move beyond programmatic thinking to thinking like a shepherd of souls, that is, people walking alongside parents, grandparents, and other mentors in prayer and conversation to seek solutions that help people recover the holy ground of their lives together in faith. This will require many small steps that begin to give the home more and more positive experiences of relating to one another in faith and love. After all these years of running around as chauffeurs and time managers for their children, it will require patience and persistence for parents and children to see and experience the joy and hope found in the fruit of the Spirit (Galatians 5:22–25), renewing and enlivening relationships in the home.

Clarifying the Language of "Home"

The home as a focus for faith formation and outreach requires defining. The concept of "home" means something distinct from "family." For many people, their experience of home will largely be understood through nuclear family life, but it need not—and dare not—be limited to one's immediate family relationships. Home as understood here is that place and community that supports people in their daily lives over time. This support has spiritual, emotional, cognitive, physical, and financial implications. The people who populate a person's home may not actually live with them. It may be that community of friends and family to which one turns regularly for sustenance.

More and more people live in configurations beyond that of a traditionally imagined family of spouse with children. Some live as single adults with or without others in one dwelling. Some live as multiple family units living under the same roof because of finances, divorce, or simply because people are recovering a sense of family that goes beyond blood and legal kinship. Some have a community of support for their daily lives that is experienced through routine gatherings of people from work, school, or community. These small groups of confidants would generally include family, friends, and mentors and could be described as "my family" or "my people" or another designation that honors a special personal and trusted relationship. These people and relationships serve as vital partners in ministry in the church, people who have more regular contact and impact than bishop, pastor, Sunday school teacher, or youth director.

Recently I heard of two young adult men in Melbourne, Australia who were discussing their own sense of home life. One declared that he was glad the language was about the church in the home instead of in the family. The language of family was problematic for him. He currently lived in a major university town hours away from his parents. The other young adult asked the first one if his current dwelling with three other young men felt like home. There was a rather long pause then a response that he thought so. The second young adult did not have that sense with his housemates. As they discussed their different views and experiences, a significant difference for the two was that the one man had meals with his housemates a couple of times a week. That made the relationships feel a lot more like home. The other acknowledged no such shared mealtime in his apartment. That void contributed to a lack of a sense of home for him and, he believed, for his housemates.

Another man joined the conversation. He was a pastor from Denmark and a decade older than the other two. He discussed his experiment years before with an intentional community, some of whom lived in the same dwelling and some of whom simply joined with that community on occasion. That group experienced a sense

Shepherding in the Home   111

of "family" by sharing evening meals together. He described it as a kind of agape feast. They would read the words from 1 Corinthians 11:23–26:

> For I received from the Lord what I also handed on to you, that the Lord Jesus on the night when he was betrayed took a loaf of bread, and when he had given thanks, he broke it and said, "This is my body that is for you. Do this in remembrance of me." In the same way he took the cup also, after supper, saying, "This cup is the new covenant in my blood. Do this, as often as you drink it, in remembrance of me." For as often as you eat this bread and drink the cup, you proclaim the Lord's death until he comes.

For the pastor, this ritual at the evening meal was the glue that bound the community together. After years of this intimate life and commitment to one another, people eventually left the community and established new homes and places of work or study. However, instead of a total termination of the home environment, people would periodically return as a whole or in smaller groups and continue the sense of commitment and care that was so important to who they were. In other words, the sense of "family" continued.

This pastor's story gives another example of how people today need and want an experience of family that gives meaning, hope, love, memories, and a sense of security in a world where people can otherwise feel lost and alone. It also relates to the two young adult men who reflected on how eating meals created a sense of home. That element of breaking bread together (see Acts 2:42–47) helps to establish not only a feeling of home but a community committed to one another as shepherds of souls. The tragedy for today's American society is the infrequency with which people in the same home have meals together, especially dinner. The good news is that there is a recovery of mealtime traditions with greater attention to the ritual of putting a real meal together . . . together with others. As an example of this, cooking shows, magazines, and websites are gaining in popularity.

A Biblical Lesson on Shepherding Faith at Home

The role of the home in the life of faith has a long history. It is easy to overlook the fact that the biblical faith of the Old Testament emerged out of the life of an extended family. The God of Abraham, Isaac, and Jacob is the God of a parent, child, and grandchild. The history of that extended family contains the allegiance of God to the family over generations in the midst of Abram's disloyalty to Sarai, Sarah's jealousy of Hagar and Ishmael, the bewildering sacrifice of Isaac (and Abraham), Rebecca's alliance with a younger son over an older son, Jacob's deceit of his father Isaac and his brother Esau, Laban's deceit of his son-in-law Jacob, and the jealousy of Jacob's sons against their brother Joseph. Other intriguing and less-than-honorable stories fill in the family history, but in the end God's will is done to continue the covenant God has with God's chosen people. What people in the lineage of Abraham, Isaac, and Jacob intended as evil was, nonetheless, used for good (Genesis 50:20). Clearly, dysfunctional family life was not a problem for the God of the Bible. Jacob is able to give a blessing to his sons as the next chapter of Israel's history unfolds with the life of Moses whose mother is faithful during a difficult time, and his sister Miriam and brother Aaron play key roles in the unfolding of God's promises to the people.

Modern eyes read the Bible and easily miss the cross+generational basis of faith's transmission, but it is definitely present in the biblical narrative. Deuteronomy 6:4–9, known as the *Shema*, part of which Jesus quotes to name the Great Commandment, has been read morning and night by Jews for more than two millennia. It states clearly, "Keep these commandments that I am commanding you today in your heart. Recite them to your children and talk about them when you are home and when you are away, when you lie down and when you rise" (vv. 6-7). Not only are the commandments to be recited and talked about daily in and out of the home, they are to be made into ritual symbols that are visible on hands and foreheads, on houses and gates (vv. 8–9). These verses and others in the Bible have directed God's people throughout the ages to pass on the faith in and through the home.

Shepherding in the Home   113

The twelve tribes cross the River Jordan and take stones from the river to create an altar. The reason for this altar and these stones is made clear in the story: "When your children ask in time to come, 'What do those stones mean to you?' then you shall tell them that the waters of the Jordan were cut off in front of the ark of the covenant of the LORD" (Joshua 4:6b–7a). The existence of these stones would prompt opportunities to talk about the people's unique history with the God of their ancestors. Along with this biblical ritual of using an altar of stones, a tradition of faith talk and storytelling would meld them as God's people of related tribes again and again and again.

Psalm 78 reminds the people of a similar pattern and expectation of passing on the faith from generation to generation. God "established a decree in Jacob, and appointed a law in Israel, which he commanded our ancestors to teach to their children that the next generation might know them, the children yet unborn, and rise up and tell them to their children, so that they should set their hope in God, and not forget the works of God, but keep his commandments" (vv.5–7). This biblical supposition regarding the role of the home to tell the story and live in faith throughout the generations also reoccurs in the very final verses of the Old Testament: "Lo, I will send you the prophet Elijah before the great and terrible day of the LORD comes. He will turn the hearts of parents to their children and the hearts of children to their parents, so that I will not come and strike the land with a curse" (Malachi 4:5–6). At the conclusion of the Old Testament, the home—not the temple or the synagogue or the congregation—gets the last word as the community that nurtures faith in God.

Yes, the history of the people of God is a very checkered history, but that very history prompts the people to give praise to God with a song: "O give thanks to the LORD, for he is good, for his steadfast love endures forever" (Psalm 136:1). That steadfast love would lead a peasant couple named Joseph and Mary to travel from Nazareth to Bethlehem. That family would regularly return to Jerusalem for the Passover. When their son Jesus was twelve, they followed the tradition again, but this time Jesus became the cause of concern for parents and the amazement of the teachers who heard his questions and

114 Shepherd of Souls

conversations. This time there was a bit of role reversal as the child surprised and confused the parents, leading Mary to ponder and treasure "all these things in her heart" (Luke 2:51b).

And so the Christian faith that emerges from the New Testament narrative remains woven in the tapestry of the home and the faith heritage of the Old Testament. Disciples are called by Jesus who are fellow students, siblings, neighbors, and friends (John 1:35–51). Jesus shepherded this tightly-knit familial group for three years and modeled their own future shepherding with countless conversations and reflections on God's word, all of this done within the context of Jesus' attention to servanthood (Matthew 20:18–28), caring for the healing of bodies and souls. Clearly Jesus mentored his family of disciples in such a way that helped them and the early church develop daily and weekly patterns of faith formation (e.g., Acts 2:41–47; 20:7). Saul (who became Paul) could boast of his family lineage (Acts 23:6 and Philippians 3:4–6). He could also affirm in Timothy the same faith that was first in his grandmother Lois and mother Eunice and also shared through Paul's own laying on of hands like a spiritual father (2 Timothy 1:5–6). There is the faith in the household of Mary, Martha, and Lazarus (John 11:1–44), the households of Lydia (Acts 16:14–15), the Philippian jailer (Acts 16:25–34), Prisca and Aquila (Romans 16:3–5a, 1 Corinthians 16:19), Nympha (Colossians 4:15), Philemon (Philemon 1–2), and the faith assumed to be present in many other household communities throughout the New Testament church and beyond.

The Difficulty of Letting Go of the Primacy of the Pastor

When Martin Luther wrote his *Treatise on Marriage* in 1522, he elevated a church heritage not dominated by the institutional, hierarchical powers of Rome. In so doing, he challenged and redefined the authority of the church in his day. When Luther wrote, "Most certainly, father and mother are apostles, bishops, and priests to their children,"[4] he lifted up the role of the home. Luther emphatically extolled people who were mostly peasants and uneducated to be the primary source of authority for teaching and nurturing the Christian faith to the newest generation. That was a bold and dramatic shift, especially given the challenges and sufferings of these people who lived precariously because of starvation, deadly disease, and other factors that compromised an empowered sense of life. When he wrote, "Whoever teaches the Gospel to another is truly an apostle and bishop,"[5] he included not only parents but also a whole cadre of trusted people who influence faith and daily life. This could include an individual's grandparents, godparents, friends, mentors, colleagues and, in Luther's day, masters working with apprentices. One can imagine the words of Jesus who reordered a sense of power and authority when he said at the end of the parable of the laborers in the vineyard, "So the last will be first, and the first will be last" (Matthew 20:16; see 20:26–28). The real authority and impact in one's life may not be determined by the ecclesiastical elites but by people who are there day in and day out for others. Luther's words assert the formidable reformation theme of the universal priesthood or the priesthood of all believers, something that legitimately might be described as part of the unfinished Reformation.

Many in the church today still reverence the priestly life of clergy over parents and other caregivers. The life dedicated to the visible church structure that relies on clergy still seems to be present today. Luther's radical reappraisal is still waiting to be fully acknowledged. Similar to the priesthood of all believers, the role of the parent as apostle, bishop, and priest and the one for whom there is "no greater or nobler authority on earth"[6] remains part of that same unfinished Reformation.

An Abundance of Evidence

Perhaps Luther was simply wrong. In his desire to distance the Saxon church from the papal grip of Rome, perhaps he went too far. Perhaps it could be argued that Luther speaking of parents in such glowing terms is more hype than reality. But numerous research studies since the 1980s dispute that. They found that no category of people has the influence in a person's faith like that of a mother or father. Whether it is Australia, the United States, or Norway,[7] research continues to show that parents are the primary influences in a child's faith. One might say that parents are the primary shepherds of souls to their children. Yes, grandparents, other adult mentors, and a host of other people—including siblings, children, spouse, friends, and pastors—have their place, but no one surpasses parents as persons who influence one's life of faith.

 No category of people has the influence in a person's faith like that of a mother or father.

The psychologist Alfred Adler observed generations ago that children see in parents a kind of god, someone who is all-knowing and all-powerful. In the experience of children, parents know things in a way that is uncanny, and they can do things that previously were unimaginable. To children, parents have magical powers. They are also some of the first faces children see and voices they hear. Parents utter the sounds that will become the words that express the thoughts that convey the realities around the children. In other words, parents and the life of the home cannot avoid passing along core experiences, values, and faith to the child, whether that faith is a traditional religion or the cultural trust in materialism, nationalism, or hero worship. Most of the religious experience of people's lives has a link to the life of the home in the early years.

It is time that the larger church recognize this notable role of parent as shepherd of souls, a role that extends to the larger experience of the home through grandparents, other trusted adults and siblings, children, and later, spouses and life partners. Some church leaders would argue that not all parents believe the Christian faith or know the basics of the faith, even if these leaders want to affirm and support the role of the home. All that may be true. But the church cannot ignore the influence of the home in shepherding souls. Plus, it is legitimate to ask whether all in the congregation (and even leaders) understand the basics of the Christian faith and truly claim Christ over national flag or pocketbook. It is time for the local congregation to work with the home to offer a vision for the home as a

Shepherding in the Home   117

community of faith. The home is deserving of all that the Christian church can offer to equip the home to nurture the Christian faith. For it is the church in the home that daily addresses the gospel to real issues, real needs, and real lives. A good shepherd of souls wants others to be "at home" with faith, so why not focus on relationships in the home?

Luther did. His reform efforts made the home a centerpiece of faith practice. And he practiced what he preached. In 1530, he wrote a personal letter to his four-year-old son Hans, a letter initiated by a letter from Hans' tutor, Jerome Weller. It is worth noting that the letter was written while Martin Luther was secluded at the castle in Coburg during the Diet of Augsburg. Luther could not attend this historic gathering because he was an enemy of the empire and could not safely attend an official assembly that represented Holy Roman Emperor Charles V. The result of the gathering was the presentation of what came to be one of the most important Protestant confessions of faith, the Augsburg Confession. In spite of the intense moment, Luther was able to write a very fatherly letter to his son:

"To my beloved son Hans Luther in Wittenberg: grace and peace in Christ.

My beloved Son:

I am pleased to learn that you are doing well in your studies and that you are praying diligently. Continue to do so, my son, and when I return home I shall bring you a present from the fair.

I know of a pretty, gay, and beautiful garden where there are many children wearing golden robes. They pick up fine apples, pears, cherries, and plums under the trees, and they sing, jump, and are happy all the time. They also have nice ponies with golden reins and silver saddles. I asked the owner of the garden who the children were. He replied: "These are the children who love to pray, learn their lessons, and be good." Then I said: "Dear sir, I also have a son. His name is Hans Luther. May he too enter the garden, eat of the fine apples and pears, ride

118 Shepherd of Souls

> *on these pretty ponies, and play with the other children?" The*
> *man answered: "If he likes to pray and study and is good, he*
> *may enter the garden, and also Lippus and Jost [two of Hans'*
> *friends]."*

Luther continues his description of the tantalizing garden, then concludes,

> *"Therefore, dear Hans, continue to learn your lessons and*
> *pray, and tell Lippus and Jost to pray too, so that all of you*
> *may get into the garden together.*
>
> *Herewith I commit you to the dear Lord's keeping.*
>
> *Your loving father, Martin Luther.*
>
> *And greet your Aunt Lena for me, too."*[8]

Over the years this letter has been read publicly to a number of church audiences and received a wide variety of reactions. Educational psychologists and teachers have stated how deeply they admire Luther's intuitive grasp of the thinking processes of a four-year-old. His letter fits nicely into the pre-operational stage of a two- to seven-year-old, a time when a child does not understand concrete logic and learns through play and pretending. However, the letter has also troubled those who expect Luther's law-gospel theology to be evident at all ages and in all circumstances, including this letter. These people ask, "Where is grace here? It sounds a lot like law, not gospel." As one person put it with a touch of humor, "It just goes to show you, once a Catholic, always a Catholic."

However, if one can accept that writing or speaking to a four-year-old has its own joys and parameters to communicate God's love, then a closer look at the letter can reveal a father's heart for his son's faith journey. Using the Four Key Faith Practices, one can detect a literary style that presumes a caring conversation, not only as a thoughtful dialog contained in the epistle, but also as a prelude to a later conversation when Martin gets home. Second, the letter promotes prayer, learning, and good moral behavior, the kinds of things that reflect a devotional life through prayer and a life of service through education and "being good." The formal yet loving salutation and closing words of the letter indicate a way to honor Hans through rituals and traditions that speak of the peace of Christ and bless the boy with the protective care of the Lord. All of this models and fits into a lifetime of faith practices. And all of this is contained in a whimsical story to Hans that suggests a heavenly reward for a little boy. The real resolution to this letter can only be revealed with the father's homecoming and the questions Hans must have had about the magical place his father described.

The letter is an engaging example of Martin Luther as a shepherd of souls to his own children, but it is certainly not his only example. Sitting around his table at home with family and friends he said, "Though I am a great doctor, I haven't yet progressed beyond the instruction of children in the Ten Commandments, the Creed, and the Lord's Prayer. I still learn and pray these every day with my Hans and little Lena."[9] Being a shepherd of souls allows one to walk alongside another person and grow in the grace of God together. A great biblical scholar and pastoral theologian of the Reformation could do this. It is an example for parents today who often feel they don't know enough to be a spiritual guide to their children.

Luther gives ample examples of his conviction that the home should be a centerpiece of Christian formation, especially under the leadership of parents. He wrote his Small Catechism for the "head of the household" and urged parents to lead the home in faithful conversations, prayer, service, and daily Christian rituals and traditions. He understood that the historic core of the catechism, the Ten Commandments, the Creed, and the Lord's Prayer, were meant to guide one's "conversation, conduct, and concerns,"[10] the experiential focus of a shepherd of souls. He playfully chides his wife Katie for her worries over his health when he traveled to another town and wonders if worrying is what she has learned from her catechism. (He did die a week later, so there was wisdom and valid concern in what Katie wrote.) He learned the faith and prayed the faith at home not only with his small children, but with other family, friends, students, and guests. His home life could include dozens of people at one time, who all received his shepherding as head of the household. And whether at home or away, he had the desire and ability to keep the life of faith at the center of his children's lives and his relationship with them.

In Luther's letters, you see his desire to speak the gospel to real issues, real needs, real lives. Luther is wanting to help people be at home in faith. And he did this personally, relationally, addressing individuals with the hope and promise of the gospel in creative—if sometimes unorthodox—ways.

The home has shepherded some rather notable Christian leaders over time. Monica, the mother of Augustine, remained in constant prayer and wept for the soul of her son. At the end of her life she was able to give thanks for his Christian leadership in the church. Monastic communities over the centuries took on the nomenclature of the home by shepherding the religious people under the guidance of holy mothers and fathers. Luther's home seems to have reflected his own monastic life as his domestic life in Wittenberg had its own routine that undoubtedly would have included readings from Scripture, the catechism, hymns, service to others (including guests), storytelling, and the "mutual conversation and consolation of brothers and sisters."[11] John and Charles Wesley had life- and faith-shaping instruction and practices in their childhood home, a typical experience for the home of their day. In the Wesley home, the children had a rather exceptional experience, learning Latin and Greek and being able to quote large portions of the New Testament by heart. Their mother, Susanna Wesley, led daily reviews of their lessons and weekly reviews of their spiritual lives. At one time when their father was away for an extended time, Susanna conducted Sunday afternoon worship services in their home. Others were drawn to these services and large crowds began to join in services of prayer, praise, and sermons that she would read. The Wesley children, ten of nineteen who lived beyond infancy, gained much through the discipline, education, and faith formation that was routine in the Wesley home under the tutelage of their mother.

Over the centuries, small groups of devoted Christians have likewise gathered to read the Bible, pray, and serve others. It is

Shepherding in the Home   121

a model similar to what Philipp Jacob Spener recommended in *Pia Desideria* and what pietists have done since the eighteenth century.[12]

Shepherding Souls through the Generations

Of course, there are countless further examples from people's lives over history, narratives that are most often not recorded in a public document. One family I know talked about the letters a great-grandfather sent his children when they moved from Germany to Australia. He reminded them of the importance of their Christian faith and how much that faith meant to him. Reading those old German letters still brings tears to the eyes of the man's daughter. She is now translating the German letters into English, the language of her children and grandchildren and generations yet to come. These letters will shepherd his family lineage as they recall and read about his care, his faith, his prayers for them, and his enduring presence in their lives. It is a gentle, rather one-sided form of shepherding, but one filled with love for people yet unborn, not so different from the shepherding letters of the New Testament.

In another instance, Duane, a man in his eighties, told of being a small child growing up on a North Dakota farm. They were tough times. His grandfather had died and his grandmother moved in with Duane's family, meaning that as a small boy Duane gained a new roommate, his grandmother. He recalls tiptoeing partway up the stairs to sit and listen to his grandmother reading in their bedroom. She would read her Norwegian Bible aloud for several minutes at a time. And then, she would pause, begin to rock in her chair and pray aloud based on what she had just read. In those prayers, she would include thoughts and intercessions for neighbor farmers, their safety, and their economic, physical, and spiritual wellbeing. She would pray for her new homeland in America and the wellbeing of the people there. She would pray for her motherland, Norway, and the safety, economic, physical, and spiritual wellbeing of the people there, too. She would pray for the work of the church around the world. Interspersed between these prayers she would read more from her Bible, then return to rocking and praying.

122 Shepherd of Souls

When Duane reflected on the importance of his grandmother on his life and faith, he was not sure she ever knew he used to listen to her reading and praying. He then reminisced on his own life that led him to the seminary and on to the mission field to study languages in Paris, then serve in Madagascar for years. Over time, he learned eight languages in addition to English: Hebrew, Greek, Norwegian, German, Malagasy, French, Papua New Guinean, and Hawaiian. He taught, he preached, he prayed, and he served in numerous places around the globe. In the midst of all his travels, family life, and work, he always recalled his grandmother, her Bible reading, her prayers, and her sitting in the rocking chair in their bedroom.

When Duane died, his family of four generations gathered for his funeral service. His children (including a son-in-law) spoke of a man who seemed to them bigger than life, a father, grandfather, and great-grandfather who had done much to influence them with his gentle voice, winning smile, and strong faith. They celebrated life and faith in a service Duane had planned with hymns he had selected. They quoted him and they told stories about him and his faith in Christ. That day, no one mentioned his grandmother and childhood roommate, but in so many ways her story was lived out in his. The worshipers left that day shepherded in hope, faith, and love in a manner that few will ever know in the twenty-first century, receiving a living faith from at least six generations of conversations, reflections, prayers, and lots of service to others.

Children can also make valued contributions to the faith life of the home. What they learn in a congregation can be brought home to bless relationships there, too. I heard of a three-year-old who was attending her first year in a Catholic preschool. One day she asked to give the table grace. She paused for a long time, trying to remember what she had learned. Then she prayed, "In the name of the Father, Son, and Holy Spirit. We pray for joy and peace and happiness to all the children around the world. Amen. In the name of the Father, Son, and Holy Spirit." She began and concluded the prayer by making the sign of the cross over her body as she named the Triune God. The table grace was deeply appreciated by the three generations of family that had gathered together for a special occasion. Making the sign of the cross was a bit of a surprise for this Protestant family, but a ritual received with smiles and joy at the emerging life of faith of a beloved three-year-old.

Next is a story of three generations of family faith formation, family members shepherding one another in faith active in love, a faith and a love that touched not only each other over the generations, but others, too. A father writes the following:

One of the things we did while our kids were growing up was that we would make caramel popcorn, bag it up, and then, as a family, go out caroling to the homes of people who had experienced a family death that year. It is something that our grown children often talk about as being a very meaningful part of their faith journey—faith in action. In fact, the first year we were in Annandale [Minnesota]—and our girls were in college—they got us to make caramel popcorn—and we went out caroling around the neighborhood. People were wondering who this "strange" family was that had moved into the neighborhood!

For me personally, [what influenced my faith] was watching my dad befriend a special needs man in our congregation. If you've seen the movie Radio—I can't help but see my dad in that movie. My dad would take John with him when he went hospital calling. John would wait in the lobby, and then after Dad was done with his visits, they would both go out for coffee. John was often a guest at our house (especially after his parents died), and John would come along with us to the Minnesota State Fair. Watching my dad care so tenderly for John—and welcome him into his life—taught me so much about the unconditional love of Christ.

And just this past Thanksgiving, our kids were home (and thus our two grand dogs), and so the Friday after Thanksgiving, Diane, my wife, got up and took the dogs for a walk. It

124 Shepherd of Souls

was a cold morning—and as she walked, she passed a house where there was a crew of men sweeping the snow off the roof so that they could replace the shingles (our development got hit by hail this past summer). She came home and made a pot of soup, and then at lunch time, she took it down to the house. They asked her why she was doing such a thing? She said, "I saw you working in the cold, and figured you probably didn't have anything warm to eat—and so I made you this." The man asked her: "Do you know God?" She said, "Yes." "Do you know Jesus?" "Yes," she replied, "I do know Jesus, do you?" He said, "No." But I think that day, he met Jesus in my wife! And her actions made a difference in my life, and the lives of our grown children![13]

With stories like these, perhaps it is not so surprising that there is an abundance of research that indicates that families and couples that practice faith together have a higher level of satisfaction in the home.[14] They share a desire to be together. They find comfort and strength in each other's presence. They experience a sense of the divine, the holy, that leads them beyond a narrow vision of daily life to imagine something more. That something more bonds lives and gives hope, meaning, good courage, and a desire to shepherd others in the love of God.

Eavesdropping, storytelling, and letter writing are but a few of the ways that generations past bless generations yet-to-be. Other often heard examples include the accounts of children remembering family devotions read out of published devotional books and seeing a parent or grandparent reading their Bibles in another room or hearing their elders pray in their bedroom with the door closed or overseeing them on their knees in prayer, sometimes as a last resort as a life, a farm, or a job is slipping away from their grasp. In each case the impact is often not immediately felt by those who witness the faith in action. People often talk about being annoyed by the need to sit at the kitchen table or in the living room and listen to readings that seem disconnected from their everyday lives. Or they recall watching a parent or grandparent praying or reading the Bible without much thought about its significance for the elder or for them. But then, in later years, some of these same children grow up knowing that parents and grandparents lived with a faith for which these children could only hope. It sometimes gets the children on a journey to explore what it was in reading and praying that could mean so much. Shepherding can look like this.

The goal, of course, is not to annoy children of today with things that seem to them uninteresting or without meaning to their daily lives. What is worth retaining from these examples is the commitment to the practice of faith in the home that includes thoughtful conversations, a devotional practice that touches lives, service that makes the faith real in its consequences for others, and rituals and traditions in the home that name what is important, *what is good and acceptable and perfect*. Shepherding can look like this, too.

How to Promote Shepherding in the Home

Whether they are the homes represented in the Bible, famous Christian homes, the small groups of pious Christians gathering for edification and service to one's neighbor, or the countless undocumented experiences of the cross+generational life of families, the domestic life of the church in the home has made a large contribution to the witness of the faith to the world. As today's congregational leaders gain a new appreciation of this history and the possibilities for the contemporary church, a critical question emerges: "Where do we start?" How do we as the congregational leaders committed to this direction get the attention of homes, of parents, of grandparents, of mentors and others, and what suggestions do we make to them? It is a legitimate and sobering question. After decades of neglect, most parents, grandparents, and their congregations don't know what to do or how to begin.

The first answer to this critical question is not a list of ideas on how to get others involved. For those committed to nurturing faith in the home, whether as a congregational leader or someone who wants this life for their own home, understand this important point: "Start with yourself. It begins with you." Whoever you are, you live in a home as an individual or as part of a larger community. You have trusted relationships that sustain you within or beyond your residence. Whoever you are and whatever home life you experience, start there. It becomes your laboratory for learning and will give you credibility as one who walks the talk.

The important step of starting these faith practices in one's own home will often lead to a confession that they have not been part of one's own life either. The church cannot ask or expect others to begin to be shepherds of souls in their own daily lives if those who make the recommendation—leaders in a congregation or in a home—are not walking the talk, too. In fact, leaders who commit to walk the talk are the authentic leaders to be trusted and the ones who are learning as they go, gaining the wisdom and the credibility to promote faith formation and shepherding souls in the home. The leaders will learn what works for them and what does not, what comes easily and what is hard to adopt. They will have the stories that will enlighten and encourage others to join the movement that believes that the church alive and well in the home is the church alive and well for the world.

The challenge is that an inordinate number of congregational leaders—including pastors—have not experienced much in the area of faith nurture in their own homes. Pastors who dare to explore the task of equipping homes for faith formation often ask for help as to how to begin this ministry in their own homes. Often, other staff and governing boards are honestly too embarrassed to mention that they haven't a clue as to what this would look like for them. Therefore, the first real step for congregations to equip homes for shepherding souls will be a candid confession of ignorance and neglect. Once this hurdle has been crossed, a humble and loving journey toward shepherding souls in the home can begin.

Even before specific suggestions can be made for nurturing faith in the home, a number of hurdles are often articulated within the congregation that need to be addressed. One of the great anxieties parents express is the difficulty of beginning to nurture the life of faith in the home with children who have not experienced it as part of their home life from the beginning. This is especially true with older children. When this is the case, one of the best things to do is

Shepherding in the Home 127

be candid and acknowledge that the family is moving into new territory, new territory that the parent or parents (or other community that considers itself a home) desire to be an important part of the quality of life in their home. It is okay that a parent or grandparent is nervous, and that he or she is not sure what will work or how it will work. Encouraging families to make this newfound faith life an adventure and experiment is an important step. Such candor and such desire to do this together are themselves important contributions to healthy family life.

Another common concern is how to promote this in a home where one parent does not participate in the life of the congregation, or, more dramatically, is not a Christian. One initial response is to ask congregational leaders what the congregation currently offers those homes. How are adults who parent the faith in the home with a non-supportive partner being supported by the congregation? Most often the response is something like, "Well, that's a good question. I am not sure we do anything." Offering faith practices that enrich family relationships and foster faith formation are at least a start.

One wife and mother spoke of her fears about bringing the faith life in the home because her husband did not like anything that sounds like it came from the church. Anything that reeks of liturgy or something rote is definitely not okay. Anything that reminds him of the public church and the hypocrisy he believes he experienced there is forbidden. That makes this wife and mother rather fearful of trying anything related to faith formation in the home. However, after explaining how anxious she is to try using something like Taking Faith Home with her family, she began to reevaluate her situation and her husband's attitude. She recalled that when the children came up with their own prayer at mealtime or their own thoughts about the Christian life, he was quite accepting of it. Though the liturgy from the public sanctuary is not welcomed in his home, the liturgy from the lips of his children is. She began by using the Caring Conversations related to specific Bible passages as a way to bring faith talk into the home. As the children became excited to try different service ideas connected with biblical themes, the dad was more than willing to join in.

It is helpful to recognize that many an uninvolved parent is not necessarily against God. More often, that person has had a negative experience in congregational life and has chosen not to participate anymore. Other parents have simply had little to no experience with a congregation and feel awkward participating. At other times, a self-professing atheist or agnostic can still be willing to support the family's desire to practice some form of spirituality at home. This is especially true at Christmas or Easter, but it can also extend to such routine moments as a table grace or nighttime prayer. Few parents are adamantly against any spiritual life in the home, even if they are a nonbeliever. Some parents who resist association with the congregational church and are adamantly against anything that feels "churchy" are often surprisingly open to the spiritual life, the "church" life of the home.

One pastor recently described to me a sixth grade Milestone experience in his congregation. The sixth graders had a Saturday night sleepover, followed by taking active roles in the Sunday worship service. Many of the youth were given different parts in the service to help lead the worship. They were small but important parts of worship like giving the opening greeting, reading a Scripture text, or contributing to the prayer of the church. When it was all over, one father came up to the pastor to make a comment. The pastor was fully attentive to this dad because the dad had made it quite clear he did not believe in or support the Christian faith. However, after seeing the youth and his own daughter leading worship, he thanked the pastor for a very beautiful worship service. Who knows exactly what the dad was thinking or what he had objected to in the past. But the story reminds us that it is best not to make assumptions about what parents (even non-believing parents) will or will not support in the life of the home—or the congregation.

Pastors are not necessarily clear about how to nurture the faith and promote faithful shepherding in their own homes either. It is not uncommon for pastors to ask me—often in private—for help when the faith life of the home is presented as a vital part of the church. This is especially true with older children or when the children have left home and may have started a home life of their own without the routine of Christian faith practices, including attendance at worship services. One reason pastors that are not more in the forefront of promoting the faith life of the home and the role of shepherding disciples of Jesus in the home might be that these same pastors are not experiencing it in their personal lives either. Some feel guilty for the lack of involvement in the faith life of the home. Others, because of their own experience, assume that targeting homes as a place to shepherd faith is not realistic. If it isn't working for them, how can it work for others? The pastor willing to try or start over and try again is the pastor who can be a shepherd to others as he or she is also being shepherded in nurturing a vibrant life of faith in the home.

Couples have sometimes lived together for decades before they ever explore the richness of intertwining their lives of faith in the home. Some of those who have begun to pray together, do acts of service outside the home together, or simply take time to engage in meaningful conversations about life, faith, and core values have expressed their delight at the deeper bond they have come to enjoy. Whether it be a young couple or a couple in their later years, a single adult living alone or with others, a grandparent living far from grandchildren, a single parent with children, or a multi-family community, all can benefit from entering the uncharted waters that leads to shepherding one another in faith. These same households will often need the assistance of a faith community—of other shepherds—to take initial steps and stay on course. These initial steps I call shuffle steps.

Shuffle Steps

A basic rule of thumb is to start with easy and brief faith practices in the home and with trusted relationships. A good resource for this is Taking Faith Home, introduced and explained in chapter 2. With a number of options presented, individuals, couples, small friendship groups, and larger family units and households can experiment and find out what works for them. Starting with Caring Conversations establishes a nonthreatening tone that builds trust and makes it easy to expand from there. The small commitment it takes to have just a few minutes of conversation makes a successful beginning more likely, and often people will want to continue to talk beyond the initial time slot.

Quickly, the practice can start feeling like a success and motivate you to expand your repertoire of practices. Perhaps you can incorporate the Mealtime Prayer from Taking Faith Home into your household's routine. Someone may wish to use A Blessing to Give with friends or family. A Prayer for the Week and A Scripture Verse for This Week all add simple faith practices that can build upon the Caring Conversations. Sections entitled Devotions, Service, and Rituals and Traditions all offer fresh ways of thinking, reflecting, and acting that build on the biblical material for that particular week. As people become more comfortable with these simple practices and they discover how easy they can be, additional options also become easier to use.

One such option is *lectio divina* or divine reading. It's a way to meditate on the Bible that has given innumerable Christians a way to shepherd souls in the Christian faith. It entails a straightforward reading of a short biblical text in a small group setting (or for individual prayer and reflection), preferably not more than four to six verses. It is read slowly followed by silence for reflection. The text is read a second time followed by more silence. This time the individuals identify a word or phrase in the reading that stood out for them. No comments are solicited. The words or phrases are uttered, then the text is read a third time before individuals comment on how the word or phrase they identified speaks to them. The text can be read a fourth time with silence then discussion on how the text will impact their lives in the days ahead.

Children from elementary school age—and younger—as well as octogenarians—and older—can use *lectio divina* to reflect on God's word in Scripture. This approach to reading the Bible can also help small groups of Christians to encourage one another in faith with prayer and conversation.

No matter what the resource or model used for home faith formation, a benefit of this kind of experimentation is discovering what works for individuals and larger groups of family or friends. Such experimentation creates a sense of ownership of the journey instead of it feeling forced. One family liked the weekly blessings and expanded them with caring conversations into a Sunday tradition. Before bedtime on Sunday evenings, each of the children had

Shepherding in the Home 131

individual time with the parents, who discussed the upcoming week while cuddling their child between them. In turn, each child talked about his or her concerns and excitements, feelings and interests. The parents then concluded the time by offering a blessing for the child that incorporated some of that child's comments. The family practice used caring conversations, had a devotional moment that blessed the child with God's word and expressed God's love for them, served the child with attentive listening and supportive responses, all of which developed into a ritual and tradition that the family looked forward to. It represents a form of shepherding that includes conversation, reflection, and prayer.

Another family that developed a meaningful devotional time with children has added a playful piece to their ritual to encourage the children to pray. After reading a Bible story and discussing it, the family concludes by having each person offer a prayer, often praying for people in their lives. At the end of each prayer, the person praying says the name of another family member. That person is next to pray. That pattern continues until everyone has been given the opportunity to pray something. The lighthearted anticipation about who will be next keeps the time of prayer engaging for the children. This is especially true when grandparents or other guests are present to take part in the prayer rotation.

Some college friends developed the tradition of attending a weekly evening chapel service on campus. Afterwards they adjourn to a dorm room, coffee shop, or some other setting to continue to reflect on what they have experienced. Sometimes they light candles to continue the sense of being in the presence of holiness as they talk.

Coworkers can develop a sense of "family" and care for one another through a shepherding model. They can find ways to support one another in the life of faith in a way that affects their work together. A group of public school teachers gathers together each Monday morning to pray for their school, students, staff, and families. They pray for each other and the concerns expressed by the group. Their pattern exhibits the Four Key Faith Practices without them even articulating them explicitly. They engaged in caring conversations, experienced a devotional life through prayer, served one another with

132 Shepherd of Souls

active listening and care that sometimes led to supportive actions beyond their time of prayer, and the weekly pattern established a meaningful Christian tradition for the group.

Whatever practice it is that you try, don't burden yourself with a sense of guilt for not doing it more often or thoroughly. Yes, routine is helpful and blesses the faith journey and shepherding relationships. However, setting up goals that lead to guilt and disappointment does not help anyone. People are pleasantly surprised by how they can be blessed by bonding in the Christian faith through the Four Key Faith Practices even when the experiences are not done with absolute consistency or perfection.

Remember that the primary goal is to be drawn to an experience of the holy in life with others as well as alone. Routines, patterns, and schedules help this happen in a cherished community. People and groups can be encouraged to discover what feels right and good and beautiful and do it when one is able to without self-judgment for not doing more or doing it more frequently. Freely and intentionally returning to faith practices in the home when one can and when one remembers to do so is enough. Grace-filled reminders from the group become all the accountability that's necessary. Affirming the desire for God's word in one's life is an important part of shepherding others in the love and peace of God.

Using Milestone Moments for Shepherding

Milestones ministry (see chapter 6) provides a helpful model for shepherding souls in the home. It takes actual experiences in the lives of people and makes meaningful connections to the life of faith. For example, one mother talked about her son going away to college in the month ahead and was grieving over his impending departure. A milestone for her son was going off to college. A milestone for the mother was letting go of her son. She was encouraged to do a simple "milestone" event for going away to college. Without much effort, she put together some conversation starters around his life and faith story so that her son and the rest of the family could reflect on this occasion together. The family used a number of Bible passages that were meaningful to them. They blessed the son and served him

Shepherding in the Home 133

by supporting him during this passage from living at home to living away. Afterwards, the mother wrote about her experience to the couple that had recommended doing the milestone event.

"Oh my! I just wanted to tell you what a wonderful evening we had sending our son off to college with a milestone celebration at home. We opened with prayer. I shared his faith formation story (highlights from baptism to confirmation). His sister read his confirmation verse (Isaiah 40:30–31). We gave him a watch and his dad read the verses from Psalm 121 as we told him we'd enjoyed "watching him grow" and that "God would continue to watch over him." I shared one of my favorite verses (Jeremiah 29:11)— reminding him that God has great plans for his future. We closed with the Colossians blessing [Colossians 3:16] and took turns making the sign of the cross on his forehead as we each said, "God bless you." It went very well and he was obviously very moved that we did that. Thank you so much for reminding me of the way to use the milestone celebration! What a blessing! I'm sure you won't mind if I share the idea with some friends . . . it was such a gift to me that I want to pass it on!!!"

In another comment made later, the mother added that she wished she had known about milestone ministry years ago. Yet even if they started somewhat late in their family's life, it is clear that this family was able to take a significant moment in their lives and rather easily adopt the Four Key Faith Practices and the milestones ministry model with great success.

Like this family, a common fear people have is how to start being shepherds to one another in the home when they haven't done it in the past. Starting with a meaningful family moment like going to college, cramming for final exams, graduating from school, starting school, a birth or celebrating a birthday, learning to ride a bike, starting a vacation, enduring a hospitalization, getting a job, losing a job, grieving the death of a loved one, and a host of other possibilities

134 Shepherd of Souls

make good prompts. For these are occasions on which people can be made more aware of a sense of the divine in their lives and in their connection to one another.

A couple that had become accustomed to using the Four Key Faith Practices with milestones in their home were given the opportunity to be shepherds to a friend, a mother who was very anxious caring for the younger of her two sons. He was a depressed college graduate who had recently attempted suicide, and it wasn't the first time. He had struggled with depression for years, been in counseling and on medications, and now he was again experiencing a dark time in his life. The mother and the son were both receiving professional help with his depression. His mother was caring for him at home at the same time she was having serious difficulties at work. It was a job she would soon have to leave.

In the midst of these challenging times for her and her son, this couple invited the mother over for breakfast to care for her and offer what support they could. As part of their time together, they used the Taking Faith Home for a Bible reading, conversation, and prayers. When they sat down to eat, they lit a candle on the dining room table and said, "Jesus Christ is the lamp to our feet and the light to our path." They ate, talked, laughed, listened, and prayed together. Afterward, the mother sent them the following message:

> *"Dear Tim and Cindy, thank you for your hospitality. I enjoyed the delicious breakfast. Thanks also for listening to me and all my challenges in life. I appreciate that so much as I'm alone and often have no one to tell my stories. Reading the Scripture together brings peace for me. I did reflect back on the reading when I got home. I also appreciate the prayers for my boys and me. Thank you. Thank you. Thank you."*

Caring for others does not always bring a cure. But it can break through some of the isolation of going through tough times and offers the healing power and peace of Christ. Shepherding can look like that. It can be as simple as initiating conversation, consciously placing God's word into the moment, serving that person or group of people with love and care, and using Christian rituals and traditions like prayer and blessings or lighting a candle for a moment of silent reflection. These basic Christian practices do bring a measure of God's hope into daily circumstances.

Being away at college is a significant time of transition for emerging adults. It brings with it occasions to learn, question, doubt, and wonder about the deeper meaning of life and one's place in the world. One college student was struggling with these very issues, wondering whether it was even worth remaining in college. On more than one occasion she gathered some of her close friends together late at night, lit candles, and engaged in meaningful, reflective conversations. She later wrote to her dad that he would be surprised at the level of theological reflection that took place during those late-night sessions. Having come from a family that placed God in the center of its life and was devoted to "what is good and acceptable and perfect" (Romans 12:2b), this daughter already had a good grounding that helped her through a time of questioning. She was comfortable with shepherding that invited in trusted friends and family.

The Ultimate Spiritual Moment of a Home: Death

Dying well is a treasured spiritual practice. Death represents that moment in a person's, family's, and community's life that requires a response to the question of meaning, the presence of the divine, and what the future holds for the dying person and the grieving community. The sadness of death only becomes magnified by gathering family and friends together without a sense of how to face death with honesty and the future with hope. The family and friends that do this well are often the ones who have had practice with meaningful conversations in the past, the ones who have been able to talk about God and who pray to God together. They also tend to be the ones who have served others knowing that life is about more than meeting one's own needs and interest, a way of life that believes there is a greater good out there in the universe and a gracious God who orchestrates it with goodness and mercy. And, they tend to be the ones who have established meaningful Christian rituals and traditions to face sadness and hope in the same breath. They tend to be the ones who have prayers to pray, songs to sing, words of comfort from the Bible, and a robust worship life, faith practices that have taken place in the home as well as in a congregation.

Nathaniel and Grace and their children Evan, Samuel, and Tammy are one such family. They were on a vacation to visit Grace's family in Charlotte, North Carolina, a long fifteen-hour drive. But Nathaniel and Grace decided it was important to take a detour to visit Grace's Uncle Harold, with whom she had had little contact for years. Now he was dying. Evan, Samuel, and Tammy were ages seven, nine, and eleven and really didn't know their great uncle. They were not too pleased by the side trip, and frankly they were also a little nervous to see someone who was dying.

When the family arrived, Aunt Millie received them warmly. The six of them visited awhile before being taken to the place where Uncle Harold was lying in bed. Evan, Samuel, and Tammy stayed closer to the entrance to the room while their parents walked up to either side of Harold's bed, held his hands and started a conversation. Nathaniel and Grace asked him how he was doing. They talked about Uncle Harold's life, and reminisced about his many contributions to others over the years. They talked about the challenges of his illness and the care of God in the midst of them all. Nathaniel and Grace closed by praying with Uncle Harold and with Aunt Millie at the bedside. They prayed for the Holy Spirit's healing touch, for the ongoing presence of Jesus, and gave a word of thanks for Uncle Harold's loving life with and for others.

As Nathaniel and Grace stepped away to leave, Nathaniel noticed the faces of Evan, Samuel, and Tammy. Their expressions communicated intense interest in what they had just witnessed, for facing death with faith in Christ was something they had not experienced before. The rest of the drive to Charlotte felt different to everyone in the car. The children asked questions about Uncle Harold and showed an interest in the family history that had not been present earlier in the trip.

Conclusion

There exists a long and revered history in the church of nurturing the Christian faith in the home. It goes back to biblical times. That nurturing was emphasized in the Reformation through people like Martin Luther, the Wesley family, and the pietistic tradition. Research from recent decades makes it clear that parents and other caregivers have a unique and pivotal role to play in the faith formation of children. The challenge for the church of today is to reclaim that history and build upon that research as vital components of a vibrant church, one that partners the ministry of the congregation with the ministry of the home. To make that shift will take congregational leaders valuing and equipping the home to be the shepherds of souls for individuals, homes, and the larger community. These same leaders will want to begin with their own homes as a place to experience God's grace with others. Once this shift has solidified itself in the life of congregations, we can expect more homes to experience the joy of life together, evangelism within Christian homes, and the love of neighbor—all neighbors—to reach out to the larger world through the church in the home as well as through the church in the congregation.

Questions for Reflection and Conversation

1. How has your congregation equipped you to practice faith in your home?

2. What is something your congregation could do to help you express your faith in your home and daily life?

3. Who would you consider to be part of your family that does not live with you in your home?

4. How does your congregation honor and equip parents as those who have the greatest and noblest authority on earth?

5. Have you experienced a small group of Christians meeting in a home devoted to study, prayer and service? What was that like?

138 Shepherd of Souls

6. If your congregation has an active small group ministry, what are some of the suggestions in this chapter that can support those small groups?

7. Who in your extended family life or "home" has influenced your life of faith?

8. What gets in the way of homes with children experiencing the life of faith in the home? What can congregations do to help these homes?

9. What next step would you like to take in making your home a place for Christian shepherding?

10. What daily life or family milestones do you experience as a faith moment (e.g., birthdays, anniversaries, graduations)? What other moments would seem to be natural to make into milestones ministry experiences for your home?

5

THE LAY LEADER AS SHEPHERD OF SOULS

> Now there are varieties of gifts, but the same Spirit; and
> there are varieties of services, but the same Lord; and there
> are varieties of activities, but it is the same God who activates
> all of them in everyone. To each is given the manifestation of
> the Spirit for the common good. *1 Corinthians 12:4-7*

In addition to the pastor, other congregational leaders are called both
to shepherd one another and to shepherd individuals and families
in the congregation and beyond. Offering support to servant leaders, whether paid or not, whether the decision makers or those who
implement the decisions, is an often-overlooked area of ministry, and
one that can be remedied by affirming the shepherd of souls as a vital
leadership function. Once these servant leaders have gained confidence in being cared for and in caring for one another as a shepherd,
these same skills and sensitivities can be shared with other people in
the congregation as well as with family, friends, and the larger world.

The focus of this chapter is to expand the task of shepherding
souls within a congregation beyond the pastor, and to support lay
leaders in this role. By extending the network of shepherds, shepherding care can promote and develop the daily life of faith of many

140 Shepherd of Souls

more people through caring conversations, reflection, and prayer. Such shepherding can not only promote the life of faith of more people, but encourage them to be shepherds of souls too.

Expanding the Shepherd of Souls Ministry to Key Lay Leaders

That the shepherding ministry of lay staff and key leaders from the congregation is essential is something Jesus himself recognized when he noted that the people were like sheep without a shepherd, for although "The harvest is abundant… the laborers are few" (Matthew 9:37). Because the church needs an abundance of shepherds in the world, extending the ministry beyond that of pastor is critical. Including other congregational leaders is a strategic starting point to expand shepherding in the congregation and beyond.

This chapter focuses on staff members—both program and administrative—and governing board members as the first leaders to train. Members of the governing board (here referred to has "council" but in other denominations and congregations variously called *board, vestry, session, elders,* or *deacons*) represent those elected people who serve the congregation in leadership by guiding the vision and mission of the congregation, serving as models of faith and practice, and playing an important role in the staffing of the congregation. These shepherding leaders also serve other people serving on committees, teams, and task forces. Their identification as leaders in the life of the congregation does not necessarily imply they are the most gifted shepherds in the congregation, only that they are significantly placed shepherds who have the ability to impact the larger faith community with a shepherding model.

Staff members who work directly with the pastor(s) in program positions include worship leaders like music and choir directors, faith formation directors who work with Sunday school supervisors and other Christian education program leaders, and youth and family directors. (The faith formation and youth and family work in congregations are overlapping and, at times, one and the same.) The efforts of program staff work best when informed and guided by the congregation's articulated vision and mission in conjunction with the

The Lay Leader as Shepherd of Souls 141

pastor's own work in the congregation and community. Otherwise, independent ministries can emerge like isolated silos that eventually work at cross purposes, creating alienation, factions, and a ministry that goes nowhere. However, program staff that work in concert with the goals and shepherding care of the congregation and pastor(s) will have a better chance of serving people with a consistency that is reliable, trustworthy, and faithful to the Great Commandment and the Great Commission. While periodic reviews, evaluations, and administrative support are very important, caring for these people with the shepherd of souls ministry is also integral to the life of the congregation and the work of the larger church.

The care of souls ministry offered by a pastor to staff and key lay leaders in the congregation can certainly be broadened by a similar shepherding ministry offered by staff and other congregational leaders. As these leaders work on teams and projects with people from the congregation and larger community, they too can engage in *caring conversations, faith-filled reflections, and prayer.* This approach to ministry certainly adds to the health of the larger congregation and surrounding community.

The perennial challenge to the shepherd of souls ministry is the temptation to be focused on congregational goals, tasks, deadlines, and outcomes at the expense of the very people assisting in the work of the congregation. This tendency to overlook each other's needs and faith formation afflicts clergy and laity alike.

Here's a story about how this can play out. A budget committee met to decide on staff salaries for the following year. Although the local economy was not stellar, both the staff and most of the committee members assumed that staff members would get raises. However, one member objected strongly, suggesting that the congregation's members could not afford to give more. The rest of the committee capitulated to his stern words and persistence; salaries remained the same, and the group felt frustrated with the one outspoken member and disappointed.

The following day, that same vocal committee member came to the pastor's office for a conversation. He told the pastor he regretted his comments from the evening before and confessed that it

142 Shepherd of Souls

was directly related to what had happened to him that day. He has a small business and his one employee demanded a raise or said he would leave within two weeks. The business owner didn't feel he could afford the raise but also acknowledged he could not keep the business going without his employee. He had come to the meeting determined not to give in to any other pay raises.

If the budget committee meeting had started with a shepherding model of caring conversations, it might have given the agitated committee member the opportunity to get his frustrations off his chest without dominating the subsequent agenda. He could have been heard, supported, and prayed for prior to the budget discussions. Some people argue that committees do not have the luxury to start meetings by checking in, having devotions and prayer. Others have learned that, in the long run, productive and efficient meetings in the church do not have the luxury of beginning without the shepherding care of checking in with one another and offering the support needed to work as a community of faith.

Paying attention to those partnering in the work of the gospel is itself vital ministry. Those who show up and do the work of the congregation also deserve and need care. Lay leaders—staff, elected, and appointed—benefit from encouragement and guidance. People, as well as programs and projects, need to be the recipients of care. Supporting one another's faith practices, home life, and relationship to God, church, and larger world are worthy of such care. So too are their needs, disappointments, and frustrations with the ministry and community they serve. Ignoring personal needs and painful experiences that occur while serving in leadership positions can do harm to the leaders as well as get in the way of effective congregational ministry. It can even drive them from the church. Staying in touch with congregational leaders is vital to the spiritual and emotional health of individuals and, as a result, to the health and ministry of the larger congregation.

Checking In with Leaders
The pastoral model of checking in with staff and council members described in chapter 2 can motivate and equip staff and other leaders

The Lay Leader as Shepherd of Souls 143

to check in with and care for one another. People's daily experiences both support and challenge their lives of faith. Family and work issues, personal interests and hobbies, relationships with friends, colleagues, the sense of the divine in one's life or the absence of that sensation, and one's emotional wellbeing all have an impact on one's faith journey. Providing a safety net of care that includes meaningful contact and the openness to prayer can prevent a minor scrape from becoming a major abscess in one's life and in the life of the community of faith.

Indeed, an ounce of prevention is worth a pound of cure. It is best not to wait for someone to express hurts and disappointments before intervening with care and prayerful attentiveness. It is best not to wait until an individual or household has left a congregation to discover what was distressing him, her, or them. Once someone actually cries out for help or makes it apparent that something is seriously wrong, it can be difficult to undo the hurts and be open to the healing that is so necessary. Routinely checking in with congregational leaders to see how things are going with their work in the congregation and their life in Christ is thus an important practice. Even those not experiencing particularly difficult situations are still challenged by the demands of life and the deeper questions and issues that shadow most all disciples of Christ. Investing a little time to check in with others can offer support, encouragement, and that added sense of joy in being a part of the Christian community.

This approach to caring for and supporting faithful disciples can appear basic and even expected. Yet it is the exception for many congregations. For example, council members express disappointment that their pastor has not reached out to them with the kind of personal care that she routinely offers others. The reason sometimes given is that the council members do not need the attention because they obviously are doing well. The evidence for their doing well is that they show up at worship and assist the pastor and congregation by being on council. Council members will groan with disappointment because of such a pastoral perspective. In these cases, the pastor has little idea of the questions, issues, and pains as well as joys and dreams that go untended. Other servant leaders in the congregation

144 Shepherd of Souls

similarly groan at the disconnect between the public life in the congregation and the personal journey of every Christian disciple.

With a congregational culture that promotes and equips the shepherding of souls, the sense of spiritual abandonment need not happen. Simple questions can open a shepherding conversation with others in the congregation and be sustained outside the confines of the congregation. Questions like the following can easily be part of the routine of all ministry teams in the congregation. For team leaders (including program staff as well as elected and appointed leaders) to ask the following questions periodically in a confidential setting with each individual or with the group will benefit the lives and work of ministry teams in the congregation:

- "How are you doing?"
- "What is it like working on this team/project? Is it meeting your expectations and hopes?"
- "How do your efforts here give you a sense of delight or frustration or challenge?"
- "How can I/we support you in your efforts here?"
- "What do you need from me?"
- "How does your participation as a servant leader impact your faith life?"
- "How can I be praying for you these days?"

While such questions are helpful, it is critically important that the genuine care for each team member be kept distinct from simply caring about the job they are doing.

As the culture of shepherding becomes ingrained in the congregation, team members will become more comfortable with and adept at checking in with each other (including the team leader) with similar conversations, reflection, and prayer.

The amazing and often unasked question is this: As communities of faith and compassion, why is it so novel for our congregational leaders to be engaged in this kind of attentive and prayerful support of one another? The deeper question might be, "Why is soul care not the standard way of life for our congregations and leaders?" Once this rhetorical question—or one like it—is articulated, the congregation is already on the road to shepherding souls.

The Value of Not Overlooking Support Staff

In our shepherding of souls ministry, we ignore support staff, people working in office administration and custodial work, at our peril. First of all, they have applied or volunteered for these positions for a reason, often a reason greater than an income. Program staff and council members do well to understand something about the interests and reasons support staff want to work in a congregation. That thoughtful understanding contributes to an increased satisfaction for support staff. And, when the support staff's interests, desires, and interactions impede the larger work of the congregation, then the intentions and plan for their work need to be known and redirected. Support staff have an understanding of the life of the congregation and larger church and their role in it. Their own understanding, their own assumptions, expectations, and vision for their work need to work in partnership with those their work supports, including the important work of shepherding souls.

Support staff are particularly well placed to shepherd souls. For they often have direct contact with a number of people from the congregation and community. Their interactions reflect on the ministry of the congregation and can either greatly enhance or diminish those efforts and impressions to the larger world. Their initial greeting to someone who steps into the church office or calls on the phone can make all the difference as to what happens next. A warm greeting on behalf of the ministry of Christ can facilitate meaningful ministry, whereas a curt one can stop a relationship in its tracks. Even the way someone hands out food or donations to others can convey a lot to people who are already sensitive to their own vulnerability. And, yes, all of this has a bearing on shepherding.

For example, the congregation's custodian who cleans up after the messes left by others serves the ministry of the congregation well by understanding the importance of the presence of the mess-makers. It helps if that custodian knows and remembers that his or her ministry is more than keeping walls, windows, floors and bathrooms clean during the week. Offering a sense of gracious welcome and hospitality to those who use the congregation's facility also provides an atmosphere conducive to shepherding souls. Recognizing the importance of the work of custodians, some congregations use the term *sexton* as

146 Shepherd of Souls

the title for their work. The term comes from the middle ages and represented a form of ministry in the church that had responsibility for sacred things. One congregation considered changing the title of their custodian to sexton once members learned that when he unlocked the doors to the church facilities each day, he prayed for all who would enter through the doors. With or without a formal ministry title, acknowledging the significance of the custodian and other support staff can enhance the shepherd of souls ministry offered through the congregation.

Support staff go through bad times too. Perhaps they are experiencing a tough personal crisis or simply not feeling well. In either case, they can benefit from some personal intervention and support. At other times, support staff may understand their work in a way that does not mesh with the goals of the congregation, and such difference can cause consternation or even a crisis. Besides the usual management tools to address such situations, we can draw upon shepherding to bless and care for support staff.

Sometimes we undervalue or ignore the work of the support staff, its impact on the lives of others, and its implications for shepherding souls. We appreciate them for getting assignments done but are less likely to recognize their impact on others who are the agents and recipients of the congregation's ministry. Offering support staff the same soul care given others presents another opportunity for the congregation to be a community of faith, healing, and hope.

Shepherd of Souls and the Congregational Council

Members of the church council have a unique and important role in the life of the congregation's faith formation ministry, including soul care. In recent years, more and more church councils have gravitated toward this understanding of their work, often with the encouragement of the pastor. However, many councils remain stuck in a model of leadership that perceives their role as that of any other non-profit organization: make sure the doors are kept open, the bills are paid, and staff members and committees are doing their work.

This model of congregational leadership assumes that council members oversee the work of others rather than take an active

The Lay Leader as Shepherd of Souls   147

part in the ministry itself, including the soul care of one another. Council members subscribing to this approach to leadership would likely be shocked to read their own congregation's constitution, a document that likely speaks to their spiritual leadership. A typical constitution will point out that the purpose of the congregation is to nurture lives in the word of God so that people may live their faith in Christ daily, and council members are to support, equip, and even challenge people in the congregation to live this faith daily. A well-written congregational constitution will also encourage council members to be examples to others of those who lead this life personally and corporately, the life expected of all the baptized. As members of the priesthood of all believers and examples to the flock, council members are spiritual elders guided by the word of God and the congregation's confessional commitments and spiritual practices.

Strikingly, on rare occasions one can find council members who do not even bother to show up to worship and yet feel justified as a fully authorized council member. These people may have little or no sense of the spiritual dimension of the congregation and their own leadership. If the bills are paid and the congregation's cemetery is cared for (especially true in more rural settings), that is perceived as enough. Other council members show up regularly to worship, yet would confess their lack of biblical knowledge, basic Christian concepts, and personal faith practices in daily life. Therefore, reflecting on the mission of the church and the pivotal role of church council can help awaken council members to the need for the Christ-centered, faith formation aspects of their work. That awakening will impact how council meetings are run, how agenda topics are addressed, and, significantly, how the faith life of individual council members is maturing.

Although not all congregational constitutions speak with such clarity about the spiritual role of council, most do. Some pastors will read portions of their congregation's constitution to the council in order to engage council members in conversation regarding their role as spiritual leaders in the congregation—a role a few elected leaders refute while others have trouble embracing. For these individuals,

148 Shepherd of Souls

being a shepherd of souls is not perceived as part of their council member job description. On occasion pastors will hear council members saying things like, "I am here for the business of the church, not to engage in idle chit chat, do a devotional, or participate in a Bible study." When they say, "business of the church," they do not mean the business of proclaiming the gospel and serving one's neighbor in love through Christ. They mean the business of paying bills and managing the work of others. Such comments can be an opening for further conversation, not only to clarify expectations but also to address the fears and uncertainties about a council member's life of faith.

The one-to-one soul care conversations with the pastor and developing a council devotional (described in chapter 2) are both ways to help council members move beyond their fears to more active faith-filled reflection and behavior. Other strategies can also work well. Councils can begin with a Bible study and prayer. (From my anecdotal observations, more councils seem to be doing this today than ten to twenty years ago.) They can form into prayer teams and meet periodically to discuss and pray for each other's personal lives as well as the life and needs of the congregation, community, larger church, and world. Council members can go on retreat together to enjoy each other's company, learn more about one another, and practice the kind of soul care that can sustain them the entire year. Council members can be encouraged to meet individually with particular committee or task force members and commit to praying with them and for them after caring conversations and reflection. A pastor or other staff member can care for the council members as they progress along this path of shepherding souls. Participating in Bible studies and joining in local mission projects and mission trips can also enliven the life of faith of council members. All such strategies promote the soul care of council members that they may be better equipped to serve as shepherds to others.

A few simple additions to the basic council agenda can also go a long way to strengthen the identity, training, and function of council members as shepherds of souls. Such a revised council agenda would be based on the Four Key Faith Practices of caring conversations,

The Lay Leader as Shepherd of Souls 149

devotions, service, and rituals and traditions. Here is a simple agenda outline that can work for council meetings, staff meetings, or most any other working team in the congregation:

Sample Meeting Agenda:

Gathering:
> Light a candle while someone says, "Jesus Christ is the light of the world." A community response could be added: "The light no darkness can overcome."

Caring conversations (checking in with one another in groups of two or three)

Devotional time

Old Business

New Business

Review of the meeting:
> A caring conversation assessment of the accomplishments as well as how the conversations and decisions mesh with the vision and mission of the congregation

Closing:
> Closing prayer, Lord's Prayer, benediction, passing the peace, and/or other appropriate closure

The council meeting could begin by lighting a candle (*rituals and traditions*). One person could say, "Jesus Christ is the light of the world." Others could respond, "The light no darkness can overcome." This—or some other—simple Christian ritual like taking a moment of silence would remind everyone that the group gathers with the authority, privilege, and mission of the Christian community established by the word of God in Christ. The council meeting could continue with a time to check in with each other, to support each other with *caring conversations*, listening to one another's stories. This could be done in small groups of two or three that then report significant life stories back to the larger group, stories such as of birthdays, anniversaries, health concerns, or anything else that would be appropriately shared with the larger group. The *devotional* or Bible study that follows could then lift up in prayer these concerns, observances, and celebrations. The modified council agenda would therefore begin with lighting a candle, caring conversations, a devotional word or Bible study and prayer. A typical meeting agenda with old and new business would follow (an example of the *service* component of the Four Key Faith Practices). An added feature consistent with the vision and mission of the church would be to offer a prayer prior to any important decision voted on by the council. The pastor or council chairperson could ask a member to offer a prayer prior to the vote.

The meeting would then conclude with a brief assessment of the meeting itself. The group could be asked to wonder how their conversations and decisions reflect the congregation's vision and mission statements, core values, or the essential messages the congregation wants to promote. (This suggests that council members should know and have in front of them their vision and mission statements, core values, and key messages to community and world.) Did the meeting decisions reflect key themes of the mission statement? Were the essential messages promoted by the ministry of the congregation included in the council's conversations and decision making? Did the conversations reflect core values that express care and concern for people, including various—even contradictory—thoughts and feelings? Are people leaving the meeting bolstered by the word of God and the mission of the church? Or are there some concerns that need prayerful attention prior to the next meeting, concerns that will be added to the next meeting's agenda? Do people feel they leave affirmed for their life, faith, and contributions? Was a spirit of joy in God's presence articulated or does a word of confession and forgiveness need to be offered as a group? Were the lively conversations still respectful or did some participants feel that trust was breached in some way?

A closing prayer that incorporates these questions and responses would be an appropriate way to end the meeting along with the

Lord's Prayer and a benediction (*rituals and traditions*). An agenda that includes these—or similar—elements embodies the life of a council dedicated to caring for others, nurturing the Christian faith, and serving the world with the mission of the church. These are elements that various congregational councils across the country currently apply to their meetings in some way. All of this reflects the important work that equips leaders to be shepherds of souls.

A more consistent and thorough application of these steps is helpful for congregational councils. Jim LaDoux's fine book, *Surface to Soul: Coaching Spiritual Vitality in Congregations* offers a whole spectrum of leadership tools to help congregations and congregational leaders center their work in faith-filled steps, processes, and strategies. Especially useful are the tools that help congregations articulate their mission, vision, core values, key messages, goals, and covenant, the latter being a statement of how leaders will commit to work with and support one another in ways that are faithful and compassionate.[1] Establishing a congregational climate that promotes faithful, caring conversations and the pursuit of a Christian vision and mission begins with openness to one another and each other's faith stories. All are examples of shepherding souls, a discipline entirely appropriate to a church council.

As one considers these options that expand the activities of a typical council meeting, a legitimate concern is how much time they will take. Won't these added items make long meetings even longer? Not necessarily. Once the meeting is clearly grounded in the Christian faith and the goals or mission of the congregation, that focus refines the conversations and an extensive review of every committee report loses its importance. Instead of majoring in minor issues, the council conversations focus on the major issues of being the church and do so with clarity, energy, focus, and a decisiveness motivated by the congregation's mission, vision, and core values. It is amazing how much time can be saved when the council's conversations focus on the mission of the church rather than the mission of individuals who want to control agendas and meetings or who want to make every council meeting an annual audit of expenses.

Re-imaging Staff and Council Leadership

It is not so much that council members reject the idea of being spiritual elders and shepherds of soul to the larger congregation. More often, they've just not been asked or expected to fulfill that role. Thus, reflecting on the language of the congregation's constitution and installation service can present council members with an understanding of the council's identity and mission that they have not before considered in detail. With patience and persistence, councils can and do make the transition from acting like a non-profit board to being a faithful leadership team willing to participate in the mission they have promoted for others.

Once staff and council recognize and act on their supportive, mentoring roles in the life of faith of the congregation, the congregation becomes a community of faith more actively engaged with and committed to the word of God, experiencing the fruit of the Spirit that includes "love, joy, peace, patience, kindness, generosity, faithfulness, gentleness, and self control" (Galatians 5:22–23). These personal and communal qualities foster care for one another and an effective mission to the world. Congregational leaders can work together to support one another by doing a periodic check-in with those who are actively engaged with the ministry of the congregation (e.g., teams that have responsibility for worship and music, youth and family, stewardship, evangelism, property management, social outreach, global missions, etc.). The council meeting agenda described above then becomes a resource and encouragement to extend shepherding to others. Having caring conversations and prayer prior to decision making, checking in to see how others are doing in their daily life and faith, making sure that the decisions made and the way people are relating to one another reflect the core values and mission of the congregation are all helpful steps to support and train people in their shepherd of souls ministry. In other words, meeting agendas provide a model and a discipline that equip people to be shepherds of souls in their daily lives.

Over the years of working with congregational leaders I have realized that for congregations to do effective faith formation and outreach through our congregations and homes, we have to pay attention to the faith formation—soul care—of leaders. It is difficult

The Lay Leader as Shepherd of Souls **153**

to reach out to others with the good news of Jesus Christ if it is not serving, blessing, and healing the lives of those sent to others. They deserve and need the same faith formation support. Not only does their immediate home life deserve care, but these same leaders are often grandparents and godparents as well as neighbors, friends, and co-workers to others. As the gospel touches their lives through personal relationships and soul care, so too they will touch the lives of others around them. It represents the power of shepherding to do the essential work of outreach.

Staff and Councils Are Just the Beginning

Of course, the intent of shepherding staff and council members is not to be an end in itself, but a powerful beginning. Once staff and council establish the routine of providing and receiving the shepherd of souls ministry with one another, it becomes easier to extend that same care to others. As staff and council work with committees, task forces, and other teams in the congregation, they are in a position to provide a model of leadership that now includes shepherding souls as routine, not exceptional, as desired and not feared.

The structure for staff and council meetings that now include the Four Key Faith Practices can be expected of other gatherings as well, from monthly planning and annual congregational meetings to Bible studies and various service and fellowship events. People will come to expect that when they gather as a community of faith there will be caring conversations from people willing and wanting to listen and respond in faith. Meetings will no longer begin with a perfunctory opening prayer then go on to the business at hand. Instead, people will anticipate conversations that check in about their lives (caring conversations), and Scripture and prayer will wrap their life stories into the care of God (devotions). Service, whether it be the agenda for a meeting or the outcome of a Bible study or fellowship time, will be consciously present. They will come to expect that such practices will be framed with rituals and traditions that vary from lighting a candle, having a moment of silence, closing with the Lord's Prayer, passing the peace, or any number of ways to distinguish the meeting time as lived in the mindful presence of a gracious God.

In short, every gathering of the church will have a sense of Christian worship and purpose to it. There will be devotional experiences that edify people's lives with grace and mercy combined with the pursuit of justice and speaking the truth in love. There will be people who desire to serve others in word and deed. And all of this will be couched in images, words, and gestures that affirm a commitment to faith formation through Christian rituals and traditions. This is the shepherd of souls ministry. It is what identifies the uniqueness of the body of Christ in the world.

Shepherds will emerge everywhere. Brothers and sisters in the faith will engage in conversations where there is attentive listening. Praying silently and aloud with and for others will happen with a newfound desire and confidence. As this congregational culture shapes lives, people will feel encouraged and motivated to offer God's grace, mercy, and peace to family, friends, and others they meet.

Shepherding from Staff to Committee Member and Beyond

Just as the pastor engages in the care of staff, lay leaders, and the larger congregation, so too can lay leaders of every stripe. Periodically checking in with the leadership can open up meaningful topics for conversation, reflection, and prayer. For example, a faith formation director had a personal conversation with a woman on the youth and family committee who often sounded critical and negative. The conversation revealed how much she was hurting because none of her grandchildren was involved in the church though she had raised her children in the faith.

After some attentive listening, the faith formation director was able to express empathy for the woman's grief and pray with her. Periodically, the director checked in with her to support her with personal conversation and prayer and offer suggestions on how meaningful faith formation with children and youth can happen. Over the ensuing weeks and months, a new attitude emerged in this committee member. She began to see with new eyes the congregation's desire to work closely with parents and grandparents in the faith formation of children and youth.

As a result, this person learned to connect with her own grand-children in the life of faith, offering simple table graces at meals when they were together and talking to them about Bible stories that were meaningful to her. She also became more attentive to her grandchildren's interests and struggles. She began to ask them, "How can I pray for you this week?" As a result, she developed a new way of relating to her children and grandchildren. She began to understand and experience that her home was church, too, and her efforts to connect the Christian faith to her children and grandchildren did not need to wait until they were all sitting together in a public worship service. In subtle and gentle ways, this grandmother and youth and family committee member was serving as a shepherd of souls, reaching out to her own family in new ways. She even became an advocate for the congregation's faith formation work with children, youth, and families with her friends who had been more critical than supportive. What began as a shepherd of souls ministry to care for a disgruntled committee member became an occasion to care for her and in turn nurture her life as a shepherd of souls that touched the lives of many others.

Changing the Culture and Expectations of the Congregation

Many congregations seem to assume that people are spiritually fed in Sunday worship, then sent on their way into the week ahead with God's word firmly planted in their lives. The shepherd of souls ministry instead recognizes that we are called to attend to one another with God's living word on a more regular—even daily—basis.

Making sure that lay leaders are recipients of soul care will help thwart a congregational culture that assumes that occasional participation in public worship is enough to nurture lives in Christ. If leaders are cared for and fed, they will want others to know that same care and sustenance. When they serve with the care of souls ministry, they will experience the power of caring for one another with the word of God. It's a game changer for many congregations. It shows them why the body of Christ exists in the first place, as a chosen people sent to bring God's reconciling, healing, and saving work to every corner of the world and every corner of every person's life.

We are called to attend to one another with God's living word on a more regular—even daily—basis.

Questions for Reflection and Conversation
1. How are your congregation's leaders encouraged to function as shepherds of souls?
2. Give examples of how staff, council (or board, vestry, session, elders, etc.), committees, task forces, and other leadership teams support one another in their lives of faith.
3. Give examples of how these same leadership teams could do more to function as shepherds to one another in the future.
4. How do your leadership team agendas promote shepherding? How do the agendas promote doing the "business" of the church without attending to the spiritual needs of those at the meetings?
5. How would you explain to someone the benefits of including the Four Key Faith Practices in the agendas created for congregational meetings?
6. Is your congregation's support staff encouraged to participate in the larger work of shepherding souls by how they relate to congregational members and the surrounding community? If so, how does this happen? How might this happen in the future?
7. Does your congregation encourage the custodial work to be done as ministry or simply as cleanup work? Explain.

The Lay Leader as Shepherd of Souls 157

8. Do your leaders get exit interviews when they finish their work? If so, does the interview include caring for the ongoing faith life of the person leaving his or her position? If not, how might the congregation add this to future exit interviews?

9. How does the organizational structure of your congregation affect how the congregation shepherds souls?

10. In which congregational meetings do you participate? How do these meetings shepherd the souls of those who attend? How could these meetings do more to shepherd the souls of those who participate in the meetings?

6
MILESTONES MINISTRY: A MODEL FOR SHEPHERDING

Now every year his parents went to Jerusalem for the festival of the Passover. And when he was twelve years old, they went up as usual for the festival. When the festival was ended and they started to return, the boy Jesus stayed behind in Jerusalem, but his parents did not know it. *Luke 2:41–43*

In Luke 2, we read of Jesus and his family experiencing a number of memorable—even divine—moments. His parents made a difficult trip from Nazareth to Bethlehem while Mary was pregnant. In Bethlehem, their baby was born. Shepherds who had a fantastic story to tell about angels and a message filled with joyous news visited the new family. The baby was circumcised and given the name Jesus. As pious Jews, the family went to Jerusalem and the temple when Jesus was forty days old to fulfill the Mosaic law of purification. At that time, a devout man named Simeon prophesied about Jesus with such angelic words that the church has sung and prayed the recitation ever since. As the impromptu and intimate gathering dispersed, Simeon had one more word to offer: he blessed the family. Then the prophet

160 Shepherd of Souls

Anna took the celestial baton, praised God, and told anyone within earshot about the boy Jesus and the future deliverance of Jerusalem. That momentous occasion in the temple likely came back to mind every time Mary and Joseph returned to Jerusalem for the Passover festival, including the time they went with the twelve-year-old Jesus. This experience had to be a near-manhood moment (not an era to bother with being a "tween" or "early adolescent") as he sat with Jewish teachers in the temple who marveled at his wisdom beyond years. As a result, his parents saw that Jesus was growing up before their very eyes, and it would lead Mary to ponder and treasure "all these things in her heart" (v. 51). It becomes quite fitting that the narrative in Luke 2 should end, "And Jesus increased in wisdom and in years, and in divine and human favor" (v. 52).

Luke gives us most of the post-birth, pre-adult stories of Jesus' life in the four canonical Gospels. And they are told as a sequence of rituals and traditions fashioned by the Scriptures and implemented by devout people of God. Whether it was the circumcision and naming of the boy, the purification for the sake of Mary, or the fidelity to an annual Jewish festival ("they went up as usual"), Luke portrays this family as faithful to the traditions of their people, their Scriptures, and their God—and Jesus is revealed as someone clearly above the rest. He will have global impact; he is "a light for revelation to the Gentiles and for glory to your people Israel" (Luke 2:32).

Translating a Biblical Model for Today

Though some of Jesus' experiences are quite different from our own, the life- and faith-shaping events that Jesus and his family encountered nonetheless are a reasonable prototype for the lives of Jesus' followers. All of these experiences in Luke 2 fit into what is being referred to in this chapter as milestones ministry. It involves the work of the church that frames significant life moments in people's lives through the lens of the home and larger community of faith working together. These milestone moments combine Scripture, reflection, faith traditions, rituals, blessings and prayers, all for the sake of Christian proclamation and transforming souls.

Milestones Ministry: A Model for Shepherding 161

Milestones ministry is filled with ingredients that promote shepherding souls: Scripture, faith traditions, caring conversations, blessings, and prayer—all put together in a bowl that looks a lot like a community life that seeks to support and care for one another for a lifetime. As such, the result of this recipe for ministry is that people can learn to speak the faith out loud. Milestones ministry helps people move from the more passive and silent life of a Christian to the more active life of a Christian missionary who knows how to speak the faith out loud.

A congregation in Adelaide, South Australia, developed a modern example of such ministry. A team from the congregation, including the pastor, attended a workshop that offered training in milestones ministry. Each congregational team created their own milestone event, either for the congregation or for their own homes. This team decided to create something for their upcoming confirmation Sunday. Eight youth were being confirmed and the team put together an experience for the home that could bless not only the confirmands but the people surrounding them. The team filled in the template of the Four Key Faith Practices with the home of each confirmand in mind. The intent was to encourage the families to have a milestone experience for the home following the rite of confirmation in the Sunday worship service. The team recommended that the families and friends gather with the confirmand Sunday afternoon and consider doing the following practices:

Caring Conversations: Ask each person to share what has been meaningful to them about the confirmation day. How have you seen the young person grow as a result of being part of confirmation ministry? What are your hopes for their future life of faith?

Devotions: Find a Bible or your confirmation certificate and read the young person's confirmation text. Allow different people to share why they think that verse was chosen for this youth.

162 Shepherd of Souls

Service: Ask parents and godparents to recall the commitment they made to the child at their baptism. How has this been a joy or a challenge? How would you like to support the young person in their faith from this time forward?

Rituals and Traditions: Record the young person's confirmation date and text on a calendar or other prominent place to help you remember. Light their baptismal candle and ask an older member of the group to offer a prayer and blessing.

The Four Key Faith Practices were placed on a laminated card distributed at a Saturday evening event in honor of the confirmands and their family and friends. The card was entitled, "Confirmation Milestone: A basic resource to enrich your child's confirmation day in the home." Yes, the public rite of confirmation on Sunday would be memorable and meaningful, but the follow-up event would be experienced more intimately with family and friends. The sermon on Sunday would remind the families to use the laminated card at home. It would also remind the worshipping community of the importance of living out one's life of faith in the home as well as in the congregation.

The confirmation milestone event described above gave that congregation a good introduction to milestones ministry. It gave an example of how milestones ministry could instill in a congregation a culture that makes Christian shepherding a clear priority by offering active support and encouragement. It valued how parents and other caregivers can easily and significantly influence the life of faith of another and, in the process, transform the lives of many others. The faith life of the caregiver as well as the care recipient was nurtured.

Defining Milestones Ministry

A milestone is a meaningful, memorable moment in one's life or in the life of a community. It can be as momentous as the milestone of birth, adoption, or foster care, and as simple as starting Sunday school or a new school year. Baptism is the foundational milestone for a follower of Jesus. It is the milestone that defines one's whole life.

Milestones Ministry: A Model for Shepherding   163

Beginning with baptism, milestones ministry understands the various moments one experiences in life as parts of one's faith formation, the living out of one's baptism.

Every congregation does some form of milestones ministry whether it uses that language or not. In addition to baptism, other milestones recognized in congregations include confirmation, weddings and funerals, and other meaningful, memorable moments that elicit a faith response. Many congregations add other basic milestone events like a first communion, giving Bibles to children and youth, and honoring a graduation from high school as part of a person's Christian vocation. As congregations explore this model of ministry, they recognize the endless possibilities to connect daily life experiences with the presence of a gracious God, and, therefore, the opportunities to shepherd children, youth, and adults in a life of faith.

Over the years, congregations have recognized and developed particular milestones,[1] including: remembrance of one's baptism, learning to pray, welcoming children to worship, going to Bible camp, celebrating and honoring one's body as God's gift, beginning middle school, beginning confirmation, going on a mission trip, blessing a first driver's license, caring for an aging parent, becoming a parent or grandparent, getting a new job, military deployment and return from military deployment, moving into a new home, anniversary of marriage, affirming spiritual gifts, experiencing the empty nest, retirement, loss of a loved one, and joining a faith community.

In addition to milestones recognized in the congregation, other milestone events are recognized specifically in the home as moments that nurture the Christian faith and that reach out to others with the love of God. These include birthdays, getting a first cell phone, having a broken bone, leaving home for college, work or military service, going on a vacation, adding a child to one's home, divorce, preparing for surgery, enduring severe weather, getting one's Medicare card, facing chronic illness, and caring for the health needs of another family member or friend. The list is endless. People continue to come up with very creative milestones, like the loss of a tooth, riding a bike for the first time, getting braces, getting the braces off, being suspended from school, finishing chemo, and getting a first paycheck. These

164 Shepherd of Souls

milestones in life are ways the church can have a meaningful connection to people's joys, transitions, and sorrows in life by connecting those experiences with the word of God and the good news of Jesus Christ. Marking such milestones is a rich way of promoting lifelong faith formation as well as shepherding souls for a lifetime.

Milestones ministry, as an intentional faith formation resource developed by Milestones Ministry, LLC, recommends a follow-up time to check in and see how the particular life experience has affected people's daily lives and faith. These are opportunities to shepherd people in faith. Foundational to all intentional milestone ministry events are the Four Key Faith Practices experienced cross+generationally. The checking in can be done by congregational leaders or by those who participated in the event. Such follow-up shepherding opportunities elicit deeper reflection and participation in the Christian faith.

This model of faith formation contrasts with more traditional educational opportunities in a congregation that seldom do more than provide information and discussion and then send people on their way wondering how the information and recommendations pertain to their lives of faith. Milestones ministry as a faith formation model understands that others' support and ongoing care and reflection help people to develop deeper faith lives. For those willing and wanting a meaningful and deeper faith formation experience, this approach includes an element of discipline and accountability through a faithful and committed community.

Developing and Expanding the Milestones Ministry Model

No matter what the milestone, the Four Key Faith Practices equip individuals, homes, and larger faith communities to practice the Christian faith at a particular moment in life. For example, in the case of receiving a new Bible, parents, other family, and friends gather together to learn how to use the Bible with the child receiving it. This means that not only is the recipient learning about the Bible and how to use it, so are others who are with the recipient of the Bible.

Attention to the Four Key Faith Practices helps make Bible reading more of a faith experience and less of an academic exercise. As

Milestones Ministry: A Model for Shepherding   165

an example of devotions, before reading the Bible (or looking at a storybook Bible), an individual or group of people could begin with a prayer to be guided by the Holy Spirit to gain divine wisdom and compassion. One could start with a simple moment of silence to be aware of God's presence in the reading. The very act of routinely reading the Bible becomes a Christian tradition that values the Bible as a means of God's grace. By using this Four Key Faith Practices, the Bible can inform people's caring conversations, their behavior (service to others) and what they think about and value.

A congregation can offer a Bible Milestone by giving an illustrated Bible to preschoolers, a more extensive storybook Bible to primary school children, and a study Bible to confirmation students or high school graduates. Often, it is the parents who give these Bibles to their children in worship. However, one congregation changed things up a bit, and had first graders give preschoolers illustrated Bibles in worship. The first graders witnessed to the importance of this book and this moment as they were led in unison by the faith formation director to encourage the preschoolers to read the book at home with family and find the love of God in the pages. In other words, the first graders were getting simple training in shepherding others and the preschoolers were excited to have the big first graders be part of their lives. After seeing this milestone ministry exchange in the worship service, and with tears in their eyes, some of the adults admitted they were beginning to understand how important it is to have others involved in their lifelong faith formation, rather than pretending they could go it alone.

One congregation placed new Bibles at the entrance to the sanctuary and kept them there for a few weeks. Each Bible was designated for a particular child. As the worshipers walked by the Bibles, they were encouraged to open them, underline one of their favorite Bible passages, write a blessing or prayer by the passage and put their name by it. This process encouraged people to think about Bible texts and stories and their influence in the lives of others. As such, it encouraged more familiarity with the Bible in general. It also served as a motivation for the recipients of the Bibles to look up people's favorite Bible passages and the blessings and prayers placed by them. This exercise is

166 Shepherd of Souls

especially meaningful when children look up the Bible passages and prayers from close friends and family. With these steps, everyone who participates in the Bible Milestone benefits. Large numbers of people have the opportunity to do a bit of shepherding of young people receiving a Bible, perhaps their first Bible.

A pastor brought a group of third graders and their parents back together a month after the children received their Bibles. The pastor asked the group where the Bibles were kept at home, when the Bibles were used and what ideas from the milestones ministry training helped them with their Bible reading times. The pastor also asked where further help was needed so that the Bible would become a part of the families' home devotional practices. Now the parents and children were becoming the teachers, telling one another what worked for them and what was difficult. One family pointed out that the local school was challenging the students to read 1500 pages during the year. This family had added Bible reading pages as part of that count. The other families quickly saw the advantage of this, something no one else had thought of.

Making Bible reading a routine in one's life and one's home is not an easy thing to accomplish in a busy world with competing agendas and values. To make the value of Bible reading part of one's habit and faith formation, the support of others in the community of faith goes a long way. Follow-up contact helps immensely. It establishes a support community where people can learn from one another how to read the Bible in a way that is life and faith shaping.

Every Christian education experience can benefit from a follow-up contact of caring conversation, reflection, and prayer. It promotes faith formation and nurtures a community of shepherds.

Don't expect everything to go smoothly. Life's like that! One family started reading the Bible with their children using the recommended readings from Taking Faith Home, the resource connected with the weekly worship service. Unfortunately, the text they began with was complicated. Luke 20:27–40 tells the story of the Sadducees questioning the resurrection by asking Jesus about a woman who married each of seven brothers after one husband died and left her a widow to be married by the next brother. The Sadducees wondered whose wife she was in the resurrection. Jesus' answer, that in the resurrection people do not marry, totally confused and stressed the children who wondered what would happen to their parents in the resurrection. The parents, not sure how to answer, suggested the children's question needed some more time and help to answer. Fortunately, the parents were able to laugh with their congregation's faith formation director about this first attempt to read the Bible with their children. That conversation led to the recommendation of some easier Bible passages to begin with, plus a confession that the story was not the easiest to interpret, even for pastors. Encouraged and supported by the director, these parents found in a community of faith the support and encouragement to keep trying and the levity to acknowledge that a journey of faith is not plain and simple for anyone. Sometimes shepherding looks like that.

One grandfather attended a Bible Milestone training event that helped third graders and their families read the Bible in the home. His grandchildren lived over a hundred miles away and they did not attend a local congregation. He used the information gained from the training and then visited his children and grandchildren. He gave each grandchild a Bible and helped them see how easy it is to make Bible reading a part of their lives. He also promised to check in and see how he could continue to help his children and grandchildren make Bible reading a part of the life of the home. This grandfather's initiative offered a good example of how milestones ministry can be outreach to those not part of a local congregation.

In another instance, grandparents trained through milestones ministry were reading from a storybook Bible to their two granddaughters. The story was about the fear of the disciples on the Sea of Galilee during a storm. The grandmother asked a Caring Conversation question from Taking Faith Home, "When have you been afraid?" The older granddaughter said, "I am too afraid to tell you." A

168 Shepherd of Souls

bit startled by the answer, both grandparents told of times they were afraid. This freed the granddaughter to tell her story of being afraid of witches under her bed at night. The other granddaughter then told about fearing monsters in her closet. These disclosures led to some good faith conversations about witches and monsters not being real (though still understandably scary for little ones) and that God is always with them. The story found its way home to the parents who then had the opportunity to underscore the grandparents' reassurances. Shepherding looks like this, too. In this case the shepherds were grandparents and parents telling children about their own faith and confidence in God, something very important to the faith of precious little ones.

One congregation connected a public, congregational milestone with a milestone experience in the home. St. Luke's had six children going to a Bible camp, most for the first time. The children were brought forward during a worship service to receive a blessing, a blanket to remember God's embrace, and public support for their venture away from home. After that, the children were given a Bible camp mentor, someone who would connect with them, reflect on the value of the experience, and pray for them while at camp. One couple invited two brothers to their home, had donuts with them followed by a conversation about the upcoming camp experience, then shared a Bible reading and a blessing for the boys. The Bible passage was Psalm 121, a travel psalm that seemed fitting for the boys' journey away from home. They used the *lectio divina* model of reading and reflection that allowed all four to contribute thoughts about the text. While the brothers were away at camp, the couple kept them in prayer, made sure that a thinking-of-you card was awaiting them on arrival at camp, and then reconnected with them after camp to discuss what the experience had been like for them, and how it impacted their lives of faith. This sequence offered a clear model of shepherding that included caring conversations, reflection together, and prayer, all practices that present God's word to shape lives with faith, confidence, and hope.

What makes milestones ministry a means for shepherding souls is its structure that connects the generations in faith formation. The structure is simple:

Milestones Ministry: A Model for Shepherding 169

- Name a meaningful moment in one's life as a faith moment.
- Equip participants with the Four Key Faith Practices so that it becomes a faith formation experience.
- Bless the people with prayers that name the moment as an occasion to receive the love of God in Christ and the love of others from the body of Christ.
- Gift the recipients of the milestone moment with something visible to help them recall the event as a special time to connect daily life experiences with the word of God in order to nurture the Christian faith.
- Reinforce the milestone by reconnecting with the participants in the milestone event to help them continue the journey of faith formation. Checking in with people is key to both effective milestones ministry and to shepherding souls.

Milestones as Outreach

Milestones ministry not only directly supports lifelong faith formation, it also promotes outreach into the community, for milestones are not the exclusive possession of congregational members. This, too, is a form of shepherding, for it expands the reach of the church to those who have not been inclined to connect with a local congregation. Milestones ministry becomes a way to reach out to others and connect with their life experiences, even if those experiences do not include contact with the congregation. A congregation that gives Bibles to third graders can make sure that nonmembers from the community are invited to join this training. There are parents who are not members of a congregation yet still want their children to have and know the Bible. The congregation's ministry is meant for them, too. Some congregations give each third grader two Bibles, one for themselves and one to give away. In this way, the ministry of the congregation reaches people who do not necessarily worship in that congregation or anywhere else.

Another form of outreach through milestones ministry happens through milestones that take place outside the congregation's facilities and in the community. For example, milestones experienced with family and friends during the holidays like Thanksgiving, Christmas, Memorial Day, and the Fourth of July can provide occasions for the church in the home to invite others together to give thanks to God during these celebrations and remembrances.

 Milestones are not the exclusive possession of congregational members.

One congregation in a small town developed a community milestone by setting up a table across the street from the local elementary school the night of the school's first open house in the fall. The congregation invited parents and students to the table to receive a simple key chain to put on the child's backpack and a little blessing for the student. Hundreds of key chains and blessings were handed out that evening, mostly to people not connected with the congregation. Parents began to ask about the people doing this and what congregation they represented. Some even asked when the congregation's worship services took place.

This same congregation added another community milestone by holding a summer ice cream social in the town park. Along with the ice cream, the members handed out cards with conversation starters, table graces, and prayers to be used in the home. The bottom of the card read, "From your neighbors at St. Paul's." The congregation did other activities to let people know that the congregation cared about them and was ready to bless their homes with Christian resources and activities. Later, the pastor from that congregation noted that on her hospital visits she was beginning to have conversations with townspeople who were not part of her congregation yet were introducing her to their family, friends, and coworkers as "my pastor." Caring for others with simple Christian practices like caring conversations and blessings can begin a shepherding relationship with meaningful consequences.

Milestones that serve the community and larger world promote the outreach work of the church and, therefore, expand the shepherding ministry of the congregation. The church displays the love of God through caring service to others, some of whom may not have been reached before.

An Episcopal parish established an entire season of community milestones. The church building was tucked away and rather hidden in the middle of a local neighborhood. The beautiful sanctuary, church buildings, and outside landscaping were a feast for the eyes, and many people walked by the parish buildings simply to enjoy the attractive scenery. Alert to this, the vestry decided to connect with the ambulant neighbors and set up an ice cream social on the lawn in August. In September, the church blessed the backpacks for the neighborhood school children. In October, the parish offered a service for the blessing of animals that drew many neighborhood pets. In November, the church invited the neighborhood to a Thanksgiving service, and in December to Christmas caroling in the sanctuary. The vestry was so encouraged by the new contact with the neighborhood, they began considering other milestone events through which they could reach out to their neighbors at other times during the year.

Each month, the people who attended were given a sheet with the Four Key Faith Practices that included a conversation starter, prayer, service idea, and a ritual and tradition to do in the home, all related to the activity and theme for that particular community milestone. The reverse side of the paper promoted the community milestones for the following months, encouraging the neighborhood to return. At the bottom of the page the parish included a note: "From Trinity Episcopal Parish, your neighborhood church." It was the parish's way to make it clear that this beautiful parish church wanted to be more than beautiful building and grounds to be appreciated by those walking by. They wanted to be true neighbors, a community known for blessing the lives of people with the Christian faith. Within a year, a staff member from the local elementary school contacted the rector to see how members of the parish could possibly help students at the school. Who knows whether the community milestones led to the invitation, but either way, the parish was ready to be a good neighbor.

172 Shepherd of Souls

Another congregation held a community Easter egg hunt for its neighborhood on the Saturday before Easter Day worship. People gathered for a brief worship service that gave thanks for Easter and the many ways to be reminded of new life in Christ. The Easter eggs were introduced as one such reminder. Eggs have been a symbol of new life throughout human history and the church has used this symbolism as well. After the brief worship service that gave thanks for Easter and Easter eggs, the people went outside to a field and the children were let loose to find the eggs. Often the eggs had candy inside, but sometimes there was a message that the recipient had a gift waiting for them to be picked up. The gifts included Bibles, crosses, and blankets meant to remind people of being wrapped in the love of God. After the Easter egg hunt, the pastor saw a mother kneeling in front of her daughter in the hallway of the church building. Both were strangers to the pastor, people from the neighborhood who had accepted the invitation to be part of an Easter egg hunt. The pastor overheard the mother say that she had always wanted her daughter to have a Bible, and now the daughter had one. The mother's words were accompanied by tears of gratitude. It is likely that this mother and daughter had not planned on attending the congregation's Easter Day service. However, an invitation to an Easter egg hunt blessed this home with a Bible and the joy of experiencing the good news of Christ's resurrection.

Home as a Location for Milestones Ministry Outreach
Congregational milestones ministry events include a home component, that is, the milestone celebration can be done in one's home. Other milestones are intended for use primarily in the home, like the loss of a baby tooth, a birthday celebration or going away to college. In either case, the home becomes the front door to the wider community on behalf of the local congregation and larger church. For example, we have already seen that some congregations offer a Blessing of the Backpack Milestone as a way of sending kids off to a new year of school. Part of the milestone event can be done in the home, a prime opportunity to invite classmates, friends, and other relatives to a friendly and safe environment for a milestone event. In

Milestones Ministry: A Model for Shepherding 173

this way, others can participate in a faith formation event that connects directly with their own experiences, like going back to school.

Another occasion ripe for reaching out to others is celebrating Thanksgiving Day. Individuals and families from a congregation that encourages faith practices at Thanksgiving could host a Thanksgiving Day meal and invite family, friends, and also those who would otherwise be alone. The host could then offer simple Christian practices that can be gently added to the meal through a mealtime prayer and conversations that reflect on the theme of thankfulness and gratitude. A biblical text could be added to aid in the reflections. God's word can be part of the fellowship with these gentle steps, an approach to outreach that does not require a lengthy sermon or lecture about the Christian faith. All that is needed is time to reflect on a special day with others in a way that includes faith and hope in Christ and the sensitivity to do so in a way that is received as a gift of love.

Another example is that of a community anticipating a large influx of seniors through the construction of a number of senior housing units in the city. A local congregation learned that a couple from the congregation was going to be moving into one of these apartment complexes the following year. Instead of making plans simply to post signs to invite the new residents to the congregation, the outreach team of the congregation decided to do a Blessing of the New Home Milestone in the new home of the couple from the congregation. The couple plans to invite their new neighbors in the apartment complex to attend the event. This will allow the fellow residents to experience this home as a place for conversation, prayer, and blessings, a place to shepherd souls. The congregation will invite other residents to have a blessing of their new homes, too. Through such means, the congregation hopes to demonstrate to the new neighbors that their congregation is a ministry site ready to equip and bless people with the Christian faith. This is an example of a community of faith not waiting for people to walk through their doors but going out to meet people where they are and bless them with the good news of Jesus Christ, establish trusted relationships, continue to serve the needs of the new residents, and trust and pray that the people will hunger and thirst for more.

The shepherding ministry of a congregation is strengthened by the ability to reach out directly into homes in order to connect with people who may not otherwise be associated with the ministry of the congregation. Using a simple Four Key Faith Practices design, countless milestones can be celebrated or observed in homes. One older couple established their home as a place to celebrate God's presence at particular milestones like birthdays and retirements. They joined with one couple celebrating the wife's seventieth birthday. It gave the husband the opportunity to express his love and support for his wife, naming many of her accomplishments over the years. He did so to encourage her into a future—an unknown future with health issues for them both—that would be journeyed in faith. The evening celebration included ample conversations, a celebratory Bible verse (Psalm 118:24), the service of offering a tasty meal and birthday cake, and a blessing for the new septuagenarian. This same host couple has reached out to other people on their birthdays as well as those having a wedding anniversary, anticipating a surgery, or transitioning to retirement. They know that all these moments provide opportunities to shepherd people in God's providential care.

Service Activities as an Opportunity to Shepherd Souls

Whether it is the mission trip to Tanzania or El Salvador or providing meals to homes experiencing a food shortage, helping others is a way of life for Christians. A mission trip can easily be expanded to be a milestones ministry event. Participating in a mission trip in another part of the country or world is a good example of how service can contribute to the shepherd of souls ministry within a congregation. Each congregational mission trip participant can be cared for and shepherded by family, friends, and others back home.[2] Weeks before the trip happens, the congregation can organize a mission trip send-off. In addition to the mission trip travelers, family, friends, neighbors, and people from the congregation and community gather together. Each traveler will have a prayer and action partner, someone who will keep abreast of the daily activities during the mission trip, pray for the traveler and the people to be met, and, if possible through social media, stay connected with the traveler to wonder how the experience is impacting that person throughout the mission trip.

> *Serving others actually feels good, for it releases dopamine and other hormones into our bloodstream that help us feel joy and delight. Helping others changes our bodies and minds and influences our feelings and attitudes towards others and God.*

Having a prayer and action partner for each mission trip participant adds an intentional shepherding component to the trip. Once the group returns from the trip, participants and prayer and action partners can sit down and review what happened and how it all affected the participants' view of the world, their Christian faith, and their commitment to grow in grace in the years ahead. A follow-up conversation about a month later is an opportunity for ongoing reflection as the mission trip participants seek to integrate a potentially life-changing experience with life back home.

Essential Elements for Shepherding Souls
To recapitulate, milestones ministry in congregations and homes emphasizes shepherding through four essential elements:

1. The milestone event is for more than the recipient of the milestone. It is an experience that brings the larger faith village together to support, guide, and equip another person and those around that person. Therefore, congregations that do shepherding well with milestones ministry bring in other people like mentors, council members, family, friends, and more.

2. Participants in a milestones event serve as mentors to the recipients of the milestone moment and to one another. This exemplifies that shepherding often continues beyond the particular milestone event. By using the Four Key Faith Practices with others, people learn how simple

176 Shepherd of Souls

shepherding can be and this encourages them to care for people beyond specific milestones ministry events.

3. Shepherding souls includes reaching out to others with the love of God in Christ. Therefore, milestones ministry is not for congregational members only. Milestone ministry events welcome family, friends, colleagues, and other community people into the experience of nurturing faith along life's milestones.

4. Follow-up is critical for a milestone event and shepherding to be meaningful and effective. Neither works very well as a one-and-done faith formation experience. Simply having a milestones ministry event as an isolated moment is not enough. Once the initial experience has concluded, people in this kind of ministry look for ways to have a follow-up gathering or personal conversation at an appropriate and helpful time. This way, people have another opportunity to reflect on God's word and its impact on their thoughts, words, and deeds as disciples of Christ and recipients of God's eternal care.

Congregations use these four elements to assist individuals and small groups (including families as a God-given small group) to be shepherds to one another, in so doing fostering a culture that supports, equips, and cares for people as they grow and mature in the Christian faith.

Does it work? Yes! One retired bishop served short-term in a congregation that has developed an extensive milestones ministry series for children and youth. At the end of his ministry with the congregation he commented,

What most impressed me was the work being done with Milestones. Three aspects of this work stood out for me: First, you seek to work with children and homes over a period of 18 years. Second, the home involvement is so important since passing on the faith to the next generation rests primarily with the home. The church can provide some resources and a group

Milestones Ministry: A Model for Shepherding 177

setting, but the real work belongs to the home. Third, I like the way "home" is understood. It reaches out to include grandparents, aunts and uncles, and in some cases neighbors. The more support for the children and youth...the better.

It could be added, the adults that gather with these children and youth not only give meaningful support to the faith formation of the children and youth, it deepens the faith formation of the adults, too. It is a kind of adult Christian education that combines Christian reflection with action.

Milestones Ministry: Not a Program—A Way to Shepherd Souls

A pastor's involvement in the congregation's milestones ministry is particularly critical because it is about shepherding souls, about faith formation and soul care. Not only does a pastor typically have more experience in shepherding souls, experience he or she can pass along to a congregation, the pastor's endorsement of the milestones ministry as a way of faith formation rather than as a program of the church usually spurs its adoption and growth.

Such ongoing growth is what makes milestones ministry different from a program. It's not one-and-done. It's a way of being church. For it encourages people to meet together in small groups where they reflect, talk, pray, and serve one another and others through trusted relationships. They check in with one another as a means of ongoing support. This establishes a pattern of being church that is easy to continue after particular milestone events have concluded. People explore various faith practices over time to discover which are most meaningful to them. While practicing soul care with one another in a safe and guided manner through milestones ministry, people become freed to enjoy the shepherd of souls ministry whenever the need or desire arises.

The ultimate goal is to encourage and equip people to practice a way of life, a way of being that daily embraces the living word of God. Milestones ministry teaches everyone how to be a shepherd by showing them how to engage regularly in basic Christian practices. After experiencing a number of milestone ministry events in the life of the congregation and home, people become more and more comfortable remembering and giving thanks for their Christian faith and the presence of their living, gracious God. With time and practice, people will more effortlessly connect daily life relationships with their Christian faith through a community of shepherds who engage in caring conversations, prayer, and reflection.

Questions for Reflection and Conversation

1. In what milestones in the life of the congregation do you currently engage (e.g., baptisms, giving Bibles to children, weddings, funerals, etc.)?

2. What milestones do you celebrate or observe in your home (e.g., birthdays, anniversaries, holidays, etc.)? How can you make these milestone experiences a way to nurture the Christian faith? How do you currently do this?

3. Are milestones ministry events in your congregation largely to benefit children or are they to equip all generations to shepherd souls? Explain.

4. Page 169 mentions a five-part structure to make the most of milestones ministry. Which of the five does your congregation do well? Which of these need more attention?

5. How has milestones ministry in your congregation been able to reach out to people beyond those active in the life of your congregation?

6. How can milestones ministry in your congregation do more to reach out to those outside the life of your congregation?

7. How would you like to use milestones ministry to promote the shepherd of souls ministry?

8. What specific congregational milestones would you like to see added or expanded?

Milestones Ministry: A Model for Shepherding 179

9. What specific milestones for the home would you like to see added or expanded?

10. What specific milestones for the community would you like to see added or expanded?

11. Use the blank pages at the end of the book to jot down ideas of what next steps you would like to take to promote milestones ministry in the congregation and your home.

CONFIRMATION AS SHEPHERDING SOULS

You shall put these words of mine in your heart and soul, and you shall bind them as a sign on your hand, and fix them as an emblem on your forehead. Teach them to your children, talking about them when you are at home and when you are away, when you lie down and when you rise. *Deuteronomy 11:18–19*

Note: This chapter is the collaborative effort of David Anderson with his longtime friend and partner in ministry, Pastor Mark Asleson. Pastor Asleson recently retired after thirty-eight years of parish ministry. Over the years he has developed clear and effective pastoral leadership for faith formation through milestones ministry and particularly through the significant milestone of confirmation ministry. His work has been fundamentally shaped through what he calls "home-based ministry," a cross+generational approach to faith formation that brings together members of one's family as well as other personal, trusted relationships along the journey of faith. When the first person singular or plural "I" or "we" is used later in this chapter, it references Pastor Asleson's own voice that articulates what he witnessed, learned, evaluated and implemented in an approach to confirmation ministry that shepherds souls into Christian discipleship.

182 Shepherd of Souls

Over time, the church has used a great variety of ways to mark confirmation, and even today the curricula, schedules, and expectations for confirmation have varied from congregation to congregation and pastor to pastor. The lack of standardization and clarity in confirmation ministry seems almost staggering to imagine and a bit bewildering to congregations.

In August 1979, brand new pastor Mark Asleson sat down with the parents of his first confirmation class to find out what they wanted and hoped for in their children's confirmation. When asked what they wanted, the first answer was, "Well, Pastor, you went to seminary. Don't you know?" Neither the parents nor the new pastor was sure.

David Anderson also started his first parish call in August of 1979. Confirmation was to begin in September. He decided he would start with the existing confirmation program in the congregation and over time make adjustments based on his strengths, preferences and emerging assessment of what a successful confirmation program would look like. Unfortunately, within a week of his arrival, the chairperson of the Christian education committee told him the former program had not worked for the confirmation families, and he would need to create an entirely new confirmation program. He ended up purchasing all the curricula he could find at his denomination's publishing house and by September rolled out his own concoction of a confirmation program.

Within a few years, research emerged that found that confirmation ministry was the number one reason Lutheran pastors were leaving parish ministry. And within a decade research that compared six Protestant denominations indicated that during the middle school and junior high school years, Lutherans had the highest level of youth involvement in Christian education.[1] During the high school years, Lutheran youth involvement dropped off precipitously, going from first to last among their Protestant peers. Lutheran junior high youth were involved in Christian education primarily because of confirmation classes, but once the program was over, the youth vanished. The research led some Lutheran clergy to suggest that maybe the church should drop confirmation classes so that the church would lose fewer youth! Not only was confirmation not working for the pastors, it was not working for the confirmands or their parents who largely disappeared from the congregation after their children were confirmed. What had not occurred to most pastors and congregational leaders at the time was that confirmation provides a wonderful opportunity to shepherd souls. It seems they had understood confirmation ministry largely as an occasion to teach an overview of key biblical passages and themes and to present the essentials of the Christian faith in whatever way one's own denomination taught those essentials. It seems that they hoped, at best, that confirmation students would finish their classes with a workable understanding of the Bible and what it meant to be a member of their own denomination. Confirmation appeared to be a product of Enlightenment thinking that emphasized faith as knowing and accepting certain theological propositions, and a product of denominational wars that hoped to protect the youth from foreign theologies and pieties. In other words, youth were taught what not to believe as well as what they should believe.

Certainly, maturing in one's understanding of Christian concepts is of value and part of lifelong Christian education faith formation. Confirmation programs may help youth understand the awe-inspiring goodness and mercy of God in the Bible and Christian doctrine, but for the concepts to be awe-inspiring there needs to be more than information and lectures. People need to be shepherded in faith by experiencing faith, not simply conceptualizing faith. To "be doers of the word, and not merely hearers who deceive themselves" (James 1:22) is a guiding principle that can prevent Christian education leaders from deceiving themselves and fooling the youth into thinking that Christian concepts suffice for the Christian life and faith.

What a Shepherding Model for Confirmation Ministry Looks Like

A shepherding model for confirmation ministry does not need to be set in opposition to learning information in the Bible and about one's own faith tradition. In fact, the shepherding model proposed here suggests that by mentoring or apprenticing youth (and adults) during confirmation ministry, they will actually retain more information. For practicing the faith instills the faith far more profoundly than does

184 Shepherd of Souls

hearing about the faith in a passive, sedentary position. The addition of shepherding to a confirmation formation model emphasizes that confirmation ministry is not youth ministry but a cross+generational ministry that equips individuals and communities to shepherd children, youth, and adults in the Christian faith.

The shepherding model for confirmation envisages youth attending faith formation sessions with a mentor, preferably a parent. When parents are not available, other family members—grandparents are especially good at this—or congregational mentors can serve in the role as well. The mentor does not come to these confirmation sessions to support the youth as an observer but to walk alongside and fully participate in faith-filled conversations and activities with the teen.

In addition to a mentor who participates with a youth for the entire confirmation program (or for one year at a time), other adults from the congregation and community are also encouraged to join in the confirmation experience. It is abundantly evident that most adults in the congregation remember very little about the content of their confirmation as a youth (if they attended confirmation at all). Adults who join in a confirmation program often acknowledge how the current confirmation experience seems fresh, new, and even inspiring to them in ways they do not recall experiencing when they were teens.

An Example of a Shepherding Model for a Confirmation Class Session

The session outline for a shepherding model of a confirmation class looks very different than the typical classroom hour. The fundamental contribution of the shepherding model is to help the youth-mentor dyad (or triad or larger group if the youth has more adults joining him or her regularly) experience the faith through conversation, reflections, prayer, and service as it is developed and expanded through the Four Key Faith Practices. In other words, the conversations, reflections, prayer, and service are based on doing the word of God and not just hearing about it or talking about it. These faith experiences are intended to feed the youth and mentor for a lifetime.

Confirmation as Shepherding Souls   185

Let me give you an example from the Lutheran tradition. Let's say the confirmation group of youth and adults is learning about the eighth commandment (ninth commandment for the Reformed tradition): "You shall not bear false witness against your neighbor." In a modern translation of Luther's Small Catechism, the explanation for the commandment reads as follows: "We are to fear and love God, so that we do not tell lies about our neighbors, betray or slander them, or destroy their reputations. Instead we are to come to their defense, speak well of them, and interpret everything they do in the best possible light."[2]

The shepherding model using the Four Key Faith Practices might include the following sample outline for youth and their confirmation mentors to share around a table in class and take home to be used at the family table:

Caring Conversations (directed to youth and adults alike):

1. Tell about a time when someone spoke up for you in your defense or simply offered a kind word that spoke well of you.

2. Tell about a time you talked about someone in a way that defended them and spoke well of them.

3. When you have heard someone speak wrongfully about a different religious or ethnic group of people, how did you respond?

4. What was it like when someone said something about you that was not true and was hurtful?

5. When have you said something about someone else that was hurtful? How did you feel afterward? How did it influence your relationship with the person about whom you were speaking?

Devotions

Begin each day of the next week praying the explanation of the Eighth Commandment. "Dear God, we thank you for protecting our names and reputations with the Eighth Commandment. Help me to

186 Shepherd of Souls

fear and love you with awe and reverence by not telling lies about others, betraying or slandering them, or destroying their reputations. Instead, help me to come to the defense of others, speak well of them, and interpret everything they do in the best possible light. In the name of Jesus Christ, our Savior and Lord, amen."

Service

Take note of the comments made and heard during the week about other people. Try to avoid making negative comments about others and, at the same time, find kind and supportive things to say about others, especially those who are not particular friends.

Rituals and Traditions

Take a clothespin and keep it with you during the week, say in your pocket. When you feel or see it, let it remind you to keep your lips closed long enough to think of how your comments might hurt or encourage those around you.

A shepherding model for confirmation has three distinct parts for the time together. The first third focuses on youth and adults talking about how their use of the Four Key Faith Practices went from the prior week, in this case, the practices associated with the Eighth Commandment. Through their experiences and stories, they are now the ones teaching the Christian faith to one another. Have the participants ask one another: What was it like to have the caring conversations with family and friends? How did praying the Eighth Commandment affect their lives and their relationships during their week? What was it like to record conversations and be aware of how one talked about others? What was it like carrying around the clothespin? The second third of the time together is for introducing the next topic to be explored (likely, the Ninth Commandment), and the last third to construct or reflect on the Four Key Faith Practices to be used during the following week as a way to explore the new topic.

So, the Eighth Commandment initially would have been introduced in the second part of the class hour. The pastor or other leader

Confirmation as Shepherding Souls 187

could talk about how we honor and love God by caring for others with our words. Words do hurt and words do bless people's lives. Examples from the Bible, history, and current events could illustrate the importance of the commandment.

During the third part of the class time, the mentor group composed of a youth and parent(s) or other mentor(s) can write their own Eighth Commandment Four Key Faith Practices or use or adapt examples given to the larger class. The mentoring groups can then discuss how they will use those practices during the week. It would be appropriate and helpful to use the Caring Conversation starters during the final part of the class and close by using the Devotional prayer.

When the confirmation class meets the following week, each mentoring group (youth and parent or other mentor) could sit down alone or with one other mentoring group and discuss what it was like to engage in the faith practices that focused on the Eight Commandment. In addition to the questions listed above, here are some other sample questions that could be used to guide the conversations and process the experiences from the prior week:

- How did the experience impact your conversations and relationships with others?
- How did you sense God's loving presence in your life through this commandment?
- How were you reminded of your sinfulness when you broke the commandment or were aware of how you wanted to behave in a way that broke the commandment?
- How did praying the devotional prayer open you to love God and neighbor?
- What was it like to be reminded of the importance of the commandment by having a clothespin with you each day?
- What was your overall experience like?
- What did you learn?
- How did it impact your relationships with others and with God?
- How do you want to honor the Eighth Commandment in the future?

188 Shepherd of Souls

These mentoring group conversations generally last about ten to fifteen minutes. In the following five to ten minutes, open the conversation to the whole group to discuss how the small groups responded to these conversation starters. Once this process is used, it is likely that the first part of the confirmation hour will increase to about half the class time. The heart of what is gained during confirmation classes will typically come from the insights gained and shared with others during this first segment of the class.

The pastor or other catechist leading the class becomes a facilitator of conversations and a key person to frame the subsequent conversations. For some people may miss important points or misrepresent the lesson and the Christian faith entirely. When that happens, the facilitator can diplomatically yet clearly move the conversation into the direction of core Christian teachings and behaviors. That people will contribute comments that reflect civil religion instead of biblical and historical Christianity is to be expected. It is there in our culture and in our congregations. In what better venue could we hope to address such thoughts, feelings, and actions than in a Christian community? This action-reflection model presents an engaging format that keeps the attention of participants and directs and redirects words and deeds to reflect Christian discipleship. This is shepherding in action.

A number of observations can be made about this shepherding model of confirmation faith formation:

- It reduces lecture time and adds to learning through personal involvement, trusted and caring conversations, and shared experiences.
- Confirmation lessons impact the whole week, not simply an hour of religious education.
- Each lesson gets two weeks of attention instead of a "one-and-done" approach.
- Repetition of a message with some variations over two weeks reinforces what is learned.
- What is really learned is how to speak faith out loud.
- Confirmation promotes the Christian faith as a way of life instead of propositional concepts to be mastered.

Confirmation as Shepherding Souls 189

- Cross+generational learning takes place during the hour together as a class as well as at home, at work, at school and other daily-life settings.
- The youth and adult students become the catechists as they tell one another what they experienced during the week and how those experiences and reflections have impacted their understanding of God and the Christian life.
- The youth and adult students become witnesses to the faith on a regular basis.
- Confirmation leaders and students become shepherds to one another.
- Confirmation leaders become shepherds more than teachers.
- Attentiveness during the class hour stays high as all students are actively engaged in the faith formation session.
- Youth and adults become more adept at seeing all of life through the life of Jesus Christ.
- And, it has been reported that youth have been known to go to school the next day excited to talk about their confirmation experiences.

One Pastor's Experience in Confirmation as Shepherding: A Congregational Study

Although there has been a long history and a multitude of research to suggest that experiential and cross+generational learning—especially that which engages family relationships—has a very positive impact on faith formation, there is no direct research study that has evaluated the shepherding model of confirmation that has just been outlined. However, there are pastors who have tried a variety of approaches that simulate this model of emphasizing the role of the home and cross+generational learning through conversation, reflections, prayer, and service. Pastor Mark Asleson is one of those pastors and what follows presents his experience for its heuristic experimentation, contributions, and recommendations for others to consider.

Pastor Asleson has worked for over twenty-five years to develop a confirmation ministry that brings together youth, parents, other family members and both congregation and community in the confirmation experience. He uses the Four Key Faith Practices as a foundation for the confirmation sessions that encourages regular cross+generational conversations. (Years one and three focus on Luther's Small Catechism and year two—the longest series of the three—focuses on the Bible.) None of the youth comes alone. Instead, every youth comes with at least one caring, trusted adult who comes not to watch but to participate as a member of the class. This includes service events that can involve not only the whole class (including the adult mentors) but also small, cross+generational groups that the youth initiate on their own. Rituals and traditions occur through an opening ritual of lighting of a candle to note the presence of Christ, the light of the world. Each session then opens and later closes with prayer, in short a devotional experience. The class ends with each mentor group blessing each member in it, an example of a ritual and tradition. Interestingly, Pastor Asleson notes that each year he only lit the candle himself the first two or three weeks. After that—and without any prompting—someone would have lit the candle by the time he began the class session, a mark of how the group owned the ritual.

Prior to his retirement in 2017, Pastor Asleson had been the senior pastor of Dilworth Lutheran Church for twenty-two years. During the last seventeen years of his pastoral leadership there, he introduced and developed a home-based faith formation ministry that included confirmation ministry. Just prior to that time he had studied the Five Principles of Faith Formation and the Four Key Faith Practices (see Appendix 1) at The Youth & Family Institute of Augsburg College in a week-long continuing education workshop entitled "Family Factor in Faith Nurture," a course designed by David Anderson while on staff at The Youth & Family Institute.

Asleson recounts his own work with confirmation ministry over the years. It represents his development of what is now referred to as a shepherding model for confirmation ministry.

Confirmation as Shepherding Souls 191

Pastor Mark Asleson's Story in His Own Words

I remember well the first confirmation classes I taught as a young pastor in a two-point parish in southern Minnesota. The small class would gather weekly to learn about the Lord's Prayer, the Ten Commandments, Holy Communion, baptism, confession and absolution and, of course, the Bible. There was much to teach and so little time. After that first year, I concluded that if we spend an hour a week for thirty weeks, September to May, those thirty hours for each of the two years simply did not provide adequate time. So, over the next ten years I took part in various confirmation training opportunities that suggested new curriculum and teaching methods on how better to use those sixty hours. With the support of the congregations I served, we expanded to a three-year program that would provide ninety hours of class time. I sought to use the most current materials along with what was considered the best technologies to engage the students. I tried various class schedules: before school, after school, evenings, and even Sunday mornings. One year I tried a monthly confirmation retreat on Saturday mornings (it is not easy to lead a three- to four-hour seminar and keep young people interested or awake on a Saturday morning). The congregation then developed a mentor-based program that involved adult mentors as small group leaders. The evening would begin with music followed by a presentation on the material to be taught that night. It concluded with the students meeting in small groups to cover the material and for group discussion and prayer.

Still the results were clear. Confirmation was not doing what we hoped it would do: encourage, equip, and bless the students, their homes, and the larger congregation. Instead, the data from our congregations and the larger church reported that for all the time and energy invested, we were accomplishing very little.

192 Shepherd of Souls

It often takes serious frustration and personal pain to move one to new insights and creativity. In my case it was the typical experience of seeing countless youth go through confirmation classes only to disappear afterward, often with their parents in tow, out the back door of the life of the congregation. One experience in particular became the proverbial straw that broke the camel's back.

The boy's name was "Henry" (a pseudonym for use in this story). Henry was one of the brightest and most biblically literate confirmation students I ever remember having. He was someone the other youth in the class would listen to and follow. Henry not only asked great questions, but his questions drew the others into the conversations. I remember thinking he might even consider becoming a pastor. I recall talking to Henry about how he might continue to be involved in the church after confirmation, but his response caught me completely off guard. He said, "Oh Pastor, I'm not coming back. Do you see my parents here or my other family members? My parents wanted me to be confirmed, and I did that. No, Pastor, I won't be back." That was close to twenty years ago, and although I see him on occasion in the community, he has yet to come back to the congregation.

It was his words that not only caught my attention but moved me to change my thinking about confirmation and more generally about faith formation and discipleship. As Christians, we believe that faith is a gift, a gift from God through the work of the Holy Spirit. However, I had been under the impression that faith was something we taught. Certainly, the goal of confirmation, along with many other teaching ministries, is to instruct, but it is also to encourage faith. Henry was educated; he knew information. He had heard and learned all those lessons that the church strives to teach. However, all those lessons took up less than an hour of the 168 hours in his week, less

Confirmation as Shepherding Souls   193

than one percent of his time. I suspect he spent about fifty-six hours a week sleeping and another forty to fifty hours at school and doing homework, which leaves approximately sixty to seventy hours for his home life with family and friends. That one hour a week for about half the year and carried out for three years didn't add up to much of an impact on Henry's faith.

All of this led me to ask: "What am I missing? What do we want confirmation to accomplish? What are we expecting as an outcome?" Let me be clear: I would never suggest that Henry did not believe, that Henry did not have faith. However, what is also clear is that Henry did not see the church as a place for him or his family to be nurtured in the Christian faith. He had learned what he had to learn and now he was done. As I thought about his honest response, I realized it is the reality the church is facing with a great many other Henrys and their homes, countless people who have often left without saying a word.

As I considered how to move forward, I recalled John Westerhoff's words in his book Will Our Children Have Faith? written in 1976 when I was in seminary. Westerhoff wrote, "Faith cannot be taught by any method of instruction; we can only teach religion."[3] He goes on to write, "Faith, therefore, and not religion, must become the concern of Christian education. . . Experienced faith, therefore, results from our interactions with other faithing selves."[4] I was now getting a greater understanding of what Westerhoff meant. It connects to the first of the Five Principles: Faith is formed by the power of the Holy Spirit through personal, trusted relationships—often in our own homes. Yes, information is important, but as a community of faith we are to speak the faith out loud. Our human voices are part of the work of the Holy Spirit that nurtures the Christian faith. We are to speak in order to share our experiences and understanding of faith with one another. Faith spoken out loud encourages faith, *not only for youth but for the whole community of faith, for the congregation, for every home, for all God's people even those beyond the doors for the congregation.*

To accomplish this, I knew a couple things to be true. First, this is God's work accomplished among us through the power of Holy Spirit. Second, the task is about more than me (the pastor) and my ability to teach, speak, and encourage. Third, the task is too big to be done alone; we (the congregation) need parents, extended family members, and other faith mentors along with the support of the congregation.

I had to adjust my thinking about the ministry of the church and how the church nurtures faith in the lives of people. It had to be about more than public worship and a classroom presentation and the use of instructional models that were far removed from people's life experiences and relationships. Due to my own experiences and frustrations with the confirmation ministry over the years, I decided to commit fully to a model that shepherded both the youth and their homes through the active involvement of parents, grandparents, and other mentors. I guided the congregation through a faith formation process that used the Four Key Faith Practices as a foundational way for people to speak, practice, study, experience, and encourage faith. I referred to it as a "home-based" confirmation ministry, one that fully incorporated the shepherding model presented here.

Almost immediately I began to notice a difference. I especially noticed the engagement of the mentors: these parents and other congregational adults were not standing at the back of the room watching the children learn as they might have been before. I didn't use the word at that time, but what I was watching was the shepherding of souls. It was amazing to listen and hear not only what the adults said about faith and life, but how the young people both listened and responded to the parents and other adults in the room. Yet it was what I noticed next that really caught my attention and my heart. The parents and other adult mentors began to engage one another in faith conversations and encouragement after class. They were beginning to speak the faith out loud, shepherding one another. They were actively engaged. I also noticed that I wasn't teaching as much as I was listening and watching as youth and adults told stories of life and faith with each other. Again, I didn't use the word at that time, but what I was doing was "shepherding."

Dealing with Resistance

Transitioning to a home-based confirmation structure that asks parents and other adults to engage in faith conversation and instruction with youth had its challenges. Initially, it was difficult to get parents to come. It was not uncommon to hear a parent respond with something like, "Been there, done that; ain't coming back!" So instead I asked such parents along with their children to name a mentor, a trusted, caring adult who would commit to coming regularly with the confirmation youth.

I will never forget the mother who came to me when we first began our home-based confirmation ministry. She obviously didn't want to attend with her daughter. Her comment to me was, "I want my daughter to have the same experience I had with my pastor when I was her age." As we visited, she told me that her own dad had died when she was young. Her family lived next door to the parsonage and the pastor's daughter was her best friend. She remembers many a night at the dinner table of her friend and even going with them on family vacations and outings. As I listened, I began to understand that the pastor and his family were a second "family" to this woman. She was not seeking a program of education for her daughter; instead, what she wanted for her daughter was a relationship like the relationship she had known with her pastor. The difficulty was that I could not give her daughter that same experience. I was not the next-door neighbor. I was not the father of a best friend. I could not be a father figure to her daughter. In short, I could not be the family she wanted me to be for her child . . . but she could. I hoped this mother would understand that someday, and provide the kind of faith nurture that would stay with her daughter for a lifetime.

This is an example of how difficult it is for some people to see the work of the church as theirs rather than as that of the programs and leaders of a congregation. What this mother could not see was how she could be a part of her daughter's faith formation, of how her faith spoken out loud could and would bless both of them as well as the community around them. The mother could not see that the home next door to hers when she was growing up was actually a living church for her where "faith is formed through personal, trusted relationships." However, for this mother, that could not be church. And yet, as I listened to her story, it truly was an expression of church for her. I have had a number of occasions over the years when people have resisted seeing the shepherding ministry going on around them.

This has been confirmed by my own informal confirmation research. Over the past seventeen years, I have met with eighth graders and their parents or mentors at the end of each eighth-grade year (for us the second year of confirmation). One of the questions I asked was simply this: "Would you prefer to come just with your friends, or continue to include a parent or mentor in the confirmation process?" I always assured them that they will continue to come with their friends and classmates no matter how they answered the question. Would they still choose to include parents and other mentors?

Over three hundred young people went through the home-based confirmation classes. Once the parents, grandparents, and other mentors are included, that means that over 750 people have participated. Out of over three hundred youth, only seven teens said they would not want the adults present in confirmation! That means 98 percent of the teens answered that they wanted their parents or mentors present in the confirmation classes.[5]

However, when we first began the new home-based confirmation, I had a number of parents who said that their children would prefer to come to class without them or that a mentor would be better. One particular mother who said this told me that children need the opportunity to talk freely among their classmates and friends, away from the watchful eyes and ears of parents. However, during the eighth-grade confirmation interview with her child, I asked my standard question and the daughter's response caught her mother completely off guard. The daughter responded, "I would want my parents there." The mother responded, "Why, why would she say that?" And the daughter simply and candidly said, "There are things that we need to talk about that I can't talk about in front of my friends and classmates." That evening, the mother's whole perspective about our home-based ministry changed.

Over the years I have had adult members like her who would not come to a Bible study or even dare to speak out in a congregation meeting out of fear that they might somehow reveal their lack of knowledge of things related to the Christian faith. These fears can develop into resistance to cross+generational faith formation and be communicated in a number of ways. Like this mother, some will suggest that it is better for their child to go through confirmation with another adult, just not them. They may say that their child would not want them there, but this is an opinion that is rebuffed by 98 percent of our confirmation youth.[6]

The Importance of Milestones Ministry to Home-Based Ministry

Shepherding, meaning encouraging faith and a life of faith in one another, begins at baptism. Baptism is the first and most essential milestone of the church. In response to God's promise and claim in Holy Baptism, we call on parents and sponsors to encourage infants and small children (most often) by telling them of God's promise and love. As a result, after baptism, the second milestone event we offer is when the child is two, the year before they can begin Sunday school. This early milestone event helps parents, the extended family, and also the congregation do just what they promised at baptism: to nurture, encourage, and bless these little ones in Christ. The congregation developed a total of thirteen milestones—including baptism and confirmation—to help the home over the years to engage actively in their child's faith formation.

There is not much to be afraid of when the focus is on the emerging faith of a small child. An important benefit of milestones ministry is that parents (and other family members and friends) experience faith formation together with their children and discover that many of their fears and anxieties about faith and life are not uncommon.

However, the real blessing and gift of milestones ministry is that it builds a community of faith, fellowship, and trust not only in individual households but also across the larger congregation. Households that have participated in the milestones ministry series often become more involved in the life of the congregation prior to and beyond the confirmation years. Milestones ministry, including confirmation ministry, has deeply impacted the life of the congregation over the past seventeen years. Along with nurturing the faith of our youth and adults, it has also strengthened the vitality and mission of the congregation. In a congregation of 1,100 baptized persons, a majority have been engaged in training for shepherding through milestones ministry. It has allowed the pastors and other faith formation educators to serve as shepherds, encouragers, and teachers as they equip others to be shepherds as well.

The challenge for the larger church is to believe that confirmation ministry is best understood as a ministry that is experienced for a lifetime. It begins in baptism and is best lived out through a cross+generational emphasis that encourages faith spoken out loud. Confirmation ministry shepherds faith in all God's people and results in blessing the home, the congregation, the community, the church beyond the local congregation, and the world. What I discovered in inviting households to be involved in confirmation is that we were not only nurturing, teaching, and encouraging children and youth, but also the adults. I cannot tell you how often I have heard adults tell me, "I don't remember any of this from when I was in Sunday school or confirmation." Truly, nurturing, teaching, and encouraging God's children in the Christian faith is for everyone.

Shifting the Paradigm of Confirmation from a Youth Focus to a Home Focus

A mother and her son came in for their confirmation visit at the end of their second year of classes. I asked the young man my standard question: "If you could do the first two years over again, would you choose to come just with your friends and classmates or would you still want your mother to attend with you?" This usually very quiet boy turned to his mother, smiled, and said that he would still want his mother to be there. The boy's words caught his mother completely off guard. In fact, she sounded a bit agitated as she looked at him and said, "Don't you realize how difficult this has been for me, how much time and effort it has taken to reschedule work each week so that I could attend with you, how busy our life has been with all the family and home issues that have impacted our home over that last year?" She went on to describe the challenges of their home life in great detail. Her young teenage son seemed quite embarrassed by the fact that his mother was saying all these things in front of the pastor. When the mother had regained her composure, she turned to her son and asked, "Well then, why would you answer the way you did?" The son looked at his mother and responded simply and quietly, "Because each week I knew I had you." The mother looked at her son and began to cry as she realized that her Wednesday nights with her youngest son was the glue that was holding their relationship together. After that, they both kept coming, but not because she had to. Instead, she came and continued to come because she wanted to. As she told me later, that conversation in my office was one that neither of them would ever forget.

There was also a father who came with his daughter. One night the father came up to me after class and said, "I think I know what you're up to, Pastor. You're not after my daughter; you're after me." I paused for a moment and said; "No, I don't think so. I think what I'm after is your grandchildren." The father looked at me and said, "But she is only fourteen. What do you mean you're after her children?" I responded, "What do you think she will remember about confirmation? Do you think she will remember who came with her and—assuming she does—will she come and bring her children as you brought her?" That was over fifteen years ago. Recently that daughter and her husband, along with her dad and mom, joined together in the baptism of her child. The father who is now the grandfather and I looked at one another and gave each other a knowing smile.

The critical role of shepherding faith in our children, youth, and adults has become more and more obvious to me. Every week, as part of our confirmation class time together, homes are given opportunities to reflect on what faith means to them. One night a mom, who is well respected both in the congregation and the larger community, shared openly with the group about some of her struggles in seeking to be a good and faithful mom to her children. I watched as her son listened to his mom talk about what her faith meant to her in the midst of her doubts and challenges. Of all that he remembers about confirmation, I doubt he will ever forget his mother's willingness to stand up and bear a public witness to her life and faith. It was also amazing to watch what happened after class that night, how the other parents—especially the other moms—gathered around her, thanked her, and began to share their own stories, struggles and all. That night something changed in the congregation: certain barriers came down, the barriers that keep us from supporting and encouraging one another, the barriers that make us think that we are supposed to have everything under control. That night blessed not only the class, this mother, her son, and the other homes, but also the larger community as precious conversations like hers spilled out into other fellowship settings in the congregation and community!

I have watched the eyes of the teens, those youth whose parents have stood up and spoken of their faith out loud. I have seen the teen's eyes glued to their parents as they responded to a question or shared a concern, doubt, or belief. Of all the things the youth will remember from confirmation (and other milestone events), they are most likely to remember the words, convictions, beliefs, and core values their parents, grandparents, and mentors articulated to them. Is this not faith formation? As I have often found myself saying, "What is the worst thing that will happen if the home takes the time to talk about faith, values, and life, and in the midst of it all, to do service activities that communicate the love of God in Christ?"

Confirmation and the other teaching ministries of the church are intended to promote lifelong faith formation. Research, personal experiences, and congregational trial-and-error strategies are teaching us that Christian formation is strongly aided by the intentional practice of shepherding souls, souls who are often in one's own home. These souls walk alongside and take the information of the faith and give it flesh and blood so that the Christian faith becomes the source of trust and hope for a lifetime. If Henry's parents had been a part of his confirmation experience, would Henry, his brothers, and his parents be in the church today?

The Dynamic of Changing Family Configurations Participating in Confirmation

Divorce is not an uncommon event in the lives of the homes throughout the congregation and larger community. Parents may get divorced, but Mom and Dad never stop being Mom and Dad. As a result, I began intentionally to invite divorced parents to attend with their children. It was a bit of a concern at first because tensions are often high between divorced couples. It was not unusual for couples to tell me that it was not easy to come, and yet some—if not many—agreed it was important for their child. The truth of that conviction became even more evident as I watched the positive responses from their children.

There were also the single parents. I had a single mom who came with her daughter. The mom had never married and had decided to come with her sister, her daughter's baptismal sponsor. The father of the child, who is from a different Christian faith tradition, asked if he could come also. All four of them came together regularly on Wednesday nights for three years. In addition, during the year in which we focused on the Bible, they gathered once a week to talk and pray about the week and the lesson. Not many church leadership or faith formation models will mention the possibility of this kind of healing and new day for parents and children, but with an inclusive approach to home-based ministry, it has happened.

It is also not uncommon in a congregation to have homes where marriages are in trouble. However, what I have noticed is that the

202 Shepherd of Souls

homes involved in our home-based ministry (including the many milestones ministry events before and after confirmation) tend to be more willing than others to seek help in the midst of those troubles. In the past, couples who were getting divorced often ended up leaving the congregation and losing the support of the faith community. However, because of the connections homes make with other homes through our home-based ministry, many of the couples that are going through tough times have found support and encouragement from the other parents and homes. As a result, some of the couples who have become divorced have found a way to remain in the congregation. I am not suggesting that this always happens, but I have witnessed the reconciling power of faith active in love as we have sought to shepherd a community of faith with the ministry of reconciliation.

An Ecumenical and Cross+Generational Environment for Shepherding Souls

Like many other congregations, we have a number of homes that include persons from a variety of faith traditions. It has been instructive to listen to the conversations that occur during confirmation classes, especially from adults who have come from a Christian background different to that of our denomination. Topics like Holy Communion, baptism, worship, and Scripture bring out a rich variety of thoughts and perspectives. Topics that often divide homes because of loyalties to various theologies and pieties (and the families that nurtured them) seem to diminish in significance thanks to the caring, supportive, and candid conversations that take place.

What I have come to discover is that many adults have not had the opportunity to engage in open conversation about what they believe or believed. A big part of shepherding faith is to allow them to give voice to their faith stories, to have the opportunity to tell their story for both their home and the other homes in the class to hear. Such open discussions and even revelations encourage other homes to share their faith stories and their questions about the meaning of what they do and do not believe and do. Most of all, their questions and the conversations that follow enrich the whole confirmation experience. It is interesting to see who is listening: everyone! There is no longer idle chitchat about who is playing in the ball game Thursday night or who is dating whom. Instead, these cross+generational and family groups are using confirmation classes to encourage one another actively—to shepherd one another—in the lifelong journey of faith.

It is wonderful to watch children's faces as they listen to adults talking about their lives of faith and the questions and concerns they have. Their faces seem to say, "They really believe this!" This strikes at the core of what God calls the church to do: to make disciples and to build up the body of Christ (Matthew 28:19 and Ephesians 4:12). I suspect the young people—and maybe many of the adults—will not remember a lot of the information taught, but I am convinced they will never forget who they came with and the witness of faith they experienced and shared. They will leave confirmation with the ability and practice of having real conversations about real issues about faith in daily and family life.

Other Mentors

There are times when, for a whole host of reasons, parents cannot be a part of the class. When this happens, parents and child together choose a mentor. When we first began the home-based confirmation ministry, many mentors were congregational members. However, over time parents and youth began to invite other family members or even trusted neighbors to be the mentor. The only requirement we asked was that the mentor had to be a baptized member of a congregation. Time and again mentors have stated how they have been blessed through this ministry. Likewise, it is apparent that the congregation—and especially the young people—have been blessed as well. How do I know that? Because about four years into the home-based confirmation ministry I began to notice that most of the mentors—especially those who were not family members—were present not only at the High School Graduation Milestone Blessing in the congregation but also at the graduation receptions. And not only were they present, parents and graduates acknowledged them as honored guests. These mentors subsequently often step into leadership roles in the life of the congregation. These new leaders were often in that thirty-five to forty-five-year age group that is lacking in many congregations.

I have also noticed that grandparents (and other older adults) seem to have a special impact on the young people they mentor. Conversely, the experience has an impact on these older adults as well. I know grandparents who have driven up to an hour-and-a-half one way once a week for three years to attend confirmation sessions with their grandchild. One particular grandmother even came every Wednesday night for a year while she was undergoing cancer treatment. Another grandparent came with the student's parent and not only for the Wednesday sessions but also took an active part in the many service projects that the teens, parents, and mentors do every year. Their gifts of time, commitment, listening, and storytelling are something these young people will likely never forget.

Pastor and Catechist as Shepherd

As a result of our home-based confirmation, I found myself teaching less and listening more. This was apparent not only in the class sessions but also in the sessions I had privately with each home. Before the actual rite of confirmation, like many congregations we ask the young people to write a statement of faith and then meet to discuss it with the pastor along with their parents and mentors. These sessions have been truly amazing, for youth and their homes share not only the faith papers but so much more about life and faith. This became particularly evident as I learned to listen beyond their faith statements to them and to their family experiences. Repeatedly, parents would say about their children's faith statements, "Pastor, I could never have written what my child wrote." Again and again these parents expressed a sense of awe and pride in a child who expressed a faith and a life of faith that far outdistanced what the parents could have hoped for.

I recall the young man whose dad had died rather suddenly the year before. He began his faith paper by saying; "I believe; I believe in God. I believe in Jesus. I believe in the Holy Spirit. I believe in the teachings of the Bible." And then he looked at his family and then at me and added, "but it's hard." After a moment of silence, I simply asked him to explain what he meant by "hard." This quiet and very reserved young man began to bare his soul as those who cared for and nurtured him listened. Our meeting became an opportunity to stand with him in the midst of his grief and to talk about how God is still with us even when life is not easy. Faith in Christ can indeed be difficult and yet hopeful. That night was not about assessing how well he'd written his paper or expressed his faith. It was an occasion to shepherd this child and his family.

This and many other examples have taught me the importance of speaking the faith out loud. That represents a different goal and understanding of faith formation. Instead of getting children and youth to attend Sunday school classes or instead of getting youth to finish confirmation classes or instead of getting high schoolers to remain part of a youth group or instead of focusing on having pews more full than empty on a Sunday morning, I want people to speak their faith out loud. That is something many—if not most—of our parishioners have not been able to do in the past. However, our home-based ministry has opened hearts, minds, hands and mouths to speak, to wonder, and to serve with compassion and to express faith, hope, and love with prayers, blessings, affirmations and candor in a way I had never experienced before in my life. All those past standards of a successful congregation are no longer central to this congregation's ministry. And our Sunday school, confirmation ministry, youth ministry, and worship life have all been blessed and empowered in ways we could not have imagined.

 I want people to speak faith out loud.

To shepherd faith is to encourage the life of faith to be experienced in daily relationships. I have been blessed to watch homes of confirmands along with others in the faith community engage in caring conversations about faith and values that then enrich lives. What was amazing was how this engagement also caught the attention of

206 Shepherd of Souls

other homes outside the congregation who began to ask if they were welcome to attend. Apparently, the homes in the class were speaking faith to their neighbors and community friends. This is a particularly exciting part of the shepherding ministry. This is the ministry to which I have been called: to encourage, equip, support, and bless God's people—children, youth, adults, homes, and families—which in turn blesses the entire congregation, the community, the world, and the mission of the church to make disciples. Faith is the power of God at work in us. To speak faith to each other, to share our experiences of faith in daily life is how we encourage and shepherd one another in the grace and love of God.

Questions for Reflection and Conversation

1. If you went through confirmation classes, what was your experience like? How did it shepherd your soul?

2. What is working well in your congregation's current confirmation ministry? What appears not to be working well?

3. What are your expectations and hopes for confirmation ministry? for the confirmand?

4. How much of confirmation ministry should be informational? How much should be formational?

5. In what ways might adults benefit from participating in confirmation classes?

6. In what ways would youth benefit from parents and other adults participating in confirmation classes?

7. In Pastor Asleson's home-based confirmation ministry, 98 percent of the youth wanted parents and other adults to be a part of the confirmation ministry. Why do you think so many parents believe confirmation ministry (and youth ministry) would be better off without them?

8. How can the home-based confirmation ministry contribute to the health and wellbeing of a diverse family life, including divorced parents, single-parent homes, and other family structures?

Confirmation as Shepherding Souls 207

9. What ideas from this chapter are part of your congregation's current confirmation ministry?

10. What ideas from this chapter do you want to incorporate into your congregation's confirmation ministry? Write down your thoughts on the blank pages at the end of the book.

8

CONGREGATIONAL LIFE EQUIPS SHEPHERDS

O come, let us worship and bow down, let us kneel before
the LORD, our Maker! For he is our God, and we are the
people of his pasture, and the sheep of his hand. *Psalm 95:6–7*

This chapter expands the influence of shepherding souls to most everything a congregation does. In addition to what has been covered
by addressing pastors, lay leaders, the role of the home, milestones
ministry, and confirmation ministry, a still broader application of
shepherding will help congregations understand who they are as a
thoroughly shepherd-of-souls community. For congregations to accept their shepherding role more fully will require that they give attention to soul care through such ministry areas as worship and music,
Christian education, service activities, and fellowship opportunities.
Yes, some suggestions echo ideas in earlier chapters, but they do so in
a way that broadens their application to more people and settings in
the life of the congregation on behalf of the ministry of Christ.

Clearly, shepherding souls is not an "add on" element to the work
of the church or something that pastors and other congregational
leaders are assigned to do occasionally, as needed. No: shepherding
addresses the heart of the Great Commission that seeks to make

209

followers of Jesus. It is lifelong task, not something that is concluded in baptism or some audible declaration of allegiance to Christ. Shepherding also addresses the heart of the Great Commandment that understands love of God and neighbor as mutually inclusive commitments to care for the whole person under God, including their sense of meaning, hope, and faith.

The Critical Element of Checking In with One Another

This shepherd of souls ministry of the congregation involves checking in with one another all along the journey of faith. The vast majority of the work of faith formation is follow up, reconnecting with people to see how God's word and the Spirit of Christ contribute to one's Christian life, one's daily dying and rising. Such checking in or follow up can happen in many contexts, whether it be as a participant in a Christian education faith formation event, serving on a leadership team, or greeting someone after a worship service. Such occasions and contexts present perfect opportunities to explore with people how God's living word is affecting their lives, how God's word is slaying the old self and giving rise to a new person, a new life, a new soul (see Romans 6:3–4).

Just being alert to who is present and how they are present is a vital shepherding quality. One woman missed Sunday worship for a number of weeks. She had been an active part of the congregation and a member of the adult choir. She became aware that no one seemed to notice her absence. No one from the worshiping community checked in to see how she was doing. No one shepherded her by valuing her and showing concern for her absence. She didn't come back for more than a decade and then her return was due to another family member who wanted to attend.

Once leaders have become accustomed to noticing who is present and who is not and to check in with each other at staff, council, and other team meetings, the next step is to branch out and check in with the recipients of the ministry of the congregation to discover how the ministry is impacting their lives and the lives of their loved ones. Who is benefiting? Who seems not to be connecting? Who is getting overlooked? However, that is a big leap for many congregational leaders. To check in with each other and to attend prayerfully to each other in trusted relationships is one thing. To go out and ask how the larger community of faith is doing as a result of the congregation's ministry is something quite different—and can feel intrusive and awkward. Hence, the ubiquitous congregational survey has emerged as the escape mode dressed in the clothing of the shepherd. Surveys can assist, but they do not shepherd souls.

> The vast majority of the work of faith formation is follow up.

Ironically, even congregational staff express frustration that they do not get regular feedback regarding their work or their personal experiences in ministry. Nor do they hear from members of the congregation. Sure, people make the occasional complimentary comment or a snide and hurtful comment, but a thorough and organizationally supported check-in is more the exception than the norm. An associate pastor I know said that she had only one supervisory conversation with her senior pastor and lay leaders about her ministry in her six years in the congregation—and even then, she not only had to ask for it, the request took eighteen months to fulfill.

There remains something deep in the psyche of many of our congregations and leaders that prevents them from evaluating or correcting the direction of ministry. And yet, one of the most supportive things leaders can do is to sit down with other congregational leaders to assess how the work is going for the individual and the larger congregation. Shepherding in a congregation looks like this. Not having the conversation and working in isolation as a staff member or other congregational leader can be very disheartening and lead to anxiety, fear, and displeasure with what could otherwise be a joyful ministry.

And yet, to evaluate the work of individuals, leadership teams, and the congregation at large and to assess the benefits of various ministries is to further the work of the church and its loving, healing service to the world. An honest and caring evaluation and assessment can be a loving act of kindness that leads to a stronger and more effective ministry, and represents a form of shepherding that blesses individuals and serves the larger ministry of the church.

Reclaiming the importance of shepherding souls will undoubtedly reshape the identity and work of many a pastor, lay leader, and leadership team. It will bless homes and the faith formation of congregations, exemplified through milestones ministry. It will energize confirmation ministry, and it will renew the life of congregations to look less like a country club and more like a lifesaving station caring for those in danger on the seas.[1] And, yes, if shepherding souls into the reign of Christ is to be clearly evident as the reason for being, then everyone in the church—whether on congregational membership lists or not—is at some level a shepherd of souls. For such shepherds are followers of Jesus, the Good Shepherd.

> An honest and caring evaluation and assessment can be a loving act of kindness that leads to a stronger and more effective ministry.

Everything the church does—whether in the home, the congregation, in society, or in the wider world—should have this understanding of shepherding as central to its purpose, goals, and values. What follows is a description of how the larger congregational life can benefit from the ministry of the shepherd of souls. Congregational activities such as worship and music, educational faith formation, service, and more contribute to the work of soul care beyond the confines of those congregational occasions. Emphasizing soul care within these specific areas of congregational ministry strengthens the impact of those congregational ministries. Foundational to all of the shepherding is the Christian spirituality of the Four Key Faith

Congregational Life Equips Shepherds 213

Practices: caring conversations, devotions, service, and rituals and traditions. These foundational practices promote a Christian spirituality and shepherding of one another that can easily be juxtaposed to the daily and weekly activities of the congregation. Just as the Four Key Faith Practices shape and promote a vital faith formation through congregational meeting agendas (see chapter 5, "Lay Leaders as Shepherds"), so can those same faith practices deepen the faith formation of worship, music, education, service, and fellowship.

Worship and Shepherding Souls

Worship is that foundational act that binds the community of faith together as a people of God. Gathered around God's word and sacraments in public worship gives people an experience of the holy, that which gives birth to—and nurtures—faith in Jesus Christ.

Any way one can bring the message and practices of Christian faith home to one's daily life serves as an important resource in the shepherding of souls. Shepherds need to have the words, phrases, ideas, and actions embedded in their own lives to benefit another more fully with caring conversations, reflection, and prayer. If it is not part of one's own consciousness, language, and practice, it is difficult to bless others with God's word and living presence. Debbie Streicher at Milestones Ministry says, "We assume that everyone coming through our doors is fluent in the language of faith. Fluency in a language does not happen in one or two hours a week. It happens through immersion and involves the congregation and the home." Debbie calls the task before us learning "faith as a second language."[2] One does not truly learn, digest, and become fluent in a language without using it and becoming immersed in it regularly. The church has always had a balance between the public and the domestic expression of the faith (see Acts 2:42–47). The symbiotic nature of the dance between weekly worship and daily practice of the faith goes a long way for Christian disciples to become fluent in the language and thinking of the Christian faith that, in turn, shapes how one experiences the gospel of Christ in the world and in relationships with others. Worship resources that equip lives as shepherds include Bible, worship books, hymn books, bulletins and inserts like Taking Faith Home.

The use of the liturgy (even so-called non-liturgical worship has its own order, texts, and emotional tone that intend to go home with the worshipper) offers a script for our daily lives, one that encourages and promotes praise to God, humble confession and forgiveness, gratitude to God and for one's neighbor, and the giving of God's peace to others as it has been extended through hands and voices in worship. Being a shepherd of souls includes speaking and hearing in such a way that God's presence is acknowledged and passed on to other. This can be communicated in a number of ways by using phrases such as the following: "The Lord be with you." "Thanks be to God." "The peace of the Lord be with you." "Create in me a clean heart, O God." "I confess to you, my brothers and sisters ..." These and other verbal exchanges used in worship are all sayings and language of faith worthy of repetition, if not verbatim, then at least in spirit, as part of one's shepherd of souls ministry.

Children in Worship and Soul Care

Actively engaging children in worship is another important element of soul care. It recognizes the cross+generational nature of shepherding, a ministry of the church that reaches out to children through generations of adults and to generations of adults through children. Research on faith formation since the 1980s has made this so clear that even evangelicals who have prided themselves on segmenting youth and children away from adult worship have begun to change their stance.[3] Just as we learn language, the importance of relationships and core values from the beginning of life, so is the language and life of faith to be experienced in worship and other cross+generational communities from the beginning of life.

Congregations are experimenting with various ways of making Sunday worship more cross+generational. One congregation makes worship child-friendly by using children on occasion to bless people after receiving Holy Communion. People are touched by the words and touch of the children who make the sign of the cross on their foreheads. The children are touched in return, both figuratively and literally by a caring, safe, and faith-filled community. Other congregations have children work with a parent or other adult to offer prayers used in worship. Even silently standing by a parent as that parent offers prayers in worship sends a powerful message about faith and prayer experienced in a cross+generational community. More and more congregations are having children and youth read the Scriptures for worship. Involving children in worship leadership is another way of learning the language of faith, the language that helps a shepherd of souls speak and act in a way that reflects the gospel. Some congregations have added a "pray-ground" in the front of the worship space. It provides small tables, chairs and quiet activities to keep children directed to what is happening up front instead of being distracted in the pew. The senior pastor in one congregation was thrilled to actually hear one of the children in the pray-ground joining him as he was singing the pastor's part of the liturgy.[4] Worship that involves and delights children and youth sends a strong message about their worth as children of God and importance to the community of faith, another important ingredient to serving others and training others in soul care. We do well to remember that children are not just the future of the church: children *are* the church!

We at Milestones Ministry recommend a Taking Faith Home Moment, a time in worship that focuses on the children and how to bring the faith home through the Taking Faith Home insert. Young and not-so-young alike are encouraged to practice some portion of the resource together as a way to stimulate further use of foundational faith practices once the worshipers return home. Pastors and others can check in with people during the week and report back how living out the faith through the Four Key Faith Practices has blessed as well as challenged people's lives. Reporting back what has worked for people and what has been learned further equips people and encourages people to continue to make faith practices in the home a habit of the heart.

Shepherding Souls through Music

Music has long been a faith formational tool of the Christian faith and life. The vast majority of people throughout most of Christian history have been illiterate. Even if Bibles had been available—though for many they were not—these Christians could not have read them or any other material for Christian edification. Music and the visual arts like statues, paintings, murals, mosaics, architecture, and stained-glass windows have taught the faith to millions. Music in worship offers more than a moment of audible inspiration on a Sunday morning. It provides devotional material, scripts for conversation, and melodious themes to sustain and embolden the shepherd daily. The words and tunes personify the life of the shepherd and the faith of the shepherd. Music speaks its own language that reaches deeply into the soul with emotion and images that words cannot always convey. All of this, too, serves the ministry of the shepherd of souls by presenting and modeling a faith-filled, Spirit-filled presence that in turn shapes conversations, reflections, and prayers of the shepherd. To hear the words of Christian hymnody and liturgy in the daily conversations of the saints is an all-too-infrequently heard blessing. To hear those same words sung—something experienced even less today—offers a blessing to others that words alone cannot always approximate with the same depth of feeling and meaning.

Choir members and praise bands have an added advantage in benefiting from music. As they rehearse the music, they receive the words and music of the faith like a mantra to be repeated again and again. Choir and band directors can encourage their members to pray and discuss with others the verses during and after rehearsals. All of this aids in Christian identity and the practice of shepherds. Combining multiple generations from childhood to the most senior in rehearsals and in worship actually creates a setting in which soul care can take place as the generations greet, talk, and support each other through a ministry of music.

Once this element of rehearsing is appreciated, it is a short step from the edifying words and tunes in hymns and praise songs to an actively cross+generational environment for shepherding. For example, congregations can and do bring the generations together for mass choirs. That creates an opportunity to have cross+generational "choir buddies" by pairing older and younger choir members. They can have conversations to get to know one another better and to pray and care for one another in safe, structured relationships for faith formation.

Congregational Life Equips Shepherds 217

Faith Formation Education

Christian education in recent years has been intimately linked with the language and focus of faith formation. However, it is important to note that most every ministry in the life of the church forms the life of faith, including—and especially—worship. The emphasis on faith formation through education means that Christian education is being recognized for more than the dissemination of information. Christian education at its best becomes formational, shaping the life of the Christian in community, and that community faith formation is an example of shepherding. Therefore, faith formational education embraces faith practices that take the content of the faith and helps it come alive in a person's "conversations, conduct, and concerns." Being able to recite Scripture and defend doctrines and theological positions is not enough. Faith gives meaning and direction to one's life, not just to one's philosophical views of life through a particular theological lens.

If faith formation education is practical and consequential for conversations, conduct and concerns, it needs to connect with daily life experience; it needs to include an action-reflection model that helps people reflect on what they have learned in the context of lived experiences. Whether it is attendance at Sunday school, confirmation class, vacation Bible school, an adult Bible study, a congregational pre-school, or participating in milestones ministry, the faith formational aspect of the educational activity is not complete without exploring how the initial experience affected the individuals who participated in it. This is true not only of the recipients of the experience, but also the providers of the experience.

Kathleen, a director of faith formation, led a women's retreat on forgiveness and reconciliation. She was asked to record what difference the retreat made in the lives of the retreat participants. How was it affecting their life of faith and their personal relationships following the weekend retreat? This meant she needed to get the feedback of the participants, explore what they experienced, and wonder with them how their experiences at the retreat might continue to shape and inform their lives following the retreat. In other words, she needed to serve the retreat participants as a shepherd of souls. Such

218 Shepherd of Souls

an investigation, a valuable form of research within the congregation, could also impact how the director would lead other retreats in the future. The feedback could confirm the importance of the retreat activities or it could lead to adjustments and larger changes.

Interestingly, this director, like a lot of program leaders in a congregational context, resisted doing the follow-up contacts to learn vital information that could benefit future retreat participants. The director feared that such inquiry would not be appreciated by those who attended. People were not accustomed to being asked about how a congregational experience changed lives. She also had some concern regarding what would be learned and was both somewhat intimidated about making the calls and worried they might be experienced as intimidating too. However, as an assignment that required a report back to the staff, she grudgingly made a couple of calls the night before a staff meeting.

The next day she reported that she was quite surprised and pleased by the responses. First of all, Kathleen was delighted by how happy the women were to be asked how the retreat went. They actually wanted to give her feedback. They felt affirmed for being valued for their thoughts and opinions and, in return, the director was affirmed for her efforts of putting together the retreat and for seeking the follow-up feedback. In fact, she began to get feedback not just about the retreat but about other events from the past, events that had left a positive impression. These women wanted to convey their delight in current and past faith formation experiences in the congregation.

Kathleen had anticipated that if the retreat had had a lasting impact on these women, the results would have shown in their relationships with family and friends. To her surprise, a couple of women talked about how it was impacting their places of work. One woman was a human resources director and had already implemented some of the activities from the weekend with the personnel with whom she worked. The HR director found ways to use some of the weekend exercises to improve the working environment of her company. Another woman who attended the retreat talked about a strained relationship with a co-worker in her office. The retreat gave her the

Congregational Life Equips Shepherds 219

courage to take the initiative and try to redirect the relationship in a positive way. She used some of the retreat material that talked about how to gift the lives of others. She took this in a very literal way and placed a little gift on the desk of the other person and made it clear she was hoping to have a more positive relationship with this other person in the future. She reported to Kathleen that the results of that effort had been very positive and the woman thanked the director for a retreat that made her think differently about a particular person at work and gave her the motivation to do something about it. For this office worker, forgiveness and reconciliation had real consequences in her daily life that she had not anticipated.

When Kathleen reported these accounts to the staff, she talked about her fear of initiating the follow-up inquiry and how thrilled she was by the conversations that emerged from her phone calls. Although she had been encouraged to do the follow-up work and told that it would serve her well in her work, she had been hesitant. She had not anticipated that people would want to talk about their experiences, including reflections on other faith formation activities from the past. The director had not imagined how the retreat on forgiveness and reconciliation would enter into the women's lives in the workforce. Kathleen's checking in with them opened her eyes to how the Christian faith had consequences far beyond her initial hopes and served as another form of shepherding souls.

Kathleen had called retreat participants to see what follow-up support people might be needing or find helpful and to learn what worked and what didn't work at the retreat for future reference. It turned into an example of how shepherding others can be quite simple and direct. Her contact reinforced themes central to the Christian faith and encouraged people to continue to pursue the life of forgiveness and reconciliation. Instead of being a wonderful retreat weekend that ended when the people returned home, she gently yet assertively supported these women in their ongoing desire and attempts to make their lives and the lives of others a bit richer through the love of neighbor that Christ brings to their lives. In turn, some of the women had served as shepherds to the director by encouraging her for her efforts and giving her ideas and motivation for future events, events that brought the Christian faith and daily life—including one's work life—together.

Bible Study as Soul Care

Those who attend Bible studies are motivated by many things: the desire to learn more about the Bible, God, Christianity, and their own lives of faith. Most are also motivated by the desire to reconnect with the study group itself. Another valuable motivation—though often not articulated—is repentance. The Reformation theme of the church continuously reforming itself implies personal repenting and beginning each day anew. As Luther stated in his first of ninety-five theses, "When our Lord and Master Jesus Christ said, 'Repent' (Matthew 4:17), he willed the entire life of believers to be one of repentance." This should remain as an underlying goal of biblical study as well: to be addressed by the living God who draws us to God's grace through judgment, repentance, and forgiveness. It contributes to a way of life that shapes one's "conversation, conduct, and concerns" with humility and faith grounded in a love of God and neighbor.

With personal renewal through repentance and forgiveness as a foundational objective of reading and learning from the Bible, approaching Bible study as a means of being shepherded in faith becomes an integral component. One way of enlisting this approach to Bible study includes the use of the Four Key Faith Practices. Another would be the use of prayer and action partners in Bible study groups.

A Bible study using the Four Key Faith Practices takes biblical material and places that material into the lives of the students in a way that intends to educate by shaping one's life in the word of God. This means that a biblical passage can be studied and explored in such a way that it leads the learner to be informed and formed by the biblical text. This occurs as the student uses the words and messages from the biblical text to engage in daily conversations and actions. The Bible passage becomes the source of daily prayers that draw upon biblical themes to connect the person with the divine. A Bible passage encourages reflection on how God's word leads a person of faith to the needs of one's neighbor with compassion and hope and an empathy that seeks to see the world from another person's perspective.

Congregational Life Equips Shepherds 221

This means being able to understand the hurts and needs of another in a way that responds with love. All of this will be aided by biblical images and convictions that suggest Christian rituals and traditions that reminds the Bible student of a way of life filled with faith, hope, and love.

In this way, Bible study that is faith formational seeks a life that does not conform to the convictions and prejudices of the current age but is changed by an encounter with the living word of God. Paul writes, "I appeal to you therefore, brothers and sisters, by the mercies of God, to present your bodies as a living sacrifice, holy and acceptable to God, which is your spiritual worship. Do not be conformed to this world, but be transformed by the renewing of your minds, so that you may discern what is the will of God—what is good and acceptable and perfect" (Romans 12:1-2). Bible study guided by such a principle then becomes a "form of spiritual worship," and that takes the study beyond gathering information to presenting one's self "as a living sacrifice, holy and acceptable to God."

One can make a Bible study into a form of worship and living sacrifice by seeking to understand God's word by living the text, by experiencing the message in one's daily life. Using the Four Key Faith Practices does this by turning study into an experience of the word of God, a form of worship of God, that speaks, prays, serves, and symbolizes the word of God as foundational to one's daily existence.

Romans 12 can be used as an example to study the Bible in this way. The chapter follows immediately after a discussion of the election of Israel that Paul admits involves a mystery. He wants the church in Rome—and beyond Rome—to wrestle with an election of Israel that does not easily fit with election of those who claim Jesus as Lord. To be clear, this is a challenging passage for the church. Even the biblical text in Romans 11:25-36 is based on a number of early manuscripts that offered some different wording that can impact how to best interpret his message. However that passage is read and understood, Paul moves on to words of praise and glory to God by stating, "How unsearchable are his judgments and how inscrutable his ways" (11:33b). Paul acknowledges that the election of Israel involves a mystery. He then offers words of praise to God and moves in the

222 Shepherd of Souls

next chapter to how we then live as believers, those who live with the mystery and praise of God. Paul does not attempt to solve the mystery introduced in Romans 11. He rather seeks to live into the mystery as those who have been transformed by the gospel to give praise to God and serve others in love.

With this as the immediate background, one could study Romans 12 and encourage Bible study participants to reflect on the chapter in a way that lives the text through conversations, devotions, service, and rituals and traditions. For example, Bible study participants could reflect on this section of Romans and leave to engage in conversations that wonder with others what it means and what it is like to be transformed, to have one's mind renewed. In the context of mystery and praise to God, how does one discern what is good and acceptable and perfect? How might this relate to Paul's exhortation that one not think too highly of one's self (12:3)? Raising such questions in conversations with others during the week could result in some fascinating observations and understandings, the kind that involve a consciousness raising in one's relationships to others and to God.

Bible study participants could be encouraged to pray portions of Romans 12 in the morning or evening or both. Words and themes could be used in table graces. People could pray, "Dear God, you who ask us to rejoice with those who rejoice and to weep with those who weep, we thank you for freeing us to live beyond our own self-centeredness and in harmony with one another. Help us not to be haughty but to care for the needy and not depend on our own wisdom. This we pray through Jesus Christ, our Savior and Lord. Amen." One could pray at mealtime, "Dear God, just as you give us gifts that differ from one another to serve the whole body in Christ, we thank you for serving us with the gift of this food today. In Jesus' name, amen."

Romans 12 is filled with ideas for service: show hospitality to strangers; use one's God-given gifts to serve others; show compassion to those who rejoice and those who grieve; make a financial contribution to the work of the church far from home; show restraint with those who you think deserve condemnation and let God be the judge.

Congregational Life Equips Shepherds 223

Students could commit to some specific act of service prior to the next Bible study using these examples and others from Romans 12. People could use some form of Christian ritual and tradition to recall and experience being a living sacrifice of God's mercy. To reflect on spiritual worship and being transformed by the mind of Christ, people could commit to lighting a candle daily and sit in silent prayer. People could make the sign of the cross and say to one's self, "By the mercies of God, may I be transformed by the renewing of my mind." It could be a blessing extended to family and friends during the week, "May the transforming power of God's love and mercy, renew you this day."

All of these examples of the Four Key Faith Practices taken from Romans 12 could present very interesting observations and reflections at the following Bible study session and offer new understandings regarding Romans 12, Bible study conversations, confessions and admissions that might sound very much like spiritual worship. The students might discern how living with the text has made their lives a laboratory of learning what God's word in Romans 12 might mean to them. People could discuss how living with the text during the week had shaped their conversations, their behaviors, and what was important to them. They might reflect on how their relationship with someone changed during the week and how this might say something about how that transformation fits with Paul's message.

This form of Bible study requires that each lesson is not a self-contained study that begins and ends in a session. Biblical learning and faith formation take place throughout the days and weeks and presents a biblical awareness that can be discussed and imagined with others, including at a future Bible study session. Each Bible study session would begin with a discussion of what people learned about God's word following the last session. They would check in with one another as shepherds of souls. How were lives transformed as well as informed by living God's word through the Four Key Faith Practices? What new insights and actions have been gained as the Bible material was converted into a lived experience? This approach has the possibility of helping biblical material go deeper into one's life to transform one's gratitude, thinking, and behaving with others and before

224 Shepherd of Souls

God. It presents a model that shepherds souls through a Bible study group that learns, questions, challenges, repents, and reflects together on God's word.

Prayer and Action Partners

A second element to this form of study involves students as prayer and action partners (see chapter 6, pp. 176). Each student can confide in another student what commitment is being made to practice during the week to reflect on and live out the Bible passage. The confidant becomes the prayer and action partner who knows what Four Key Faith Practices the person plans to do. The prayer and action partner prays for the other person and for the commitments made to live out the Bible passage with particular Christian practices. Between Bible study sessions, the prayer and action partner can help remind the other person to fulfill his or her pledge by simply asking how the person's efforts are going. All of this reminds the students that one does not live the faith in a vacuum but with a community of saints that can even reach out as a shepherd of souls to offer prayerful and engaged support as a sojourner in faith.

Sunday School and Confirmation

Other traditional Christian education programs can also be guided by a focus on faith formation via faith practices. Lessons can be transformed from information-laden learning to faith-forming experiences that combine information with exploration through faith practices. For children and youth, it is very helpful for the content and lifestyle of the Christian faith to be brought home where parents, the primary faith influences on children and youth, can positively impact children's faith formation. When parental involvement is not feasible, other mentors can be added to be part of a shepherding community.

Pursuing this direction in Christian education and faith formation also requires a church culture that values the role of parents and seeks to equip parents rather than be satisfied with a status quo that ignores, belittles, or is frustrated by parents for not doing enough. Inspiring and encouraging parents with a call to be shepherds of souls in their own home can have a positive impact on the church and on the level of family satisfaction experienced in the home.

Confirmation ministry has so much potential to move from informational dogma to a formational and shepherding process for students, families, and larger congregation that another chapter is dedicated to it (chapter 7). Granted, not all denominations and congregations even offer confirmation as a part of the baptismal journey, but for those who have retained this form of Christian education, a formational focus can make it a joy for confirmands (both youth and adults) and catechists alike.

Preschools and Day Schools

Why not shepherd souls through a congregation's preschool or day school program? Too often there exists a great divide between the perceived mission of the school and that of the congregation. What a sad development when this has happened! The Christian educational setting can offer what other educational institutions can't: the spiritual dimension of child development, something that impacts not only the child but the child's family as a whole. Introducing faith practices to the home through the faith formation work of the school can add to the delight of family life itself.

The child and the child's home can be shepherded by the school by providing the home the Four Key Faith Practices through Taking Faith Home and by emphasizing seasonal faith practices at Advent, Christmas, Epiphany, Lent, and Easter, special times in the church year uniquely available to bring the faith home, both literally and figuratively. These high church season times can foster a desire for something more to happen in the home, something that impacts the spiritual life of the home and the relationships within the home. Occasions can be provided to check in periodically with the home and see whether the faith practice suggestions are getting home and how they are contributing to the life of the family and its faith life. Friends of the school from the congregation can make occasional phone calls or some other form of communicating can be used to express the desire to support the life of the home and its spiritual quest.

At times a level of frustration from congregational leaders can be heard in the comments from pastors, council members, and others regarding the disconnect between school families and participation

226 Shepherd of Souls

in the life of the congregation. However, that concern represents the wrong starting point, one that does not reflect the importance of shepherding souls. The starting point for evaluating the success of the school's faith formation impact on the children and their families is not attendance in congregational worship or any other activity of the congregation. The better starting point is to assess whether God's word is reaching the children and their homes through faith formation practices that teach the faith by living the faith in the home. Of course, the hope is that families that discover a faith community invested in them and providing them resources that bless their domestic relationships and the spiritual life of the home will want more. Over time some of the school families will, thus, find a church home with the local congregation. However, the real goal is not membership in a congregation: it is meaningful and sustained faith formation for the homes of the school children. This does not happen simply by accepting children into the congregation's preschool or day school. Shepherding children and families by providing resources and occasional follow-up communications with the home to support these families is important too. Feedback from parents as well as children can help the school and the congregation determine what support is most helpful and what kind of care is most appreciated. Starting with the needs of families instead of the needs of a congregation to grow its membership exemplifies the intent of the shepherd of souls ministry.

Shepherding Souls through Other Ministries

The manner in which shepherding souls can take place through worship and education also happens in other congregational ministries. Whether it be youth and family ministry, outreach to others and their needs (i.e., mission trips and food banks), fellowship activities, vacation Bible school, Bible camp, or any other activity of the church that brings together people to love God and neighbor, a shepherding component remains central. These various occasions give opportunities for people to learn, experience and take to heart essential practices of the Christian faith. They provide a community experience to care for others on a personal as well as a collective basis. They can

Congregational Life Equips Shepherds 227

encourage follow-up contact to continue to shepherd others in the love of God. Any time the body of Christ gathers together, people can be equipped with faith practices, prayer and action partners, and community support that checks in with one another to promote and develop a life together where people engage in caring conversations, reflect on the Christian faith and life, and experience a relationship to God through a life of prayer.

The Value and Challenge of Checking In

Congregations have become accustomed and expected to offer events and programs, activities that bring people to the congregation for some kind of faith formation experience, whether it be worship, education, youth or young adult group, fellowship, or service activity, hopefully in an environment that is pleasing, safe, and populated. By the end of such activities, we hope that the participants go home having received something positive for their daily lives, especially their lives of faith. But, what happens next?

What begins in a community of believers typically ends up by sending people off on their own, and a fundamental part of soul care is often missed: checking in with one another to see how the event or program actually impacted people and their faith formation. However, in our individualistic age, checking in can feel daunting and intrusive to some. A major source of the resistance is the fear of prying, of meddling in the lives of others. The norms and values of our very individualistic society have crept into the life of the church and stalled the shepherding of souls.

In addition to being part of an individualistic culture, a second deterrent to checking in with others is the fear of what the leader or fellow participant will learn. People can fear being judged or criticized for their efforts. Perhaps people will express dissatisfaction with the ministry, the programs, or the leaders themselves. For most congregations and leaders, sitting down to discuss how the ministry of the congregation is impacting and blessing others is a step too far. At best, leaders will ask for another survey to do the work for them, a tool that rarely gives much clarity or promote the personal, trusted relationships needed for the care of souls.

A genuine motivation for checking in with others—and one that can move away from a sense of judging or maligning the Christian life of another—is the desire to learn how ministry can be done better. The Bible study leader, the team leader, the worship leader, the retreat leader, the youth group leader, and others who represent those and other ministries can go back to the people they serve or work with in the congregation and ask, "How is it going? What is working for you and what is not? How can I/we be of more help to you? Help me do a better job of walking alongside you." The idea of helping the one asking the question can go a long way to shifting the focus from the one being asked. This perspective puts the one being asked in a position of positive influence, one of helping another soul who is not sure how to be the best partner in the gospel that he or she might be. People do appreciate being asked their opinions, and, surprisingly, when asked what is working often try hard to emphasize the positive, even to the point of expressing thanks at being asked.

Finding a Larger Biblical Perspective for Soul Care

Since the care of souls ministry, described here as the shepherd of souls ministry, has not been a prevailing image for every Christian, a good exercise would be to see in the Bible the very warrant for shepherding one another in love. For example, the four Gospels are filled with accounts of how Jesus worked with his inner circle of followers, pursued them, taught them, corrected them, and sent them out to make more disciples. This is also true in the rest of the New Testament. In Galatians 6:1 Paul writes, "My friends, if anyone is detected in a transgression, you who have received the Spirit should restore such a one in a spirit of gentleness." The faithful are to seek out and care for one another with a determination to strengthen and edify people in faith, yet without being arrogant or rude, to use Paul's love language in 1 Corinthians 13. In Colossians 3, Christians were to commit to a number of faithful characteristics and practices, including the directive to "teach and admonish one another in all wisdom" (3:16b). In this passage Christians live in community in a way that promotes compassion and harmony while also being willing to guide and correct people within the community. Hebrews 10:24–25 states, "Let us hold fast to the confession of our hope without wavering, for he who has promised is faithful. And let us consider how to provoke one another to love and good deeds, not neglecting to meet together, as is the habit of some, but encouraging one another, and all the more as you see the Day approaching." Here there is a sense of urgency and value in supporting each other in the life of faith as time permits.

These biblical examples and images and others like them are not passive models of leadership or shepherding. They indicate the necessary and active qualities needed to care for others in a way that brings repentance, healing, and hope to people day in and day out. Noting such Bible passages can aid in one's discovery of many others passages that guide one's life to the care of others. It can also help one to see that the very purpose of the Bible is not only to teach basic truths about the God-human relationships but to envision a way of life that cares for every soul. It leads to an appreciation that the words of the Bible shepherd us in divine love.

Congregation as a Center for Soul Care

The culture of a congregation offers a valuable context for the shepherd of souls ministry to the world. While congregational events like Sunday worship and faith formation education throughout the year may seem to be the primary avenues to nurture the Christian faith and model the shepherd of souls ministry, most any experience that connects one with the Christian faith and life as part of the body of Christ can benefit one's faith formation and be a training ground for shepherding one another in faith. That larger culture of the community of faith also becomes the ground on which other souls who live without faith in Christ are touched with the love of God. Having people in the Christian community willing to walk alongside others, pay playful and thoughtful attention to others, and check in with others on occasion explicitly to see how others are doing in their daily lives makes the body of Christ a healing and hopeful community that expresses the love of God and the love of neighbor.

Come Holy Spirit, bless and enliven your people that this may be our experience today, tomorrow, and always.

Questions for Reflection and Conversation

1. How do sermons, hymns, prayers, the overall liturgy, bulletin announcements, and the community life of worshipers support you as a shepherd of souls?

2. What more could your worship community do to prepare you for your role as a shepherd of souls, help you learn the language of faith, and bring it into your daily life?

3. What do your choirs, praise teams, and worship leaders do that helps them in their life as a shepherd of souls?

4. How are faith practices part of your congregation's faith formation education? What could be added?

5. What kind of follow-up contact is made through faith formation education in your congregation? Does your Christian education ministry use some form of prayer and action partners? What could be added?

6. What groups like Alcoholics Anonymous or Boy Scouts or programs like a preschool or day care program use your facilities or are directly part of your congregation's ministry and outreach? How could your congregation be available to these people and their homes as shepherds of souls?

7. Who do you have as a shepherd of souls in your life? Who do you have who checks in with you and supports you in your daily life of faith? Who could you ask to be a shepherd to you?

8. Whom do you serve as a shepherd of souls? To whom could you reach out as a shepherd of souls?

Conclusion

Shepherd of Souls: The Life of All Christians

Shepherding souls is what Christians do. Shepherding is what the body of Christ, the body of the Good Shepherd, has to offer a world in need of care instead of indifference, of hope instead of despair, and of light instead of the darkness of sin, death and evil. It is what Andrew did when he reached out to his brother Simon Peter with the news that he had met the Messiah, and what Philip did when he found his friend Nathaniel and announced, "'We have found him about whom Moses in the law and also the prophets wrote, Jesus son of Joseph from Nazareth'" (John 1:40–42 and 45). Lydia, a newly baptized follower of the Lord Jesus, shepherded the community of faith through her hospitality (Acts 16:15, 40). Priscilla and Aquila shepherded Apollos by taking him aside and instructing him more fully as he became a noted teacher of the faith (Acts 18:24–26). This essential work of the church involves everyone who claims the name Christian. It represents the life of one who follows Jesus, the Good Shepherd. It identifies a way of life that fulfills the Reformation theme of the priesthood of all believers. It is the calling of all Christians, the essential work that needs the attention of the reformation of the church today.

...stic focus to shepherding. Why? Because
...ouragement to "walk by faith, not by sight"
...here are lots of sights and sounds that surround
...tions contrary to the reign of God. To be part of
of saints is to be pointed in the direction of Jesus
...t assistance to see Jesus in life is what shepherds offer
...er and the larger world. It involves more than a momen-
...oclamation; it involves caring conversations filled with listen-
...o the deeper movement of the soul; it involves mutual reflection
...n daily life experiences, struggles, hopes, and aspirations; it involves
prayer that seeks a life divinely embraced by undeserved kindness,
mercy, and peace.

Much has been written and discussed about outreach as essential
to the church's work of evangelism. There is also the need for in-
reach, touching the lives of those who are part of the church now.
Many of the children of the church—and the parents, grandparents,
godparents, siblings, and uncles and aunts of those children—have
simply walked away later in life, disappeared from the community
of saints. With more active shepherding of those within the church,
many a soul might still be part of the community of faith as people
upheld in their daily struggles, overcoming their indifference, and
having their joy restored. The church is uniquely capable of being
that community where parents shepherd children, friends shepherd
friends, older children shepherd younger children, older men and
women shepherd younger men and women, and, of course, where
children, youth, and younger adults return the grace and favor and
shepherd their elders in faith, hope, and love. All Christians need the
support of shepherds to walk the life of faith for a lifetime. Evangelical outreach is not only for those who have never received the good
news; it is for those whose life of faith needs to be fed daily. It is the
ministry that builds up the body of Christ.

Returning to an emphasis on the care of souls by all Christians
presents a necessary corrective to what has been called the "church-
ification of Christian ministry,"[1] what I have called "playing church."
This malady of the body of Christ has been diagnosed for ages, but
the remedy requires more than naming the problem. It requires

reclaiming the primacy of the care of souls, the role of pastor as herd, the resources and vision to equip the saints for this vital istry, and a recovery of the life of faith in daily life, especially in through the home. It also requires a refocus of most all congregation ministries to encourage and resource the saints to be more effective in their foundational calling to love God and neighbor.

A Final Word: Shepherding Souls Happens in Community

The gift of the body of Christ is that shepherds experience this life and work together, not alone. No shepherd offers the care of souls without failures, without missteps, without sin and brokenness. Sometimes shepherds cannot hear or deal with the pain of others because of their own. Sometimes indifference and weariness overcome caregivers themselves. That is why the church is a community instead of individuals pursuing their own spiritual quests. The church serves as a loving, peace-filled army of wounded soldiers binding the wounds of one another as the very balm that binds up the wounds of the world.

In the midst of saintly dysfunction, Christ reigns and serves with the message of forgiveness and adoption as children of God. This is God's work that happens in spite of human sin, weariness, blindness, deafness, and misdeeds. The church, like Christ, heals through lives that have been broken and experiences its power in the midst of weakness. God's grace is all we need and all we can hope for (2 Corinthians 12:9). Such a life of faith and its accompanying worldview cannot be contained in institutional religion. Nor can it do its work through lives lived in isolation from one another. It needs to break out to represent and serve the God who is on the loose in the world bringing healing and hope where pain and suffering exists.

The dysfunction of persons within of the church need not be seen as "hypocritical" when shepherding. It is the very reason for and power of the work of Christ. It is the gospel proclamation that looks like weakness and foolishness but shines forth as the very wisdom and strength of the reign of the crucified Christ in the world (1 Corinthians 1:22–25). This is why we read in the New Testament the clarion

⌐hrist daily in community. Colossians
⌐ and succinctly:

⌐ ones, holy and beloved, clothe your-
⌐mpassion, kindness, humility, meekness, and
⌐ear with one another, and, if anyone has a com-
⌐gainst another, forgive each other, just as the Lord
⌐orgiven you, so you also must forgive. Above all, clothe
⌐urselves with love, which binds everything together in
perfect harmony. And let the peace of Christ rule in your
hearts, to which indeed you were called in the one body.
And be thankful. Let the word of Christ dwell in you richly;
teach and admonish one another in all wisdom; and with
gratitude in your hearts sing psalms, hymns, and spiritual
songs to God. And whatever you do, in word or deed, do
everything in the name of the Lord Jesus, giving thanks to
God the Father through him.

These words, and all of the New Testament, indeed all of Scripture, speak to those called as saints in Christ, called as shepherds in
service of the Good Shepherd. Shepherd is the description given to
the kings in the Old Testament. It is the vocation of those who first
heard the angelic message of the birth of Jesus. The Bible is the training manual for shepherds. It is the story of divine drama filled with
human failings redeemed by God's pursuit of us with steadfast love.
It presents the love and justice of God that serves widows, orphans,
and all the needy, broken, sinful souls that long for redemption. It is
the message and story of divine judgment that gives birth both to
divine mercy and to the mission of the body of Christ to shepherd
the world in love.

Notes

Introduction

1. John T. McNeill, *A History of the Cure of Souls* (New York: Harper & Row, 1951), 190.

2. McNeill, *A History of the Cure of Souls*, 191.

3. See Appendix 1 for a list of the Five Principles, Four Key Faith Practices, and the Three Characteristics of Christians referenced in later chapters.

4. See "Vital Connections in Learning: Home and Congregation in Partnership," in *Lutheran World Federation Educator Magazine* (March 1997): 57–63; *Frogs without Legs Can't Hear: Nurturing Disciples in Home and Congregation*; *From the Great Omission to Vibrant Faith: The Role of the Home in Renewing the Church;* and, *Vibrant Faith in the Congregation,* resources for congregational leaders to advance faith formation and outreach.

5. In the Four Key Faith Practices, "devotions" means more than reading the Bible or a devotional book and having a prayer. Devotions as understood here means practicing God's presence in our lives through the Word of God that is first, Jesus Christ, second, the message of Christ and his reconciling work, and third, the Holy Scriptures. In other words, reflecting on God's saving presence while taking a walk in the park fits this definition. So does participation in Sunday morning worship.

1. Reclaiming the Ministry of Shepherding Souls

1. Frank Crouch, "Working Preacher," www.workingpreacher.org, 2010, John 21:1–19

2. Theodore G. Tappers, ed. and trans., *Luther: Letters of Spiritual Counsel* (Vancouver: Regent College Publishing, 1960), 13.

mfort: Martin Luther's Letters to the De-
storal Care Today (Adelaide: ATF Theol-

ne Contemplative Pastor: Returning to the Art of
*d Rapids: Eerdmans, 1989), 56.

. (on confirmation ministry and shepherding) for
use Luther's Small Catechism and the Bible as tools for
the home.

dore G. Tappert, ed., *Luther: Letters of Spiritual Counsel* (Van-
Regent College Publishing, 2003), 107–108.

. George A. F. Knight, *Daily Study Bible Series, Psalms, vol. 1* (Louis-
ue, KY: Westminster John Knox Press, 1982), 10–11.

8. *Minneapolis Star Tribune*, April 24, 2014: A11.

9. See David Anderson, *From the Great Omission to Vibrant Faith: The Role of the Home in Renewing the Church*, chapters 2 and 3 (Vibrant Faith Publishing, 2009). In addition, www.faithformationlearningexchange. org is a good source for the most recent research in this area.

10. Walther I. Brandt, ed., LW 45:46, "The Estate of Marriage, 1522" (Philadelphia: Fortress Press, 1962).

2. Pastor as Shepherd

1. Stephen Pietsch in his book *Of Good Courage* points out that in the era of Martin Luther, melancholia represented a condition that could include depression but also included other maladies related to a soul struggling to come to grips with divine judgment and a world where death was ever present in plagues, other illnesses, malnutrition, accidents, skirmishes and war. See pp. 2–4.

2. Theodore G. Tappert, *Luther: Letters of Spiritual Counsel* (Vancouver: Regent College Publishing, 1960), 86.

3. Tappert, *Luther,* 101.

4. *The Book of Concord,* ed. by Robert Kolb and Timothy J. Wenger, "Smalcald Articles" by Martin Luther, (Minneapolis: Fortress Press, 2000), 319.

5. See www.milestonesministry.org/takingfaithhome and Appendix 2 for an example.

6. See David W. Anderson, *Vibrant Faith in the Congregation* (Minneap-olis: Vibrant Faith Publishing, 2011), 186–7 for a very concrete example of what this gift to the couple can look like.

3. A Basic Guide for All Shepherds

1. D. T. Niles in *New York Times,* May 11, 1986.

2. An alternative translation of Galatians 5:6.

3. Found in Stephen Pietsch, *Of Good Comfort* (Adelaide, AU: ₁ Press Publishing, 2016), 206. From Kenneth Leech, *Spirituality and Pas ral Care* (Cambridge, MA: Cowley Publications, 1989), 31.

4. For an even closer examination of the Four Key Faith Practices, read David W. Anderson and Paul Hill, *Frogs without Legs Can't Hear: Nurturing Disciples in Home and Congregation* (Minneapolis: Augsburg Fortress, 2003), 96–170.

5. Robert H. Albers, *Shame: A Faith Perspective* (New York: The Haworth Pastoral Press, 1995), 17–27.

6. Examples include Taking Faith Home bulletin inserts and Taking Faith Home Cards available at https://store.milestonesministry.org/category-s/1514.htm that are based on the Four Key Faith Practices. Kreativt Fokus (Creative Focus) offers sets of cards offering inspiring pictures and Bible passages for meditation and conversation (http://www.bibelkort. no). It is a Norwegian company that also offers English editions of the cards.

4. Shepherding in the Home

1. David W. Anderson, *From the Great Omission to Vibrant Faith: The Role of the Home in Renewing the Church,* (Minneapolis: Vibrant Faith Publishing, 2009), 75.

2. Sociologist Bridgette Berger noted that the American culture exhibits "virulent anti-family sentiments" in "The Family as a Mediating Structure," in *Democracy and Mediating Structures: A Theological Inquiry,* ed. Michael Novak (Washington, D.C.: American Enterprise Institute for Public Policy Research, 1980), 145. A glaring example of this anti-family sentiment in the church can be seen in a book on evangelism that references both Luther's Small Catechism and Acts 2:42–47, both of which lift up the important role of the home. However, the author in the book successfully addressed evangelism without ever mentioning the importance of the home as the intended audience of the Small Catechism and a primary location of the life and growth of the biblical church. The author had to work hard to ignore the influence of the home in the texts she herself referenced. See *The Evangelizing Church: A Lutheran Contribution,* ed. by Richard H. Bliese and Craig Van Gelder (Minneapolis: Augsburg Fortress, 2005), 71–91. As I work with pastors and other congregational leaders toward the end of the second decade

: clearly newfound appreciation for
.ver, these same congregational leaders
from the home. The reason: an insecurity
.o engage the home and a fear that it is an
.nt. Congregational conclusion: whether or not
.d leaders in faith formation for children and youth,
.o do much to sustain an ongoing effort to equip the
.g time preparing sermons, worship services, Bible studies,
.ongregational activities demands lots of time and appears to
familiar and safer terrain to sojourn.

David W. Anderson and Paul Hill, *Frogs without Legs Can't Hear: .rturing Disciples in Home and Congregation* (Minneapolis: Augsburg Fortress Publishers, 2003), 49-50.

4. *Luther's Works,* vol. 45, "The Estate of Marriage," 1522, ed. Walter I. Brandt (Philadelphia: Fortress Press, 1962), 46.

5. Luther, "The Estate of Marriage," 46.

6. Luther, "The Estate of Marriage," 46.

7. Christian Research Association, an Australian Christian research organization, stated in a September 2016 post, "The parents' faith is, by far, the largest influence on their children's faith." See http://www.cra.org.au/Pointers%2026-3e.pdf. For United States research, see Anderson *From the Great Omission to Vibrant Faith*, 40– 50. Oddbjørn Evenshaug and Dag Hallen, *Barnet og Religionen: Barnets Psykologiske Forutsetninger (The Child's Readiness for Religious Education)* 4th edition (Oslo: Oslo University Press,1992), 142. Oddbjørn Evenshaug, "Dåpopplæringen og foreldrene. (*Religious Education and the Parents*) in *Reform og Embete:* A reader in commemoration of Bishop Andreas Aarflot's 65th birthday, 1 July 1993 (Oslo: Oslo University Press, 1993), 223–8. For more research from Norway, see kifo.no for KIFO, Institute for Church, Religion, and Worldview Research.

8. *Luther: Letters of Spiritual Counsel*, 144–5.

9. Martin Luther, *LW*, 54:9.

10. Robert Kolb and Timothy J. Wenger, eds., "The Large Catechism by Martin Luther" in *The Book of Concord* (Minneapolis: Fortress Press, 2000), 385.

11. Kolb and Wenger, *the Book of Concord*, "Smalcald Articles," 319.

12. Luther even gives an example of what such a faith community in the home might look like in his Preface to the *German and Latin Mass* of 1525.

13. Pastor Dave Nelson responded to my request on the M[ ]
Ministry Facebook Page to contribute stories about "how we sh[ ]
each other in faith through the home." I went on to write, "If you[ ]
some examples/stories of how faith has been nurtured and/or how [ ]
reach has happened in your home or of those you know, please pass th[ ]
along to me." November 29, 2016 FB post. https://www.facebook.com[ ]
groups/1615599752040384/.

14. Dollahite, "How Family Religious Involvement Benefits," 2005
Sutherland J. L. & Pub. Pol'y L28, at http://www.sjlpp.org/documents/
dollahite92605.pdf. Cited in http://www.faithformationlearningex-
change.net/uploads/5/2/4/6/5246709/how_family_religious_involve-
ment_benefits_-_dollahite__thatcher.pdf

5. The Lay Leader as Shepherd of Souls

1. Jim LaDoux, *Surface to Soul: Coaching Spiritual Vitality in Congregations* (Minneapolis: Vibrant Faith Publishing, 2012), 159–61.

6. Milestones Ministry: A Model for Shepherding

1. Milestones Ministry, LLC is an organization that promotes and
developed milestones ministry for use in congregations and homes. Go
to www.milestonesministry.org for more information.

2. See the Mission Trip Milestones Ministry module at http://store.
milestonesministry.org/product-p/mtmm.htmmilestonesministry.org/
for details about how to organize the trip using a shepherding model
that includes a prayer and action partner, prayer journal, and ongoing
contact with the congregation and community back home through the
use of social media.

7. Confirmation as Shepherding Souls

1. Peter L. Benson and Carolyn H. Eklin, *Effective Christian Education:
A National Study of Protestant Congregations* (Minneapolis: Search Institute,
1990).

2. *Luther's Small Catechism*, Pocket Edition (Minneapolis: Augsburg
Fortress, 2016), 8.

3. John H. Westerhoff, *Will our Children Have Faith?* (New York: Sea-
bury Press, Inc., 1976), 23.

4. Westerhoff, *Will our Children Have Faith?*, 93.

5. On August 20, 2007, MTV and the Associated Press released findings of a seven-month study of happiness and youth ages thirteen to
twenty-four. One of the findings was that parents were seen as an over-
whelmingly positive influence in the lives of most young people and that

...oned at least one of their parents as
...ong with other caring, trusted adults,
...e and faith of their children.
...ticle published on November 5, 2014 ref-
... National Longitudinal Study of Adolescent
...ologists Christopher Bader and Scott Desmond
...ne factors associated with older teens keeping their
...dults was having parents who talked about religion and
... home. A young father said something to me a few years
...aught my attention; "My father and mother took me to church
...oke faith to me. If I don't bring my children to church and talk to
...n of faith, who will?"

8. Congregational Life Equips Shepherds

1. Pastoral theologian Howard J. Clinebell, Jr. recounted the metaphorical story of a lifesaving station on the sea coast that repeatedly got replaced by clubs that celebrated saving lives at sea. See *Basic Types of Pastoral Counseling: New Resources for Ministering to the Troubled* (Nashville: Abingdon Press, 1966), 13–14.

2. Personal email with author, February 6, 2018.

3. See the following for examples of this: http://stickyfaith.org/articles/moving-away-from-the-kid-table and https://refocusministry.org/2015/08/17/why-intergenerational-worship-and-why-now/.

4. For more details, go to Grace Lutheran Church at http://graceofav.org/prayground/.

Conclusion

1. Craig L. Nessan, "Universal Priesthood of All Believers: Unfulfilled Promise of the Reformation," in the forthcoming *Reflecting Reformation and the Call for Renewal,* ed. Claudia Jahnel (Neuendettelsau: Erlanger Verlag für Mission und Ökumene, 2018).

Appendix 1

MILESTONES MINISTRY FRAME

FIVE PRINCIPLES of Faith Formation

1. Faith is formed by the power of the Holy Spirit through personal, trusted relationships—often in our own homes.
2. The church is a living partnership between the ministry of the congregation and the ministry of the home.
3. Where Christ is present in faith, the home is church, too.
4. Faith is caught more than it is taught.
5. If we want Christian children and youth, we need Christian adults who practice the faith with them.

FOUR KEY Faith Practices

1. Caring Conversations
2. Devotions
3. Service
4. Rituals and Traditions

THREE CHARACTERISTICS of Christians

1. Authentic
2. Available
3. Affirming

APPENDIX 2

**JUNE 24, 2018
FIFTH SUNDAY
AFTER PENTECOST**

Jesus has the power to help in time of trouble.

DAILY BIBLE READINGS

These passages are related to the Lectionary texts for this Sunday.

Sunday	Mark 4:35-41	Jesus calms the sea
Monday	Job 38:1-11	God's rebuke of Job
Tuesday	2 Corinthians 6:1-13	How Paul served God
Wednesday	Acts 27:13-38	Paul and the storm at sea
Thursday	Exodus 14:5-25	Parting of the Red Sea
Friday	Joshua 3:7-17	The Jordan River stops flowing
Saturday	Psalm 107:1-3, 23-32	God saves those in distress
Sunday	Mark 5:21-43	Jesus heals and raises to life

SCRIPTURE VERSE FOR THIS WEEK

And they were filled with great awe and said to one another, "Who then is this, that even the wind and the sea obey him?" **Mark 4:41 (NRSV)**

PRAYERS AND BLESSING

A Prayer for the Week:
Lord Jesus, please replace our fears with faith; give us courage and keep us calm in times of trouble. Amen.

Mealtime Prayer:
For all we eat and all we wear; for daily bread and nightly care; for your good gifts to use and share; we thank you, Lord. Amen.

A Blessing to Give:
May God calm you when you are afraid. May you have faith to trust in God's love and care.

© 2017 Milestones Ministry, LLC. All rights reserved.

JUNE 24, 2018
HYMN OF THE WEEK
Eternal Father, Strong to Save

CARING CONVERSATIONS
Discuss in your home or small group:
- Draw a picture or talk about a time you were afraid.
- The disciples were in a boat and afraid of a dangerous storm. They thought they might drown. Jesus was with them. How would you feel?
- How do you reach out to Jesus when you experience storms in life?

DEVOTIONS
Read: Mark 4:35-41 and Psalm 107:28-31.

Find a container to represent a boat. Talk about or reflect on any worries or fears you may have today. Write these down and place them in your "boat." Pray that Jesus will calm your fears and help you to see and trust that he is with you in every storm, especially the worries and fears named in your "boat" today.

Pray: **God of creation and salvation, help us to see the storms before us, weather the storms within us, and seek shelter in the harbor of your safety and care. We pray to you through Jesus Christ who knows us, cares for us, and saves us. Amen.**

SERVICE
Even for Paul in the early church, there were tensions with the very people he cared for and ministered to with the love of Christ (2 Corinthians 6:1-13). Being a community of faith involves relationships that need to be grounded in prayer for one another, mutual love, and forgiveness. Pray for those in your faith community with whom you experience tensions or differences. Reach out to leaders in your community with words of appreciation, support, and prayer as together the community seeks to worship God and serve the needs of the world.

RITUALS AND TRADITIONS
It is easy while standing on land to forget how dangerous the open seas can be. Navy and merchant sailors, commercial fishermen, and even those sailing or motoring on the open water for pleasure can quickly be reminded of the power and danger of stormy weather. The waters of the sea and of baptism are life giving and life taking (Romans 6:3-4). This week place a bowl of water in front of you to remember not only your baptism but the raw power of water, especially for those at sea. Dip your finger into the water, make the sign of the cross on your forehead, giving thanks to God for the life-giving waters of baptism, and then pray verse one of *Eternal Father, Strong to Save*: **Eternal Father, strong to save, whose arm has bound the restless wave, who bade the mighty oceans deep its own appointed limits keep: oh, hear us when we cry to thee for those in peril on the sea.**

In addition to *Taking Faith Home*, celebrate milestones in your daily life as an effective faith formation tool. Go to: **www.milestonesministry.org**

Other Books by David W. Anderson

Frogs without Legs Can't Hear: Nurturing Disciples in Home and Congregation (2003)
David W. Anderson and Paul G. Hill

Coming of Age: Exploring the Identity and Spirituality of Younger Men (2006)
David W. Anderson, Paul G. Hill, and Roland D. Martinson

From the Great Omission to Vibrant Faith: The Role of the Home in Renewing the Church (2009)
David W. Anderson

Vibrant Faith in the Congregation (2011)
David W. Anderson

All of Anderson's books reflect his interest in faith formation and outreach to others through a living partnership between the ministry of the congregation and the ministry of the home. His efforts to lift up the role of primary relationships, especially those through the church in the home, continue to be addressed in *Shepherd of Souls: Faith Formation through Trusted Relationships*. All these books make great selections for small group ministry and congregational studies (including staff and other leadership teams).

Frogs without Legs Can't Hear, From the Great Omission to Vibrant Faith, Vibrant Faith in the Congregation, and *Shepherd of Souls,* can be ordered directly from Milestones Ministry, LLC at **www.milestonesministry.org**.